THE
BUSHMAN
WAY OF
TRACKING
GOD

THE ORIGINAL SPIRITUALITY OF THE KALAHARI PEOPLE

Bradford Keeney, PhD

ATRIA BOOKS
New York London Toronto Sydney

BEYOND WORDS
Hillsboro, Oregon

ATRIA BOOKS
A Division of Simon & Schuster, Inc.
1230 Avenue of the Americas
New York, NY 10020

BEYOND WORDS
20827 N.W. Cornell Road, Suite 500
Hillsboro, OR 97124-9808
503-531-8700 / 503-531-8773 fax
www.beyondword.com

The information contained in this book is intended to be educational and not for diagnosis, prescription, or treatment of any health disorder whatsoever. This information should not replace consultation with a competent healthcare professional. The content of this book is intended to be used as an adjunct to a rational and responsible healthcare program prescribed by a professional healthcare practitioner. The author and publisher are in no way liable for any misuse of the material.

Managing editor: Lindsay S. Brown
Editor: Julie Steigerwaldt
Copyeditor: Ali McCart
Proofreader: Jennifer Weaver-Neist
Design: Devon Smith
Composition: William H. Brunson Typography Services

First Atria Books/Beyond Words hardcover edition September 2010

ATRIA BOOKS and colophon are trademarks of Simon & Schuster, Inc.
Beyond Words Publishing is a division of Simon & Schuster, Inc.

For more information about special discounts for bulk purchases,
please contact Simon & Schuster Special Sales at 1-866-506-1949 or
business@simonandschuster.com.

The Simon & Schuster Speakers Bureau can bring authors to your live event.
For more information or to book an event, contact the Simon & Schuster Speakers
Bureau at 1-866-248-3049 or visit our website at www.simonspeakers.com.

Manufactured in the United States of America

10 9 8 7 6 5 4 3 2 1

Library of Congress Cataloging-in-Publication Data

Keeney, Bradford P.
    The bushman way of tracking God : the original spirituality of the Kalahari people / Bradford
    Keeney. — 1st Atria Books/Beyond Words hardcover ed.
        p.   cm.
    1. San (African people)—Kalahari Desert—Religion.   2. Spiritual life.   I. Title.
    BL2480.S24K44   2010
    299.6'81—dc22

                                                                              2010011394

ISBN: 978-1-58270-257-5
ISBN: 978-1-4391-7541-5 (ebook)

The corporate mission of Beyond Words Publishing, Inc.: *Inspire to Integrity*

Dedicated to those who dance the Kalahari wisdom of extreme love.
(especially Mev who is called Twa by the Bushmen)

CONTENTS

INTRODUCTION

I saw a ladder. It was more like a pole with rungs on it let down from heaven,
and it reached from heaven to earth. I was on the bottom rung,
and somebody was on every rung, climbing upward. . . .

TESTIMONY OF A FORMER SLAVE IN TENNESSEE,
COLLECTED BY CHARLES S. JOHNSON

The most extraordinary and incomprehensible fact of my life is that I entered the spiritual universe of the Kalahari Bushmen, the oldest living culture on Earth, and followed its tracks. When I came across a visionary rope hanging from the sky, I walked toward it and was lifted into the heavens. There I danced with God.

I am a university professor and practitioner of family therapy who, decades ago, was brought into the Bushman's old way of working the spirit—the original form of spirituality that predates all major religions by thousands of years. Admittedly, my experiences with them felt like I had been swept away by an alien spacecraft, shown secrets to the universe, and then brought back to Earth several decades later. In my case, I actually did work with them for a period of nearly twenty years, and yes, they took me on an experiential flight into outer space (the full story to be shared later). As incredible and delightful as this kind of experience might first seem, pause to imagine arriving home and realizing what others will think if you report the story. You might be taken to therapy.

INTRODUCTION

I have kept relatively quiet about most of my experiences. Until now, I only conveyed parts of my story, limited to excerpts that were accessible to spiritual seekers. Though I never imagined telling the whole of my learning, the Bushman elders have asked me to no longer keep it secret. With respect for their request, I am fully disclosing what I have been taught. I will share it without fear or concern about others' reactions, and without holding anything back. The world needs to know the uncompromised truth about the experiential world of these beautiful and wonderful people.

What you are about to hear may be surprising or even shocking, but be assured that it is liberating. To start, we can authoritatively say we are all from Africa. On May 2, 2009, the BBC and other major news services announced that a ten-year scientific study concluded that the Bushmen (some anthropologists call them the San or the Ju|'hoan Bushmen as well) have the oldest genetic lineage, empirically proving that they are the descendants of the ancestors for all modern humans. Furthermore, the origin of modern human migration was pinpointed as the present home of the Bushmen by the University of Pennsylvania's Dr. Sarah Tishkoff and her research team, whose results were published in the journal *Science*.

This news is timely, for it comes right when we need a long-overdue homecoming to return us to the original wisdom of the oldest ways of Africa. There, we find the source of all spiritualities. The spiritual know-how we seek was given to our African ancestors in the beginning, and it is our birthright to rediscover what has been forgotten and lost. We must return to the mother continent, the birthplace of humanity, the oldest inhabited land on the globe—Africa, home of our spiritual roots.

The Kalahari Desert of southern Africa is one of the most remote wilderness areas in the world. Amidst the dry grassland and scrubby acacias, we find lions, leopards, brown hyenas, meerkats, jackals, ostriches, exotic birds, reptiles, termites, and scorpions, among other creatures. This land is home to the largest succulent plants found anywhere, the giant baobab trees that are sometimes more than two thousand years old, and camelthorn trees, which house the haystack-size communal nests of the weavers. Resembling sparrows, these socially inclined birds live to intimately interact and embody the mysteries of being fully alive, just like the Bushmen.

The Kalahari may not look like the Sahara, but it behaves as treacherously. During the short rainy season, it becomes a vibrant oasis of lush vegetation surrounded by colorful fauna. When the rains vanish, the Kalahari becomes dry and fierce. It can rain very heavily in a single day, with immediate sweeping floods until the next day, when it returns to being bone dry. Appearances change in a moment in the Kalahari; it is shape-shifting land.

The Kalahari is an authentic place of mystery, with ancient legends and mythical tales that reach far back into the past when the great culture of the Kalahari Bushmen lived free from the disturbance of other human beings. It is presently the Bushmen's last place to survive, the final resting place of our ancestral culture.

Today we know that the Bushmen are the link to our original ancestors. From a place inside the present borders of southern Africa, modern human migration began. In the beginning, we were all Bushmen—people inseparable from the wild of nature.

Most of us assume that human culture improved and evolved since the beginning of our species. Though we are proud of technological advancement and textbook knowledge, we acquired modernity at a price. As we tamed the wilderness, we became disconnected from nature. Have we forgotten how to maintain peace? How often do we embrace ecstatic communion with one another and the divine? Are we able to track and hunt like the first people, or would we quickly perish if thrown into the wilderness to survive on our own? Have we devolved the skills that are vital for survival? Where is our know-how for nurturing emotions, natural wisdom, and raw spirituality in ways that enable us to thrive?

We have learned that we are all descended from Africa at a time when the world economy is seriously struggling, with global pandemics predicted and war littering every corner of the globe. People are feeling more uncertain, lost, and afraid of the future. Have the skills of intellect and technology failed the so-called civilized cultures?

Meanwhile, the Bushmen still dance in the Kalahari and bring forth tremendous, transformative joy. Though they have never experienced material wealth, they are spiritually prosperous. Unfortunately, their future is threatened by the recent discovery of more diamonds and special metals in their homeland, attracting the interest of a dangerous breed of scavenger driven by economic greed. They are asking and pleading that their wisdom—their original way of spirituality—be shared and taught to the world, before it is too late.

The scientific evidence clearly suggests that every one of us is a descendant of the Kalahari Bushmen. Our ancestors are the ones portrayed in the popular movie *The Gods Must Be Crazy*. Their ancient rock art indicates that they have been practicing an extraordinarily potent form of spirituality for over sixty thousand years. What the Bushmen have practiced over all these years is critically important knowledge that could benefit the rest of the world as it faces today's challenges and crises.

Finding the Original Way to God

Whereas most explorers have roamed the world looking for diamonds, emeralds, gold, and silver, different treasure is found beneath the deep sand of the oldest wisdom tradition. This book presents the recent discovery of some of the most remarkable spiritual treasure ever uncovered. It has been my life's mission to search for the original way of finding God, and I found it in the Kalahari.

There, in the Kalahari Desert of Namibia and Botswana, a small number of Bushman elders hold our most ancient wisdom. These individuals grew up at a time when there was little to no contact with technologically developed outsiders. Up until their early adulthood, they were hunter-gatherers. They chased giraffes, elands, and kudu while fighting off mambas, lions, and leopards. Living in grass huts, they made arrows out of bone and used ostrich eggs to hold their drinking water. Of all the amazing accounts about these first people, the Bushmen are most famous for their uncanny and mind-boggling tracking skills. If you want to find a lost person or locate any animal in the Kalahari, a Bushman can track it down for you.

What few people know is that the Kalahari Bushmen are also able to track God. These practitioners of the oldest way find their path to the divine in the same manner that they hunt for any other living presence. Long before there were Tibetans, Hindus, Christians, Muslims, Jews, Native Americans, Pagans, Siberians, Mayans, and Zen Buddhists, the Bushmen were walking directly into the heavens. The world's most enduring culture has been the custodian of the original way of making connection with the sacred. They have asked me to share their straightforward means of finding and entering eternity.

In the beginning of the human race, so the Bushmen say, the Creator gave them what there is to know about spiritual living. Since that time, they have conserved and embodied the original sacred mysteries, particularly when dancing on the Kalahari sand. When the Ice Age ended, the sub-Saharan land became too dry, and some of the original ancestors dispersed throughout the rest of the world. The subsequent, alleged advances of these later developed cultures generally involved taming the wild. First the plants were tamed by agriculture. Then the animals were domesticated, followed by the subjugation of women.

Along the way, complex experience was tamed with words and rational understanding, with the consequence that many human beings were left thirsting for whatever states of awe and mystery they'd had in the beginning. This encapsulation and taming of the wild fractured our connection with the divine. As we broke the bonds of relationship and interdependency with one another and disrupted our ecological matrix, our link to the divine mysteries became all but lost.

Most highly literate spiritual teachers argue that abstract philosophies and theologies represent an evolution of spirituality over the "primitives" who danced around a fire rather than sitting to read and discuss a book. The Bushmen have a different story. They believe that language, ideas, theories, and abstract thinking too easily deceive. With language games, we are led away from how our heart can be fully awakened to bridge with eternal wisdom and guidance. The Bushmen see today's world as lost and disconnected from the original mysteries given by the Creator.

The original way to tracking God, what may be called
original spirituality, **is surprisingly found through**
embracing wild laughter, syncopated rhythm,
and ecstatic love.

The Bushman way does not require books or institutionalized religions. It invites you to find the tracks that can lead you directly to the spiritual universe. Here, the spiritual tracks, called "the ropes to God," are valued over libraries, schools, and ritualized teaching. In the Kalahari, the oldest way to God is found through experiencing a journey that immerses us in the original mysteries. The oldest spiritual tradition asks us to immediately stop the pretension of pretending that we can receive wisdom through rational means. The alternative is an invitation to follow the highest bliss and joy, going past the limitations of small mind into the limitless heart and soul of Creation.

The original way to tracking God, what may be called original spirituality, is surprisingly found through embracing wild laughter, syncopated rhythm, and ecstatic love. In other words, we find enlightenment through bringing forth absurd talk, spirited music, and heartfelt embrace. These are the very avenues of expression that many well-established religions caution us about or fail to emphasize.

The message of the world's oldest religion
is to be *outrageously happy....*

The Bushmen suggest that we have turned the basic truths of living upside-down and that is why practically everything in our lives, from the global economy to our homes, schools, politics, and ecology, is in such a topsy-turvy mess. Their invitation is for us to stop spending so much time sitting still in any meditative, classroom, or boardroom stupor, and to be less attached to professed cognitive insights, explanations, and understandings. Original spirituality invites us to engage in more heartfelt caring, sharing, and daring encounters with one another. Doing so leaves us with the desire to move our body and tease our mind, rather than still our body and salute our mind.

The original way to God simply involves this unambiguous turn-about directive: start performing almost everything you have been told *not* to do. Trust ecstatic arousal more than sedated relaxation; pay more attention to irrationality than over-rationality; cultivate circular thought over linear causality; prioritize whole feelings as opposed to fragmented thoughts; seek jazzy syncopation rather than monotonous metronome-like, tick-tock-clock rhythms; become improvisational rather than ritualistic; and revere wild experience over that which is tame. The message of the world's oldest religion is to be *outrageously happy* and to do so with less seriousness, purposefulness, and know-it-all consciousness than our educators and spiritual teachers have taught. Yes, the gods are crazy, and they expect the same from us if we want to hang out with them!

Becoming a Messenger of the Original Spirituality

Sharing the message of the world's oldest religion is not without its challenges. For one thing, a background of deception and misinformation among some explorers, writers, and anthropologists has left many of us cautious about reports on previously uncharted spiritual territory.

Over the years quite a few writers—sometimes bestselling—have not told the truth about their spiritual adventures. Even some anthropologists have reported false information. There are more than a few accounts of cultural informants making up fictional replies for ambitious anthropologists. It's no wonder that caution abounds on all sides.

In addition, anthropologists easily miss the essence of Bushman spirituality because of their erroneous assumptions about how they think Bushmen experience the world. The Bushmen do not tell a person anything more about spirituality that isn't already developed and present in the person they are talking with. If you know nothing about spirituality, they tell you nothing and tease you about your desire to know, saying that too much experiential knowledge "might kill you." If you know a little, they address that little part of your knowing and still tease you. If you know a lot, they tell you everything and tease you even more.

Let me explain how I came to be a messenger of original spirituality: From a young age, I always loved science and music, specifically jazz. In high school, I was a small-town boy who, against all odds, won the international science fair and a scholarship to MIT. It was a good thing that I won the big prize because I had absentmindedly overlooked applying to college! In college, I studied cybernetics, the original science of complexity, and received my doctorate from Purdue University. I focused on explaining how change takes place in people's lives from the perspective of observed patterns of relationship rather than fantasized psychological processes. Following my mentor, anthropologist Gregory Bateson, I thought psychology's way of thinking was crazier than the clients it treated. I accordingly abandoned psychological and psychiatric thinking in favor of seeing the world through cybernetic, systemic, and ecological metaphors. My first published book, *Aesthetics of Change*, was regarded as one of the seminal texts in cybernetics by one of its founders, Heinz von Foerster.

I am trying to make clear that I did not begin as a spiritual seeker. What I knew about religion I learned from my grandfather and father, two country preachers who were kind and gentle human beings, and who simply said that God is love and that everything else said about the holy was made up. This spiritual understanding worked for me then as it does today.

All was fine in my early life, but at the age of twenty, I suddenly stopped playing the piano and told no one why, because I had no way to describe what had happened. I was not a schooled pianist but played by feelings. Music opened my heart to such an extent that it precipitated the most extraordinary experience of my life. Without any conscious guidance, I spontaneously experienced what the Kalahari Bushmen regard as their initiation to another way of being. At the time, I had never heard of the Bushmen and had no spiritual theories or metaphors to account for what took place.

INTRODUCTION

I experienced a love so big that it made me tremble and shake as I felt its pulse of infinite joy. In this mind-blowing and heart-opening experience, I witnessed a six-foot-tall luminous egg directly in front of me. It was more than a spiritual vision: it was a fountain of love that poured ecstatic happiness and deep meaning into my heart all night long. This egg hatched a love that surpassed the intensity of anything I had ever felt before. The lovesickness of romantic love, the ecstasy of spiritual conversion, and the deep togetherness of familial relations were not anywhere near this bliss zone. It was an extreme form of love.

Years later, I would learn that the Bushmen call this rare experience the deliverance of God's ostrich egg, and they believe that it brings the know-how for entering and navigating the mysteries of the spiritual universe. At the time, I was so emotionally absorbed in the experience that I didn't care about explaining it. I knew from the bottom of my heart and soul that it was completely good and came from the purest, highest, and most whole source of all that is sacred. However, I believed that the experience was so strong that if it happened again, I might be swept away and never return. That is why I stopped playing the piano. I wasn't ready to reenter that infinite bliss anytime soon.

I kept this experience to myself, telling no one for over a decade. I quieted the music, threw myself into scholarship, and moved up the academic ladder, becoming a full professor and the director of several doctoral programs. My publications, now more focused on the practice of therapy, were read around the world, and in some places, they were required reading for those seeking licensure to be a family therapist.

At the height of my early academic career, in 1992, I was invited to be a visiting professor at the University of South Africa. The week prior, I'd dreamed of visiting a band of Bushmen in the Kalahari. To my surprise, this dream showed a map of their exact location. I accepted the invitation and requested that a trip be organized to take me to the place I had seen, the Khutse Game Reserve in the Central Kalahari of Botswana, the second largest desert in Africa.

The point of my personal story is that I became an expert on the circular thinking of cybernetics and the professional practice of family therapy as a means of distancing myself from an extraordinary experience I felt I couldn't tell anyone about, only to find that my scholarship and profession provided a way for me to visit the Bushmen, the leading experts on what I was running away from. I paradoxically came full circle, and this was how I was able to first meet the Kalahari Bushmen.

I had more visionary dreams and invitations to visit remote places in the world. My dreams became a sort of mystical travel agency booking me to places I typically knew little about. I became a visiting scholar in Japan, Brazil, Paraguay, Australia, and many other places that enabled me to meet elders from the cultures I was visioning, and I often became entrusted with their most sacred healing traditions or spiritual lineages.

I finally took a sabbatical from the university to spend more time studying the global wisdom traditions. During that time, a speech I gave at a psychotherapy conference caught the attention of the directors of a foundation concerned with cultural healing practices. The foundation offered me the opportunity to continue to travel and document the healing traditions of cultures around the globe. My one-year sabbatical ended up lasting over a decade. I became vice president and distinguished scholar of cultural affairs for the Ringing Rocks Foundation and led expeditions throughout the world to help conserve the transformative expertise I had uncovered in my previous academic visits. This work was critically praised by scholars all over the world—from the American Museum of Natural History to Oxford University—and was publicly presented at renowned institutions, including the Smithsonian Museum in New York City and the Origins Centre in Johannesburg.

**I found ... that the Kalahari Bushmen,
our ancestral culture, held the original form of spirituality
and that all other traditions could be seen and
understood in relation to it.**

I found the rich samurai healing heritage of Japan, the ecstatic shaking traditions in the Caribbean, and the soulfulness of Louisiana to be especially formative and enlightening, as they revealed vibrant commonalities with the Kalahari practitioners. Overall, what I found was that the Kalahari Bushmen, our ancestral culture, held the original form of spirituality and that all other traditions could be seen and understood in relation to it. As I returned to the Kalahari over and over again during a period of nearly two decades, I began to see what was fundamental to healing, meaningful everyday living, and transformation.

I never anticipated how the key ingredients of my personal life experiences would combine to produce an accidental entrance into original spirituality. Namely, when playing music through feelings was added to precise scholarship about circular thinking, with a dash of the emotional upbringing in a country church, and then mixed together with the zesty teasing and laughter that was part of my family of origin, it made a mojo marinade that prepared me to receive a visionary ostrich egg, a dreamed map of the Kalahari, and an actual airline ticket to meet the Bushmen.

The moment I first saw the Kalahari Bushmen in 1992, they came running across the desert to greet me. The spiritual elder of the Khutse community in Botswana immediately announced that they had dreamed of my coming as I had dreamed of seeing them. Montag, an old Bushman healer, came over and said, "Welcome to your home. We have been waiting for you." He then pointed to a scraggy camelthorn tree about one hundred yards away and said, "You will live under that tree. You will dance with us, and we will feel your healing hands bring us joy. Know that you have come home. Someday you will die, and you will again return to that tree." Those were the first words I heard from the Bushmen. It might not come as a surprise that I wondered whether I was dreaming the whole thing.

I did not go to the Kalahari alone. I was accompanied by Professor Peter Johnson, whose background in qualitative field research enriched our dialogue and helped keep my experiences grounded to his astute observations. What we experienced sometimes defied logical explanation, but it was deeply familiar to my heart and the ways in which feelings had awakened my spiritual life. My first visit to the Kalahari was a homecoming for my heart and soul. There, I found others who started each day with the same spiritual breakfast—the felt presence of God's ostrich egg.

In the Kalahari, I discovered original spirituality. Its tracks lead to cultural traditions all over the planet. Most important, the Bushmen know how to find and follow the tracks that lead directly to God. The message I bring is not esoteric or complicated. It does not involve secret incantations, magic wands, or expensive potions. It has no hidden vault wherein ancient books prescribe recipes for enlightenment. It often doesn't seem anything like the organized religions of the world. It is neither old nor new age; its concern is with the timeless eternal. You might say it goes beyond spirituality—beyond the words people rely on to find the spirit.

For nearly two decades since that first visit, I have organized many expeditions to the Bushmen. I have recorded and filmed my interviews with the help of professional photographers, audio engineers, and filmmakers. I have taken other scholars into the field with me. Finally, I have shared my findings with renowned anthropologists and scientists. One of them, Megan Biesele, PhD, cofounder and coordinator of the Kalahari Peoples Fund and former member of the Harvard Kalahari Research Group, went back to the Kalahari and interviewed the elders I'd worked with. She wanted to check out the authenticity of my claims. Knowing the Bushmen's fondness for teasing, I am sure they told her that I was an unusual baboon who had the head of a rhinoceros and the tail of a giraffe. Or that they had fed me to a lion that only spat me out because I hadn't been grilled long enough. Whatever jokes they enjoyed at my expense, Professor Biesele and our Kalahari friends were serious enough about the importance of having their teachings heard that they conspired the following endorsement to help a reader trust the story that is about to be told:

> There is no question in the minds of the Bushman healers that Keeney's strength and purposes are coterminous with theirs. I know this from talking myself with some of the Kalahari shamans who danced with him. They affirmed his power as a

healer and their enjoyment of dancing with him.... He knows whereof he writes, having traveled "ropes to God" himself for much of his life....

David Lewis-Williams, PhD, founder of the Rock Art Research Institute in Johannesburg and an important rock art scientist, did not want to be left out of roasting my work. His words help explain what the Bushmen think about their way of doctoring:

> After many astounding experiences, the Bushmen accepted Keeney as a "doctor," a n|om-kxao, one who is believed to possess and control a supernatural essence or power that can be harnessed to heal people with physical and social ills.

And finally, Hans Vahrmeijer, a retired botanist and author at the Botanical Research Institute, Pretoria, South Africa, accompanied me on many trips to the Kalahari. His observations were as startling to him as they were to me when I experienced what he was talking about. He points to some of the remarkable classrooms the Bushmen use in the Kalahari:

> During the years and numerous expeditions with Bradford Keeney to the Bushmen of southern Africa, I observed an odyssey into a fascinating spiritual world. They allowed him to delve deeper and deeper until he became an accepted holder of their most important truths. I observed him being taught and trained by them to such a level over the years that even long-distance communication by way of dreams became a natural reality for him.

This book tells the story of how I, though culturally ordained as a university professor, family therapist, and even president of the Louisiana Association for Marriage and Family Therapy, found myself thrown into the mysteries of the Bushman way of spirituality and healing. In this journey, I was shown the tracks to God and led inside the spiritual universe of the original people. The extraordinary experiences described in this book have been confirmed as authentic and well-known by the most respected spiritual elders of the Kalahari.

The spiritual know-how for tracking and finding the gods has become a part of my everyday life. In this remarkable journey, I became a holder of the Kalahari way of healing. To the Bushman elders, I am recognized as a doctor who has mastered their healing traditions and who even keeps the other Bushman doctors strong. After I spent decades tracking the ultimate source of spirituality on an odyssey that took me numerous times around the world, the Bushman elders have asked me, who they call the "big doctor," to write down what is most important to know about their original way to God. I recorded their request and blessing to proceed. This book presents the teachings of original spirituality as spoken by the last remaining ancestors who actually live the oldest ways. It is written so that their ancient way, which is our original way, may be a voice of truth and a light of clarity in the midst of dark and deceptive times.

For the Bushmen, the great mysteries of spirituality are delivered through two mediums—love and laughter.

Original spirituality is unschooled and so simple that you may not believe it at first. No matter, for it has little to do with belief. It is more about getting knocked out by your heightened feelings. For the Bushmen, the great mysteries of spirituality are delivered through two mediums—love and laughter. No average feeling of love or humorous giggle will work. I am speaking of extreme love and wild laughter. From the beginning of human history, the original way of finding meaning, healing, and transformation drew upon loving and laughing yourself into the arms of the gods. My task is to help you feel this love and humor. There is nothing to understand, nor is any advanced conceptual learning required. This is an alternative to talking-head teachers. You get to the heavens with a belly laugh and a heartthrob. The main tools are inspired music for awakening your feelings and radical teasing that distracts your mind from interfering with the divine play that desires your intimate participation. This is what original spirituality is all about.

The truths of the most spiritually wealthy people desperately need to be shared with those who thirst for purpose, meaning, healing, and joy. What an irony that the home of the Bushmen, the Kalahari, means "the great thirst" from the Tswana word *Kgala*. While the rest of the world is thirsting for spiritual wisdom, the Kalahari's people have been waiting to quench it.

The Original Mysteries Revealed

This book will set forth, for the first time in written history, the oldest teachings ever given for how we can find the deepest meaning, fullest purpose, and highest joy in life. These teachings will be articulated as the twelve original mysteries. Each mystery represents one part of the whole of spirituality. These mysteries include activating the non-subtle universal life force (what the Bushmen call *n|om*), heightening emotional experience, vibratory interaction, direct downloading and absorption of sacred knowledge, extraordinary healing, activation of the ecstatic pump, spontaneous ways of rejuvenation, attending the spiritual classrooms, an uncommon range of mystical experiences, and last but not least, being touched by God. Along the way, you will be transported to other rich and diverse cultures and experiences that exemplify the essence of Bushman spirituality—spontaneous movement, gleeful absurdity, and potent life force. Together we'll explore the healing tradition of Japan, the wisdom and poeticism of Rumi's Persia, the pirate lore of the Caribbean, the infectious energy and musical qualities of church services and fabled parades in New Orleans, and glimpses of workshops and classes I've conducted around the world. Get ready, for it's going to be a wild ride—unlike anything you've experienced before.

Because you will be introduced to an array of spiritual terms and concepts, I have included a glossary at the end of this book for easy reference. If you want to dive even deeper, there is also a never-before-published dictionary of original spirituality. Although some of these terms are not discussed elsewhere in this book, the dictionary offers more detail about the Bushman spiritual landscape. To hear these words spoken by the Bushmen or to see photographs and video clips of their dancing, singing, and music making, please visit my website: www.shakingmedicine.com.

Each religion and spiritual tradition of the world has been historically familiar with some of the original mysteries, but the Bushmen hold the whole spiritual ecology. Without knowing the whole, we too easily—and mistakenly—assume that one part is the whole. We must go to the beginning, the source of original spirituality, to find the infinite ocean we have been missing and seeking in today's shower of incomplete, confusing, and frustrating wordplay. The Bushmen want to take you to the source of all vitality, creativity, and well-being. There, you are invited to jump in. Rather than talk about it, the oldest way baptizes you in its current.

In this book, each chapter will set forth a description of a particular mystery and discuss how the Bushmen understand and work with it in their original way. The ancient prophecies of the Hopi and the Zulu, among numerous others, predicted a future homecoming of the different sacred colors and directions. Perhaps they were symbolically referring to the whole of spirituality being reunited again. Without the whole, it becomes too easy to set one piece against the other. We need the interdependent relations within the whole to move past the either/or fundamentalisms of any separated parts. Seen this way, the Bushman way of tracking God seeks to bring us back together again as a global spiritual family, with relatives belonging to the same whole truth who honor and foster an authentic respect of our differences as well as our commonalities.

**The greatest mystery of all is that you were born with
everything you need in order to receive the greatest
blessings and joy life has to offer.**

Please know that finding and traversing the original track to God does not require a secret initiation ceremony, an advanced graduate degree, membership in an esoteric society, or compulsive practice of any form of spiritual (and political) correctness. You don't even have to know how to read. What it requires is your fullest humanness and a sincere desire to be willing, able, and ready to be moved by life itself. You may be shocked, you may be pushed out of your comfort zone, you may even be offended. But if you stay open to it, your life may never be the same. Perhaps the greatest mystery of all is that you were born with everything you need in order to receive the greatest blessings and joy life has to offer.

Now is the time to find your track to God and to stop taking all the distracting exits that promise fast food and quick refreshment. Stay on track, travel down the main highway, and don't stop until you find yourself embraced by the gods. They are waiting to play, dance, laugh, and sing with you. Put on your traveling shoes, for it is time to do some spiritual tracking!

1

ENTERING THE RIVER

The First Original Mystery

*Just yesterday, friend, the giraffe came and took me again. God came and took me
with him, and we left this place. We traveled until we came to a wide body of water.
It was a river. He took me to a river.... He made the waters climb,
and I lay my body in the direction they were flowing.... Then I
entered the stream and began to move forward.*

K!XAU, KALAHARI ELDER
(as told to Megan Biesele, PhD)

There are no libraries or universities in the Kalahari. Whatever
you want to learn about the sacred mysteries of the Bushman
universe is not written down and conveyed through words. Is there an
official custodian of the oral tradition, someone with perfect memory
of their cultural knowledge who eventually passes it on to the next generation's wisdom keeper? No, there is not even an oral custodian in the
Kalahari. Words are simply not trusted to hold the most important
wisdom. In the beginning, the original ancestors knew something we
have forgotten. They understood that words are inadequate for trans-
mitting spiritual know-how. You have to feel it.

"Come on, N!yae, let's go to the river," I say, standing by a
camelthorn tree in the village of Chokwe in what used to be called
Bushmanland, now known as part of the Nyae Nyae Conservancy, an
area encompassing approximately 3,500 square miles in northeastern
Namibia. This is the home of the Ju|'hoan Bushmen.

"You're already wet and ready to drown!" N!yae shouts back. She is a doctor, traditional healer, or spiritual elder—what the Bushman call a n|om-kxao, which means "an owner of n|om."

N!yae stands less than five feet tall, weighs no more than eighty pounds, and is adorned with beadwork she has hand made from ostrich eggshells. She also carries a tortoise shell around her waist filled with the same kind of medicine that her ancestors carried.

If spiritual intelligence were as abundant as Kalahari sand, all the great religions would honor N!yae as much as they respect His Holiness the Dalai Lama or the pope. She is a spiritual leader of the original form of spirituality. However, unlike the leaders of other religions, she is one of the poorest persons in the world, living on the edible plants she finds and what little meat her culture is allowed due to government-imposed hunting restrictions.

N!yae is not served meals by famous chefs nor hosted by celebrities, presidents, kings, and queens. Nevertheless, I contend that she is the highest priestess of them all, holding wisdom older and deeper than the derivative forms. What she knows, we have forgotten. What other religions talk about, she is. It is time that we seriously acknowledge the presence and spiritual authority of her tradition.

N!yae was married to the great healer and spiritual teacher |Kunta |Ai!ae before he passed away with tuberculosis. |Kunta |Ai!ae was one of my teachers. During his time, he was regarded as a treasured healer and humble human being, and the people loved him and mourned his death with great sorrow. After |Kunta |Ai!ae left the earthly plane, he returned, in spirit, to teach N!yae. He taught her by downloading something into her—what the Bushmen call n|om. The Bushmen say that |Kunta |Ai!ae became an ancestral spirit who shot n|om into N!yae's body.

"I'm going to drown you in n|om today, N!yae," I tease back. "You can never get enough n|om. You are always thirsty for it. Today I will make sure that you drown with me."

Words, the Bushmen say, are only useful for teasing one another. In teasing, we are less likely to get stuck in any particular belief, attitude, or form of knowing. This makes the Bushmen as different from the rest of the world as anyone could imagine. When they see our books and are told how we use them to teach us about life, they fall to the ground laughing, saying we are crazy. They are being kind. They really think we are spiritual idiots.

"Why would God live on paper?" a Bushman elder once asked a bewildered missionary, who confessed to me that neither he nor any other clergy he knew was able to "get the word of God" into the Bushman mind. "However, I have to say," he went on, "that God did place the Ten Commandments upon their hearts. Though they don't relate to the Bible, they truly are God's children. They relate to God."

But the missionary, his wife, and all the members of the religious organization who sent them there never felt called to dance with the Bushmen for reasons we can well understand, given their formal spiritual training. They never once made themselves available to feeling a Bushman healer's trembling hands and shaking body. Over all the years they lived in the Kalahari, they did not realize that these were the means through which the Bushmen experienced a living relationship with God.

"The white man with a paper God is a bit disturbed in the mind," the Bushmen told me at another time, when we were far away from the missionary. "He gets confused when we ask him if he'd like to meet God and dance with him. Even worse, he gets upset when we ask him to meet God's wife and dance with her. Something is not quite right about these people who come out here and ask us a lot of questions. They think words will make them understand. They miss out on having the experiences that are beyond understanding. They don't know how to drown like Bo!"

All the villagers start laughing, some rolling on the ground, with the thought of me, a white man they named Bo, being able to enter their spiritual universe. It makes them delighted, and they believe it also makes the gods happy. It is a comedic performance of the divine.

There is a river, and it is everywhere. There is a wind, and it is everywhere. They are the same except when they are different. There is a god in the sky and a god on earth that keeps changing. They are the same except when they are different. That's how Bushman elders talk and think. We can begin to see why some missionaries and anthropologists feel a bit disoriented when they try to understand or communicate with the Bushmen. The original people don't have straight talk; they speak in circles. However, their way of knowing is not simple. It is far more complex than how the rest of the world thinks.

Feeling the River Inside

Since |Kunta |Ai!ae passed, N!yae has become the strongest n|om-kxao, the ablest holder of n|om in the Kalahari. It should be no surprise (to women) that the strongest healers and spiritual teachers among the Bushmen are often the women elders. More often than not, women are less distracted by power in favor of a relational presence that is inspired by reasons and passions of the heart. The desire for power, whether you think you have it or not, distorts the track to God, even bends it, so you are led astray. The temptation of fire, as the Bushmen call it, makes us believe we can conquer our enemies and not be burned by flame, killed by lions, or harmed by the forces against life. Each Bushman sacred tracker must walk past the power-based delusions of fire and be lifted into the relational heart of the ancestors. This is where they experience the acquisition of new eyes and ears, among other enhanced ways of sensing the world. With spiritual sight, hearing, smell, and touch, they are able to find the tracks to God.

They tease N!yae and me, and call her my n|om wife. Yes, that's correct—she and I are a n|om pair. Together we can bring forth the n|om in a way that old timers claim is like it used to be in the days of their grandparents and ancestors.

Bo, my identity in the Kalahari, is also considered to be the strongest n|om-kxao in the Kalahari. N!yae and Bo together constitute what the other n|om-kxaosi dream about. Literally dream about: they see us dancing with them when they are asleep, entering the realm of the ancestors and the medicine. In dreams as well as the community healing dances, we give them n|om—that is, we shoot it inside them.

[In] the original world of spiritual mystery... anything is possible and impossible, sometimes at the same time.

There you have it: spiritually speaking, I get down with powerful grannies in the Kalahari. This kind of dancing is free from naive eroticism—it is pure and simple joy, the highest form of tender loving care. In this ecstatic dancing, or shaking, we tap into a magical, mysterious force or energy—n|om—that is an entry to a world the rest of us have heard very little about. I am speaking of the original world of spiritual mystery. There, anything is possible and impossible, sometimes at the same time.

In the Kalahari, we enter a river, a wind, a current, and a mystery that flows inside us. As Rumi poetically said, "You feel a river moving in you, a joy." This movement that takes you into spiritual mystery is inseparable from n|om. You can't say it is n|om, for n|om is more than that. In fact, you never can say what n|om is. No definition can capture it. You can't even say the word "n|om" when it is moving within you; that would be dangerous. The n|om might get too strong.

Like the Hebrews who refused to utter the name of Yahweh, the Bushmen have long known the wisdom of having respect names. These are words for holy names. N|om has a respect name, and so does God. When you feel a holy presence nearby, you respect its power and do not allow a word to set up an illusory (and potentially arrogant) knowing of something that goes past the limit of our mind's ability to understand. You use another word to distance yourself from the mirage of knowing. In other words, the respect names help keep everything a mystery.

"Bo, come on down to the river. I want to drown now," N!yae says in a kind of singing voice.

"N!yae, you are greedy. You can never get enough n|om. I can assure you that you won't be able to walk home tonight."

This, I am sure about. When she is full of n|om, N!yae looks intoxicated. Her eyes are dilated, and she can't walk a straight line. We always get drunk on n|om when we shake together.

"Come on, Bo! The river is not going to wait, and I'm thirsty!"

N!yae knows there isn't a river anywhere near the Kalahari. Yes, there are dry riverbeds, and when it does rain, they may turn into a mighty current of water. But that is a rare and momentary thing. What

N!yae means is that there is a spiritual river, and we don't have to walk anywhere to find it. We step into it by allowing our hearts and souls to be in charge rather than our minds. We allow our feelings to be stirred and awakened. When this happens, we are in the river, in the wind, in the n|om.

Rumi, who seems to have been a lot like a Bushman, once advised that we should "reach for the rope of God." This directive is actually the most important advice a Bushman n|om-kxao can give, and Rumi voices it with the same exact words used in the Kalahari: *reach for the rope of God*.

Rumi knew that purposeful will is an obstacle to be removed so that the river can move inside our heart. When will power, reason, or conscious mind takes front and center stage, there is no room for the free movement of one's heart. That is when the highest emotions stop. "Because of willfulness, people sit in jail, the trapped bird's wings are tied, fish sizzle in the skillet," Rumi wrote. The Bushmen knew this wisdom from the very beginning, as have awakened poets and muses of the heart, whether expressed or performed through song, dance, poem, or play.

Our heart dives into this dynamic current whenever it is allowed to unashamedly *feel* the full joy of being alive.

Subtle Energy Is Pretend Energy

The first mystery of the Kalahari, the wellspring of original spirituality, is natural movement unfettered by the constraints and limited manipulations of mind, but not the kind of physical exercise in which you make yourself move. We are talking about Kalahari movement—natural, effortless movement in the rivers, winds, and sands of eternity. Our heart dives into this dynamic current whenever it is allowed to unashamedly *feel* the full joy of being alive.

The rope to God takes you to the heavenly city, the "moving palace that floats in the air with balconies and clear water flowing through, infinity everywhere, yet contained under a single tent." Like Rumi, the

Bushman n|om-kxaosi open their hearts as a means of finding the rope to God which they are able to climb, taking them to the sky village home of the gods, who wait with infinite love and n|om.

I regard Rumi as a kindred spirit to the Bushman, and his poetry gracefully embodies what their original spirituality has to teach. His words help evoke the essence of the Bushman's heart. This awakened heart is the key to finding and opening the spiritual treasure everyone is seeking. The Kalahari elders hold the treasure map, the detailed directions, and the spiritual compass for how to find and bring this heart-centered way of being into our everyday life. Their invitation asks that we enter the moving stream of the heart—the movement of emotions that carries us into the more dynamic ways of being with one another.

The Bushmen say that your body must shiver with strong emotion in order to step into n|om. All the word games, grand theories, and big understandings only distract you from the spiritual focus at hand. The Bushmen would take issue with many of today's philosophically oriented spiritual teachers, warning that words, concepts, and grand theories too easily get elaborated and twisted, pulling you further away from n|om. Turn around and head the other way. Set your compass to aim for your emotions rather than your thoughts. That's where the river, wind, and n|om reside. To get there, we must remember that emotions get the motions going!

Back in the Kalahari, it is early morning and the pink streaks of dawn have announced that the sun will soon bake anyone who isn't underneath the shade. N!yae is trembling, and all the ostrich beads around her neck are shaking like a rattle. I've been holding her, and her vibrations are now pulsing inside me. We are trembling together in front of the whole community. Children, adolescents, young adults, and elders are all around us as we enter the n|om. They start to clap and sing. Twa, the chief's wife, who is usually with us, brings some water to quench our physical thirst. We and the other n|om-kxaosi who have joined us are all entering the n|om.

We are in a huddle that pulses, breathes, and shakes away our physical boundaries. We are on a Kalahari ship that is headed for the glory of sanctified n|om and spirit that the greatest of our great-grandparents once embraced. In this adventure we hope to tune ourselves—that is, align ourselves to be more in sync with the flow of the universal life force. As the river sweeps away our words and thoughts, our mind gets out of the way to make room for the waves of joy that will soon engulf us and take us on unfathomable spiritual journeys.

As N!yae and I fall into the spiritual river, our bodies trembling in unison, we begin to sing. Actually it is more than musical performance; it is the spontaneous making of improvised sound. This takes us deeper into the current. I am now nearly swept away by a tidal wave of heightened emotion. Caught off guard, I feel a tsunami of feeling immediately following the previous rush, overtaking whatever is left of my ability to consciously generate any idea about what is going on.

In this washing away of previous ways of being, I am simultaneously given new eyes and ears. This is what happens when you enter the river: you are transported to other dimensions. In this space, I intuitively sense that one of my teachers is near—Ikuko Osumi, an elder Japanese healer and remarkable master of the universal life force.

Ikuko Osumi had a healing way that was said to be rooted to the ancient samurai tradition. Everything about her was traditional, and it was no accident that her clients included some of the national treasures of Japan. She was their spiritual adviser, teacher, and healer. Though many Japanese wanted to create a religion around her, she refused and operated a simple clinic in her home. She treated people whom the medical community had given up on. Many of them recovered and devoted themselves to helping keep her work alive.

I first met Ikuko Osumi when I was invited to give a keynote address to an annual meeting of Japanese therapists. Since those first days, I have had many experiences with her family, one of the old samurai lineages. I lived with them as she taught me what she knew, and in a ceremony under the guardianship of Shinto priests, I was finally entrusted to carry on her tradition. I was symbolically grafted onto her samurai lineage.

Feeling her presence near, I realize that I am heading for Japan today. In the midst of my trembling n|om dance with N!yae in the Kalahari sand, I am spiritually traveling to Japan to be with my old teacher. In this visionary experience, I land in Setagaya, Tokyo, sitting in the front room of her house, where Ikuko Osumi serves me a cup of green tea.

We are preparing to watch a video I brought. It is a copy of the first film made of the Bushman giraffe dance, the healing dance of the men n|om-kxaosi. In the 1950s, when the film was made, Laurence Marshall, president of the defense company Raytheon, made the courageous and outrageous decision that he did not want to raise his children in a McCarthy-oriented America. He loaded a ship with trucks and supplies and went to sea, bound for Africa. He had heard of the Kalahari Bushmen, first known as the !Kung, but later more accurately called the Ju|'hoan Bushmen or San. He and his family left America to become the first ethnographers of this romanticized culture. Though untrained as anthropologists, they agreed to send their written reports and films to Harvard's Peabody Museum, where the collection is conserved today.

The son, young John Marshall, made the film that I am preparing to show to my teacher Ikuko Osumi. I start the film and, within seconds, this grandmother, a power station of ancient Japanese healing and a master of a practice called *seiki jutsu*, is clearly excited and thrilled. "Seiki! Seiki! Seiki!" she shouts and points to the Bushmen on the film, who are trembling and touching one another as they pass the body-held vibration from one person to another. N|om, like seiki, is the *non-subtle* universal force. As Ikuko Osumi says, "Subtle energy is pretend energy. The real awakened energy is non-subtle, alive, and it can toss you across the room!" N|om, seiki, chi, kundalini, Holy Ghost power, and the universal life force are different words that constitute the same pointing finger. Each is a Zen finger pointing, without words of meaning, to a mystery of nature that can never be explained.

Ikuko Osumi leans over so as to closely examine what the Bushmen are doing. Her eyes twinkle with affirmation as she sees the link between the oldest way of the Kalahari and the traditional Japanese practice of seiki jutsu. "Very good," she says. "This is very good seiki."

Seiki is the old Japanese word for the life force. Ikuko Osumi's work involves instilling it in others. As she acknowledged to me, it is the same thing that is done by the Bushmen healers—shooting n|om into a person. Both traditions know how to recognize when a person is full of the life force: they will start rocking or spontaneously moving. More precisely, when they are given the space and opportunity to move, their body will automatically start moving in a spontaneous fashion.

**For Bushman and Japanese masters of the life force,
this natural movement is the secret to a vibrant life.
It fosters healing, well-being, productivity, and creativity.**

This automatic movement of the body involves the circulation and flow of n|om. It takes you into the river, where more n|om can pour into you. For Bushman and Japanese masters of the life force, this natural movement is the secret to a vibrant life. It fosters healing, well-being, productivity, and creativity. I have met many renowned artists, inventors, scientists, and business CEOs in Japan, all clients of Ikuko Osumi. It was their belief that the seiki instilled within them was the source of their success. The Bushmen would no doubt agree.

Ikuko Osumi and I thank each other for the time we just spent in each other's spiritual presence. With that, I return to my physical body in the Kalahari, yet I feel as if we are still together. This is what it means to be a Bushman. It is possible to feel that you are in many places. In this way, you are always traveling, context shifting, and shape-shifting. The Bushman spiritual universe is multilayered and constantly in flux. They live in the very heart of unfiltered transformative process. One moment we can have the experience of being in Japan, and then, at the snap of a finger, find ourselves transported to the Kalahari and beyond.

**When Bushmen shake one another in n|om-like ways,
they believe they are shooting arrows of the
life force into one another.**

Try Some *Non-Purposeful* Movement

"I'm so happy when we can give each other n|om," N!yae and the other elder Bushman women tell me while we are resting after our experiences in the river of n|om. "Nothing is better than receiving n|om. We live for n|om, and n|om gives us life."

In the Kalahari, the Bushmen refer to this energetic exchange as giving each other an arrow of n|om. When Bushmen shake one another in n|om-like ways, they believe they are shooting arrows of the life force into one another. Like Cupid's quills, these arrows aim to pierce another person's heart, opening up the love that awakens the most precious emotions.

"We love when you come because we get new arrows. We are even able to drink the n|om," says Ti!ae, the oldest woman healer, who talks for everyone. Her brother was the star of the movie *The Gods Must Be Crazy*, and she is now in her eighties. Smaller in size than N!yae, she is another one of my n|om wives. She vibrates at such a high frequency that it can make you dizzy. Most people pass out when she vibrates them, and some fall over by simply watching her.

The Bushman elders and I are sitting around a roaring fire, sharing a meal of elephant meat. Everyone is in a good mood because there is plenty of food to share. As a fire-charred elephant rib is passed around, I can't help but laugh, for its gigantic size is absurd. It makes me want to be entertained by a Bushman story. "Ti!ae, remember the time that John Marshall brought that doctor to meet you?" I ask her to retell the story of when young John Marshall grew up to be an older man, came for a special visit, and was accompanied by a renowned Chinese qigong doctor. Marshall thought it would be interesting to introduce a master of a Chinese energy tradition to the Bushman doctors. All the people in the village of Tsumkwe were so excited that they couldn't wait to dance that night. They started dancing the day he arrived. When a couple of Bushman n|om-kxaosi touched the Chinese doctor, he passed out and remained unconscious for two days.

"Well, we thought he was a strong doctor. We didn't realize that he was just learning," Ti!ae and |Kunta Boo chime in. Then they all start laughing because they remember that the Chinese doctor woke up thinking he had died. He was convinced they had put a spell on him, and he wasn't able to believe that he had simply been shot by an arrow of n|om—something the powerful Kalahari doctors love receiving but only if they are strong. Everyone else in the Kalahari is a bit scared of n|om and leery of receiving a strong arrow.

I'm not saying that Chinese medicine pales to the Kalahari arrows of n|om, but I am also not saying that it doesn't. In the ancestral culture, we have thousands of years of accumulated knowledge and wisdom about the life force that was utilized before other cultures were born. Kalahari n|om is never subtle. It is lightning. It can knock you out, make you roll on the ground, throw you straight up into the air, and make you feel like someone plugged you into an electrical outlet.

Perhaps the Western discovery of Eastern medicine has been a preparation for our movement farther around the planetary circle until we arrive back to Mother Africa. In the first African spiritual tradition, a big bolt of n|om is inseparable from feeling a vast and mighty love. We do not find any stilling of emotion among the original Africans. Instead we find an awakening and an amplification of emotionally charged love, bringing forth heightened feelings that leave the operations of mind far behind while mobilizing our soulful interaction with others. Here, the intoxicating rhythms and creative soul of life such as jazz originate and propagate.

N|om wakes up the sitting meditator, ignites the passive contemplator, and supercharges the quiet pilgrim. It kicks opens the spiritual lotus flower and accentuates the movement in its opening.

Africa calls forth the spirit. It then works the spirit and allows it to transform our being. In the Kalahari, spirit always means movement. For the original Africans, stillness suggests someone who is asleep, getting ready for the next round of spirited movement. Stillness is a good thing but only a preparation for entry into spirited movement.

N|om wakes up the sitting meditator, ignites the passive contemplator, and supercharges the quiet pilgrim. It kicks opens the spiritual lotus flower and accentuates the movement in its opening. In the Kalahari, the gods are not ashamed to say that they are bored with stationary human beings. They want to play, and do so by stirring and shaking things up; they want us to spring into action. Similarly, in Ikuko Osumi's clinic, while there is a respect for stillness and rest, there is a reverence for seiki, the energy that teaches us through movement.

"Tell us again about the woman who sits to get her n|om," the Bushman women ask. They want me to repeat my stories about Ikuko Osumi. They love hearing about what other healers in the world know about n|om and the mysteries of spirit.

"She has a special chair, and when she sits on it, she allows n|om, or what she calls seiki, to move through her," I explain, pretending they haven't heard this before. "Sometimes she rocks gently, while at other times, she moves more strongly." I sit on the ground and show them. Then I stand up and say, "Sometimes the seiki makes her stand up and move like this." I wave my arms in a variety of spontaneous patterns.

"Very nice," the old n|om-kxaosi say at the same time. They recognize what is familiar to them. "She, too, shoots arrows into other people."

I demonstrate the sound she makes when she gives seiki. The women recognize it, not so much for the sound but for the energy it carries.

"Very good, very good. We are happy to hear about other doctors who actually know something," Twa pipes in. "Sometimes we meet people who come out here and claim to be doctors. When they dance, we see that they have no n|om. They don't even shake. What can we tell them? If you have no n|om, nothing can be said that can help. They haven't become soft yet."

"Yes, Ikuko Osumi would say the same," I reply. A person has to be ready to receive an arrow of n|om. You can't just say, "Give me an arrow. Fill me up." As the Bushmen say, you must first get soft.

Ikuko Osumi speaks from the background of my mind: "The soil must be prepared before the seed can go into it. Then the seed must be made ready, softened before germination. These things happen before there is fruit. You have to be softened and ripened to receive seiki."

Softness has to do with your heart being open, free of barriers from a doubting mind. Too much thinking, evaluation, conscious monitoring, comparing, performance anxiety, intellectual gamesmanship, and the like cover the heart with armor—the heavy metal protection of thoughts woven together as a kind of insulating fabric. You must be soft, both the Bushmen and Ikuko Osumi say, in order to receive. Otherwise, the n|om bounces off your shield.

N!yae starts laughing for no apparent reason. "Tell me again about those people who try to fake the movements."

I explain that some people use energy exercises, like those in the practice of tai chi, but that they don't mean to fake anything. Rather, they are practicing a movement with the hope that it will awaken the natural flow of n|om in the future. I know what N!yae wants to say, and she says it before I can articulate the next sentence: "They are upside-down. You aren't supposed to learn the movement. You are supposed to have a movement teach you." She pauses, getting herself ready to say it another way: "You aren't supposed to move the movement. The movement should move you!"

N!yae is talking about non-purposeful, improvised movement as opposed to schooled choreography. Many traditions of energy work memorize certain patterns of action, and after years and years of diligent practice, it is assumed that these patterns will one day spontaneously come forth. Ikuko Osumi and the Bushmen both propose that this approach is opposite to how we should find our way to being danced by the life force. They teach that you should allow *any* natural movement to come forth. It will then take you to the other relevant movements.

Ikuko Osumi's voice echoes again in my mind: "Your body is the teacher, doctor, and guide you have been waiting to meet. Allow it to take you somewhere. Just get out of the way and say, 'Please start.' When it knows you are sincere, it will start moving. With each movement is an unfolding, an awakening of the mysteries that are held within."

Unfortunately, we have learned to fear any opportunity that invites extreme spiritual excitement. The greatest taboo of our time does not concern wild sex, experimental drugs, or radically loud rock and roll; instead, we fear being too happy, or perhaps we don't know what to do with too much happiness. Even well-known spiritual teachers, and especially some respected facilitators of meditation, advise and sometimes scold students who get too excited and want to wiggle or move. I have heard too many stories about teachers advising against spontaneous movement. This is testimony about our cultural ignorance regarding ecstatic spiritual know-how.

Ti!ae has an assessment of spiritual teachers who are blind to the movement of spirit: "They need to come over here so we can teach them something. How sad that they are teaching. They haven't met God. Tell them to come see us. We'll be more than happy to shake them up so they'll never be the same. Just like that doctor from China." We all start laughing so hard that now we don't know whether it is the humor or the n|om that is shaking us.

Actually we do know. Convulsive laughter is inseparable from n|om: and the more you laugh, the softer you get, enabling even more n|om to fill you up. The Bushmen are not surprised that people are able to giggle themselves into health. They explain that it is simply one of the paths or tracks to n|om. Dr. Patch Adams, the medical doctor who dresses and acts like a clown, would find a homecoming in the Kalahari for his wild and crazy antics, particularly those that turn everything upside-down with outrageous tomfoolery.

Downloading the Message

Ti!ae, as if speaking for everyone, suddenly gets a serious look on her face and asks, "How are you going to teach these people? They are totally lost in words and have everything mixed up."

"You know what the ancestors and gods will say," I reply.

"That's what I thought you'd say," she answers back. "Good. Then get to work, but before you get started, let's go to the river again." The other women gather together and join Ti!ae and N!yae as they start clapping their hands and singing a n|om song. The rhythm of their music is believed to carry n|om. The intensity and syncopation escalate, as does our shaking. Soon we will all jump into the river, and that's where I will be given what I am to teach.

Into the current I fall. It's more like a whirling wind or a charged vortex of energy greater than the flow experience psychologists talk about. It is a super-flow experience that takes us out of ordinary mind and hooks us up to a bigger mind, a greater intelligence than we are capable of producing by ourselves. Its energy is neither the AC nor DC form of electricity; it's KC—Kalahari current. The river is a stream of electrical-like energy, but it is more than that: it is n|om, that which is too complex to explain but is readily recognized by how it moves the whole body.

The women n|om-kxaosi realize that they must really shake me good this time. They will vibrate my body so intensely that my spine will feel like it has an electrical cord plugged into a Kalahari spiritual power station. Their hands are on me and some of the women are wrapped around me as we become one love amoeba of pulsing bodies. They are wearing brightly colored scarves around their heads, and animal skins serve as skirts. Sometimes their breasts are exposed as they used to be in earlier times. Their necks are layered with both ostrich egg necklaces and strings of colored beads they have made, usually following a design given to them in a visionary dream. These women have a special Kalahari perfume that they carry in a small tortoise shell and use as a medicine for the dance. I feel their beads pressing into my body, and I absorb the sensual fragrance of these mothers of the earth, whose scent is an intoxicating summation of all the sweet smells of the wild bush country. Their bodies and beads shake me, and I feel a love that is more alive than any Hollywood love scene could ever convey. We are making love with old-school Kalahari vibrations. The frequencies take us past the planes of physical desire and eroticism. This is raw current, and it is sending me to the higher spiritual realms.

If they charge me enough, I'll be able to enter the downloading place, an experiential zone that I call the sacred library. It brings down more than visionary experience; it downloads all kinds of spiritual instruction and expertise in the form of images, words, music, dance, or more intense n|om. The Bushmen claim they have been going to this experiential place since the very beginning of their culture, thousands of years before anyone invented the term "akashic record." The latter refers to an assumed universal filing system in which records of all thoughts, words, and actions are kept. The Hindu yogis believe these records can be read in certain states of consciousness. The American mystic Edgar Cayce supposedly read them while in a sleeplike trance state.

While some scholars regard the akashic records as part of a cosmic or collective (un)consciousness, the founding members of this library were arguably the Bushmen, and they have quite a bit to teach us about it, but that is for later. Now, I will enter the library to find out what must be taught about the first mystery, the way in which a spontaneously moving body activates a healthy and invigorated spiritual life.

When you are deep in spirit, fully submerged in the river or ocean of n|om, you lose the ability to speak. If you open your mouth, strange sounds burst forth, filled with n|om. At this stage of immersion, you are essentially turning into n|om, becoming its dispenser and essence in every breath, sound, and action. The creation of sound separates itself from speech and meaning production in favor of shooting arrows of n|om through intense and sometimes startling bursts of sound. You've probably already heard this kind of sound when karate masters shout as they throw a physical kick. That sound, called a *kiai*, is a release of chi, or the life force. Similarly, a person full of n|om can only make sounds that are essentially the same as kiai—audio bolts of n|om.

Back in the Kalahari, the women have taken me deeper inside the n|om. I have lost my speech, and am making unrecognizable sounds and wild shrieks. They have done a superb job of preparing me for an entry into the sacred library. There, I will receive and bring back our first lesson about the original mysteries of the Kalahari.

I am slipping out of my body and being deposited into some kind of intense but unquestionably coherent force field. I am weightless and empty as I slowly and surely slide into the ethereal realm. There, a wetness and fog descend upon me. It is absorbed under the watchful eye of a softly glowing luminosity. Spotlights, heavenly and cabaret-like, shine through shadows and clouds, revealing contrasts that always change, bathing the known with the unknown. Here, as others have reported before, everything is less than nothing, and nothing is the essential something of everything. Deep inside, it is all felt and shown, heard and voiced, absorbed and released.

The First Mystery

The door to the mysteries is opened when you allow your body to show you that it is willing to be moved into a different way of being. It requires letting go of a mind that tries to harness the body. The body must be set free from this lower master and allowed to connect with higher mind. It matters not what you call this greater mind. It needs no name. Only your mind concerns itself with naming and does so to avoid the experience of being in the present that has no name.

Begin with the ancient Japanese tradition of seiki jutsu. It is your first step toward a return journey to the Kalahari. Find a bench or stool and take twenty minutes a day to sit on it with the purpose of having no purpose. By this I mean that your body should be given permission to move itself as it wishes without interference from a mind that observes and tries to understand what is going on. There is no need to explain or ask why you should sit and move in this way. The purpose, if there is one, is to step outside of the everyday habitual mind and allow a space for being hooked up to the mind of eternal wisdom—a mind that does not concern itself with being full of purpose, will, and even conscious awareness.

Sit, close your eyes, and gently touch each eye with your middle fingers. Slightly push against your eyeballs as if you are turning on a switch that sends a signal to awaken your body to take over. Allow your body to move in any way. Feel free to jump-start yourself. Wiggle a bit, rock yourself, and even allow a jolt to come forth. If you sit and sincerely wait, the movement will come. As it has for thousands of years for multitudes of people, so it will for you. You were born with the purpose of being awakened and activated in this manner. It is yours for the sincere asking.

Know that there are elder traditions that teach that this is the original authentic practice. The natural, effortless, experimental movement of your body is the ignition key for starting your spiritual engine. Anything that interferes with this process does nothing more than prevent your engine from starting.

Many will tell you that it can't be this simple. It must be more complicated and require years of study, textual examination, and elaborate initiation rites. If the people saying these things have visited the sacred library, they will have met its oldest custodians, the Bushman ancestors. They are the ones who built it and established how these things work. They will tell you what I am saying. It is their voice through which this directive is brought into the world.

Know that simple movement will lead to infinite possible movements, some little and some big; the size or intensity of movement is of no importance. It is the effortlessness of the movement that matters. The way it allows you to let go of habituated everyday mind, with all its patterns of mind control and body control, is what matters. Go even further and allow movement to let go of habituated everyday body with all its patterns of body control and mind control. Let the movement become nothing but movement. Know, without knowing how to know, that this is the coming into and the becoming of the spirit that moves, breathes, walks, and dances itself into God.

Allow any movement during your twenty-minute celebration. This includes the movement of your vocal cords should they want to move and make sound, whether soft or loud. Let movement move everything: all moments shall move and never cease their moving, changing, transforming, and creating.

In the movement is found the inspiration of life moving you to live with less effort, less mind, and less body. In the movement is found the wind, the river, the whirl, the vortex, the tracks, and the n|om. This is the first lesson. It teaches you the first steps in walking and tracking the spirit.

Be free to do this in a quiet environment or with rhythmic music. Listen to whatever directions are naturally called for in the moment. Though you start by sitting, feel free to stand or move your legs. Let your body be moved by your body, not the intentionality of mind. Let your mind be moved by your felt body, not the intentionality of intentional thought.

The only intention that matters here is the absence of intentionality. Say, "I surrender myself to the movement of my body. I have no purpose, no intention, no mind, and no body that matters. Let the movements take over."

If it helps to lighten things up, add this incantation: "Let the gods shake-and-bake me with their spiritual rock-and-roll. Let me fall into their web of spirited life." Ask yourself whether a chuckle is the knuckle of a giggle. Do not answer. Instead consider how it is truly a vibration; welcome it, embrace it, and allow it to become a convulsion that throws you into the arms of the laughing gods. Those are the gods that play, heal, and create. They are about life, and this life is the joy of creation, cosmic play, divine comedy, and awe-inspiring movement.

As you wiggle, vibrate, tremble, shake, quake, rock, and roll, allow joy and deep satisfaction to flood over you. Foster the recognition that you are learning to come into the river—the current that holds the Kalahari Bushmen and the ancient masters of Japanese seiki jutsu, along with all other ecstatic shamans, mystics, and spiritual masters. You will pass them as they go back and forth to the spiritual public library, carrying words inspired by spirit rather than derived from the limited, calculating mind, and unencumbered by heavy body stillness. Expect to lighten and rise. On the groundless high ground, expect them and they will come. Expect to be surprised, and then expect more of it. Move with this river, this wind, and this n|om, and make an allowance for the abundance of its flow.

Begin with the all the movements you embraced as a child. There you were, bobbing up and down, tapping your fingers on a desk, dancing, displaying silly movements and wild motions, while adults said, "Settle down and be still." You listened, and your world stopped. Now you wonder where children get all that energy.

Know that it can be returned today when you sincerely tell your body, "It's OK now. You can come out and play again."

Let your body express its body knowing. Set forth a revolution within all your cells. Expect your body to someday be in charge of your mind. Then let your body be released from itself in order to become well. You will know this is true when you fully understand that there is no mind separate from your body. They are one, and the limited idea of their being separate has short-circuited the necessary movements. Bring the movements back, mend the body–mind splits, and the world will move again. You will feel moved and will be a moving presence to others, a healing presence that treats the separations. The movements are the divine breathing—the rhythms that knew before there was any knowing that everything is about more than the name that can never name God. It is only about love.

Now I come back to myself.

Returning

When traveling in spirit, these last words are typically uttered to mark a return to everyday consciousness. Practice saying this line this very moment so you will know what to say when you are somewhere far away in the spirit world: *Now I come back to myself.* Simply saying this brings you back; that's how it works. Why? Don't ask because someone may be tempted to give you some explanation that will only distract you from jumping into the river. What you need is a baptism into spontaneous movement, not an explanation. You only need to take one step toward the river of n|om. Then it will come toward you. Your body has been waiting for your mind to get out of the way. Your mind has been waiting for your body to take charge. Your body has been waiting for movement to carry you away. You have been waiting to grant yourself permission to wed and release all parts of yourself.

When you are ready, the perfect teacher will come for you. The teacher has been ready since your date of birth, but when you stopped moving, it stopped teaching. Welcome back the wisdom carried by your whole body and the movement that waits to set it free. When it moves, it communicates, teaches, and liberates. It does so without needing words, ideas, and understandings. That said, sometimes you will receive words of meaning, but know that their veracity is truest for the moment in which they were delivered. Trust your body's movement to teach you how to know what is important about words and understanding. It knows, and its knowing can't be easily written down. Its deepest knowing is found in its most profound movements.

What You Receive Is What You Must Share

The women are still excited in the Kalahari after a day of shaking with n|om: "Your arrows of n|om were hot today! Thank you. I feel great," N!yae says to all of us. She is the one who gave us the strong arrows of n|om, but her n|om inspired and moved us to give n|om to her as well.

**The ropes of relationship are made strong and healthy
when we are moved by n|om.**

That's how it works in the Kalahari; there is no solo practice. No one sits in a cave to be enlightened. The n|om circulates in community. When someone gets a hot arrow of n|om, it is immediately sent to someone else. The person who receives it is then activated so that she, in turn, shoots another person with n|om. In the sharing is circulation, and in the movement inside circulation, the circles of life are strengthened and kept unbroken. The ropes of relationship are made strong and healthy when we are moved by n|om. This is what the oldest teachings want us to never forget.

In the Kalahari, there are no spiritual accidents or kundalini misfirings. As N!yae once put it, "Why would anyone be foolish enough to hold n|om inside? Share it with others!" If you try to hold the spirit, you breed selfishness and self-centeredness. Even working hard to get rid of the experience of self can be selfish. Holding in your spiritual energy, light, and inner gifts will give you spiritual constipation. That's what a Bushman thinks. What you receive is what you must share. It must go both ways to circulate, to move, to become a part of the current in the river.

Welcome to the first mystery—the ignition switch. When your movements are turned on and allowed to occur in your everyday life, you will notice a new form of vitality, well-being, and creativity in your life. The more times you turn on the switch, the more you will feel like a miracle is taking place. In Japan, these motions are considered an entry into the fountain of youth. Years of moving in this automatic way make people feel and look younger. Is jumping into the river of seiki–n|om–kundalini–life-force an entry into the fountain of youth? Let's ask the Bushmen.

"You need to be careful about that desire. You might come out of a dance looking and acting like a three-year-old," N!yae teases. "Why do you want to be young? Why settle for that? In the n|om, you can be everything—young and old at the same time. There is a better choice for you. That's another lesson, another mystery."

What you receive is what you must share.
It must go both ways to circulate, to move,
to become a part of the current in the river.

The Kalahari sun has retired, and the sky is a black canvas of pulsing stars so bright that they seem closer than usual. Wood has been chopped and gathered. Someone is making a fire. The sound of clapping is at hand; a song has begun. The women want to dance all night. Tonight they will enter eternity.

Ti!ae and N!yae ask, "Do your people know that you will be writing a n|om book? Do they know that reading the book can send arrows of n|om into them? Will you tell them? They might start shaking so much that the words get blurry!" Now we start laughing all over again. It's hard to maintain seriousness in the Kalahari. Everything is teased and brought down to pulsing, sometimes convulsing, laughter.

Suddenly N!yae stops giggling and looks concerned, as if there may be a problem. She slowly and somberly asks, "I'm very serious. Will you tell them?"

For a second, I am startled by how quickly she shifted her expression, her voice, and her presence. Then I can see that she is pretending to be serious. With the most professorial posture I can conjure, I reply with long deliberation and exaggerated authoritative importance: "I'll have to ask n|om how to answer your question." I proceed to make some weird sounds that are meant to be a lampoon of how both N!yae and Ti!'ae sound when they are full of n|om. This ignites an extraordinary laugh-fest. The giggles are recycled one more time, restarting the movements, reawakening the n|om, and reopening the door to all the mysteries.

The shape-shifting Kalahari with its shape-shifting Bushmen changes all the time. There is n|om behind all this movement. Here, you can meet a Bushman on his way to becoming a lion, end up dancing with Rumi, or have a cup of tea in samurai Japan. The Kalahari is everywhere. The Bushmen are everywhere. And, my friend, so are you!

2

FOR GOD'S SAKE,
SHAKE YOUR BOOTY!

The Second Original Mystery

All things in existence need to be shaken or rattled about...
[to be] agitated when they grow drowsy and torpid.

PLUTARCH

The spiritual equivalent of the Kalahari is New Orleans. This has been my other spiritual home for the last several decades, and I've come to believe that while you may not ever dance with Bushmen in the Kalahari sand, you can get a close approximation by tapping into the soul of this extraordinary destination. In this chapter, I will personally take you there.

Mardi Gras, jazz, king cakes, hurricanes, café au lait, beignets, crawfish, streetcars, gumbo, red beans 'n' rice, Louis Armstrong, Ernie K-Doe, Mahalia Jackson, Pete Fountain, Dr. John, Kim Prevost, Leah Chase, Harry Connick Jr., James Booker, Fats Domino, Jelly Roll Morton, the Marsalis family, the Neville Brothers, the Second Line, the French Quarter and its neighboring 'hoods—all beckon pilgrims of the spirit to travel way down yonder in New Orleans. Here, the motto *Laissez les bons temps rouler*, or "Let the good times roll," is amplified and glorified. Where else are there so many concoctions of delight brewing on each corner? The titillating aromas created by a Louisiana-inspired chef and the heavenly sounds of a brass band march together down the city streets. *La Nouvelle-Orléans* stirs our spirit because it is the soul of America. It is also a living, breathing embodiment of the Bushmen's second original mystery: let yourself be shaken!

Back in 1895, the Crescent City's Buddy Bolden was crowned the king of the cornet as his band started playing the first improvised jazz in dives, honky-tonks, and brothels, and at funerals. The Big Easy, the northernmost Caribbean city, still knows how to effortlessly infuse jazz into your everyday life, serving the beat that makes you want to boogie, shake, rock, and roll. Walking down the French Quarter's broken-slate sidewalks, which are saturated with decades of tap dancing, you only need a little bit of sound to get a hit of soul—the vibration that takes you to the same source of pulsing and convulsing movement found in the Kalahari.

Intoxicating Dixieland riffs and the never-to-be-forgotten, late-night eye-openers of Professor Longhair's piano still reverberate in the collective memory of those who love the classic music served in New Orleans. I think this every time I walk past Preservation Hall at St. Peter Street. Many of the band's charter members performed with the pioneers who evangelized jazz in the early twentieth century, including Buddy Bolden, Jelly Roll Morton, and Louis Armstrong. I'll never forget the moment when I had a brief conversation with Duke Ellington and shook his hand; I was in the presence of true royalty. As part of the royal soul-line that started in New Orleans, he inspired me to later become a jazz pianist, an aficionado of soul, and a resident of Louisiana.

Decades after leaving my home of origin, the renowned bass player of the Preservation Hall Jazz Band, Walter Payton, performed a composition of mine. It was a gospel song, "Precious Is His Love," performed at a church concert in the Lower Ninth Ward of New Orleans. Following the concert, we had a feast that included crawfish and sweet potato pie. Soul food and soul music: the two are always found together when you're with folks from New Orleans. Soul brings multisensory ecstatic delight, and it serves the whole of our being.

Though Katrina washed away most of the Lower Ninth Ward and some of the musicians who used to make their home in New Orleans, recordings of their music will always haunt this sultry spiritual home-land. No hurricane—whether libation or wind—can still the fact that the birthplace of jazz is the motherland for spiritual rebirth and soulful reentry. One of today's best kept secrets is that the French Quarter, or Vieux Carré, is a special ground zero for being hit by the syncopated and hip wisdom of the Bushmen, who long ago declared that it is good for us to shake our booty for God.

"You gotta get dirty for the Lord," I once heard a church mother in a sanctified Black Church tell me. She was talking about allowing the Lord to get a hold on me. This is something more than the faith-based pledge of allegiance suggested by mega-churches and multimillionaire television evangelists. Old-school Black Church, called "sanctified" by the renowned African American author Zora Neale Hurston, goes past the decisions and promises of a talking head. Here, spirit reaches down into the heart, down into the belly, and sometimes even further.

How do you know that you have n|om, kundalini, chi, or Holy Ghost power inside of you? The answer is simple: it makes you tremble, shake, and quake.

"Sanctified," "holy," "Pentecostal," and "charismatic" are all adjectives that refer to the emotional embrace of the sacred. In this spirit whirlwind, we become embraced by the kundalini-fired, chi-inspired, Katrina-esque Holy Ghost power. It spontaneously brings forth a cate-gory 5+ ecstatic storm whenever we sincerely initiate movement toward it. This is the eternally present realm of electrified spiritual experience. As it existed in the beginning, so it exists in our everyday reality now.

"How do you know when you have been touched by the spirit?" an inquiring visitor once asked a black preacher.

"It ain't about the knowin'," he replied. "It's about the feelin'. You have to feel the spirit. When you feel it and ask it to come inside you, then, Lord have mercy, it's gonna catch you. If you're lucky, it's gonna getta hold on you. Don't fight it. Let the Holy Spirit do its work." I can't begin to count how many times I have heard conversations like this among members of old-school Black Church.

It's the same kind of conversation I've heard in the Kalahari with the Bushmen. The metaphors are different, but it is about the same experience. I know because I have experienced what they are talking about—both in dance grounds on the Kalahari sand and in poor, though spiritually rich, Louisiana shanty houses of praise.

Toma Dahm, who, like his father and grandfather, was a great Bushman doctor of n|om, used to say, "There's nothing you can say about n|om. You have to feel it. Let its arrows get inside you. Once you get that arrow, you will live for n|om. You will hunt for more of it, eat it, drink it, and share it with others." This is the Bushman version of sanctified Black Church talk.

"God wants to cook you. Jump into God's pot and get cooked." This is Bushman spirituality.

Get Spiritually Cooked

How do you know that you have n|om, kundalini, chi, or Holy Ghost power inside of you? The answer is simple: it makes you tremble, shake, and quake.

Why would you want to shake? That answer is also simple: it is God's way of baking you. You shake in order to get spiritually baked.

N!yae likes to say it this way: "God wants to cook you. Jump into God's pot and get cooked." This is Bushman spirituality. We are meat for the gods to cook. They want to boil us. At other times, they bake us. Or fry us. The original people, the first hunter-gatherers, say that it all comes down to hunting, cooking, and eating, which get you ready to make love.

One of my mentors was the distinguished Cambridge-educated anthropologist Gregory Bateson. He thoroughly relished giggling over a joke he first heard as a schoolboy: "The Lord is my shepherd, but then to whom does he sell you?" I don't think that he ever realized how much truth his twisted irony held. The gods are leading us to a pot, and the spiritual journey is ultimately about getting cooked. Lost lambs, get ready to be found. You are spiritual meat looking for God's kitchen.

"God ain't a vegetarian," Mother Samuel told me in a St. Vincent praise house. "He wants to cook the meat of your soul."

If you've been cooked, you know why this is a perfect metaphor. When the spirit gets inside you, it feels hot. At first, you may think there is a fire in your belly. Or it may feel like the erupting flow of molten lava. It moves inside, and it causes you to move on the outside. Some folks will flop around more than others. While a few will be arrested, immobilized, and stunned by the current inside, others will be overtaken and find themselves unable to hold back the automatic motion of wild movement. It will fly right out of them, and they will look like they are hopping, as if trying to get airborne, over hot coals.

As |Kunta |Ai!ae once told me after a dance in Chokwe, one of the Bushman villages in northeastern Namibia, "Bo, you did good last night. You stood on the hot coals and danced over them. Your n|om is strong. You are being cooked."

Some of the n|om-kxaosi do more than walk on hot coals. They stand on their head in the fire. Of course, the people have to pull them out because their hair will burn. Though outsiders are impressed with this feat, elder Bushmen see it as an early stage of working with the n|om. Later, when the spirit lives inside you, there is no need to stand on fire because you have become a spiritual fire.

Spirit is a powerful current, a blazing movement, and a mighty wind. It easily can become a sacred hurricane that turns everything upside-down and inside-out. When the spirit is awakened, you will literally be thrown into the midst of a gale. It will not only blow your mind, it will whirl and twirl your body about. God's rock-and-roll is the extreme shake-and-bake.

The purpose of Bushman spirituality is to get fully cooked by God. It is also n|om jazz, Holy Ghost bebop, and kundalini Dixieland. It is spiritual hot sauce—a spicy awakening that is gumbo perfect. The here and now of spiritual experience, as differentiated from sideline spiritual commentary, requires stepping inside a French Quarter state of mind-in-body. Body and soul, taste and music go hand in hand in the whole holiness of soul business.

"You can't make soul music without soul food," Mother Samuel used to say. Mother Samuel was one of the most revered spiritual "Shakers of St. Vincent" on the Caribbean island that is home to one of the most active mystical cultures to be found anywhere. These relatives of the Bushmen know how to move themselves into other times and places. Mother Samuel brought people to God by fixing them a meal. I'm serious. She was a mojo chef. I don't know what else to call the way she cooked. She would take a few ingredients like peas, chicken, and a bit of spice and make the best dish you've ever tasted. Her secret? She prayed and sang spirited gospel songs while she was cooking.

"Lord God, Almighty," she explained, "whenever I pray and sing over the food, I can feel the spirit going into it. You just can't find a better seasoning than that." She cooked for me, and I can testify that her food was a sanctified feast. Cooks of the old-school way know that their love and prayers can be poured into their preparations. Home cooking means just that: home is getting cooked into the meal. It is transmitted by the soul express, delivered through songs and prayers from the heart.

Mother Samuel has since gone on to be with her Maker. In a funeral that brought out at least a thousand people to mourn her passing, we marched her coffin down the mountain in St. Vincent while singing and dancing in the streets. I was asked to do some preaching (or shouting, as they call it) and led the congregation in singing a song. I used the opportunity to praise how Mother Samuel was a special spiritual mother who taught us that prayer and song, as well as soul and taste, must be joined together. Side by side, you get a double whammy of soul. Or perhaps I should say, a double yummy.

Allow every step and movement of your everyday life to both drizzle and sizzle with soul. Not the abstract psychological soul popularized by intellectuals. I am talking about the soul embodied in the rhythmic expression of Ray Charles, Stevie Wonder, Aretha Franklin, and Janis Joplin. This soul makes you want to dance and shake your booty. It fills you with the life force, and it leads you straight to God's frying pan.

The Gods Want to Play

"Jump in! Time to get cooked!" I shout to a group that has gathered for a participatory performance of shaking medicine. We are on a stage at the Omni Shoreham Hotel ballroom in Washington, DC, and I am playing African drums while the music from my band is blaring in the background. On keyboards is Ed Prevost Jr., vocals are provided by Kim Prevost, and guitar is played by Bill Solley, all seasoned New Orleans–based musicians who have many years of improvisational experience in Black Churches, blues clubs, jazz festivals, and other musical venues. I have already explained that the only teaching that will deliver the true, authentic, spirited goods involves getting cooked by God. If a teacher gives you words and you do not feel shaken, then you haven't been cooked. That's a spiritual wind job—air has been blown to make the sound of words, but no one has shaken their booty.

"God doesn't want you to be serious. God isn't interested in talk. God wants to play and make music. God wants you to feel the ecstatic fire of sanctified and glorified joy. Get down so God can lift you up." I paraphrase what my Bushman, St. Vincent, and Louisiana elders have said to me over the decades. They never prepare for an intimate encounter with God by getting overly serious and pious. They tease their minds and loosen one another up with contrary absurdity and lighthearted, sensuous expression.

As G|ao'o, one of the oldest elders I met in the Kalahari, said, "The gods want to play. Make yourself interesting to them. Show them you are fun to play with."

You need to make yourself noticed by God.
You are the bait, and you want God to catch you.

If you were God, would you be bored with those religious rituals that have lost the zest in their fest? Would God show up to a church service that feels like a funeral? God is looking for playmates ready to be alive. God doesn't want you to have a near-death experience. A bona fide close encounter with sacred mystery is a near-life experience!

You need to make yourself noticed by God. You are the bait, and you want God to catch you. Wiggle yourself just like you jiggle a fishing lure when you are trying to catch a fish.

I recommend this immediate course of action: Attach a piece of string or fishing line to your bedroom ceiling so that it falls directly over your heart when you are lying in bed. Consider this God's fishing line. Pause for a moment and consider what new name you would like to have if God caught you, cooked you, and made you a spiritually reborn human being. Write down your fantasy of what this new nickname would be. When this is written on a small piece of paper, attach it to the end of the line as bait.

When you go to sleep each night, think of being caught by God and reeled into a pot, and then imagine being shaken by the ecstatic experience of receiving a direct transmission of God's love. Make sure that you wiggle the bait before you fall asleep. One night, you will dream a vision that suggests you were caught and then spent some time getting cooked. Set yourself up so God will catch you and toss you into the frying pan.

Shaking your booty for God means . . . you are absolutely sincere about wanting to be more connected to the spiritual current . . . and enthusiastic about anticipating the forthcoming storm.

"Stop praying! God is bored with your words." I actually say this to people to startle them into considering other ways of communicating with the divine. Pray through action and movement. Rather than talk to God, dance for the heavens before you hop into bed. God wants to know that you mean business. Your mind is so wordy that it is hard for any message to get delivered when it is wrapped with too many words.

You talk too much, especially inside your head. There is too much internal noise for a clear signal to get through. Jump twelve times for God and you'll be more likely to be noticed.

Shaking your booty for God means that you are showing God that you are absolutely sincere about wanting to be more connected to the spiritual current, and that you are happy and enthusiastic about anticipating the forthcoming storm. Like the soulful residents of New Orleans, check the sky. And when the conditions are right (or wrong), don't get scared and run away. Throw a hurricane party.

Shake to lure yourself into being caught by God. Don't just jump in the stream, wiggle and bob, and make some commotion. There is no need to say more than: "Lord, please take me and make me. Shake me and bake me." It's this simple. But we have complicated this ease of divine access by coming up with endless ways of explaining why it can't possibly be this simple.

Take a Pilgrimage to the Swamp

Join me this very moment in the French Quarter, but don't cover your eyes, ears, nose, or mouth. Open your imagination and take it all in. Don't resist being shaken. Here is the swamp of human experience. Complexity is found in a swamp; it holds many contraries including light and dark. A swamp is not crystal-clear water. It is water and dirt mixed together. It has beautiful birds soaring in the sky while snakes and alligators swim in the muddied waters. Soul, like life, thrives in a swamp.

"God lives in the swamp. That's where you need to go if you need some heavenly counsel," the old Louisiana preachers used to say to their soul-hungry parishioners. "There ain't much soul on a mountaintop with its white-as-a-sheet snow. Soul needs some dirt mixed in so we can get a nice spiritual gumbo. It's simply too cold on the high ground, and it brings on the wrong kind of shiver. You need to get closer to the ground, buried in the soil, covered with the mud before God can do some work on you. God wants you to get into the swamp. That's where the old timers found their visions."

Zora Neale Hurston, part of the Harlem Renaissance movement, conducted some ethnographic research for the anthropologist Frank Boas at Columbia University. She went to Florida and collected first-person accounts of preachers and members who were a part of the sanctified Black Church. She met a preacher, the Reverend Jesse Jefferson, who told her that he went to a swamp. There, he fasted and prayed for a vision. When he arrived, God threw him on an operating table and performed spiritual surgery. He was opened up, and several luminous balls of light were placed inside him. That's how he became a preacher. With that holy fire and light inside, he was able to shout and heal. He found what he was looking for in the swamplands.

Puritans look for clean and tidy spaces to hold the presence of God. The trouble is that God is bored with vanilla ice cream. God wants Neapolitan, a complex marbling of diversity. And God wants a lot of hot fudge, nuts, and whipped cream on top. The bottom line is that holiness lives in the swamps. Yes, the sacred is present everywhere, including Santa Fe and Sedona, but God thrives in New Orleans.

Don't believe me? Ask yourself how many jazz clubs there are in the new age meccas and how many folks there get the spirit inside them on a daily basis, bringing forth ecstatic music and dance. Are the majority of seekers just talking and sitting in a frozen pretzel posture? Is their food spicy, and does it offer a special kick? Does their music have soul? I am exaggerating to make a point, but on the other hand, I just might be understating the situation.

Do you know what it means to miss New Orleans? It is the deep longing for spirited soul. It is the intense hunger for soul food, soulful music, spirited dance, and wild, ecstatic, celebrative praise, whether it be voiced by the ghosts of former African slaves on Congo Square or by the choirs of old-time Black Churches, or the bands backing Second Line dancers, or the street music in dialogue with window shoppers and feast-ready patrons.

It's time for the next spiritual age. I am not the first to say this nor am I the first to announce that the new age is past due for a meaningful ripening and maturation. We now have the treasure map. It is time to set sail in search of the spirited gold. We need a pilgrimage to the swamp. I'll say it again so it is loud and clear: we have been looking in the wrong direction. The loot has been right behind us. Turn around and face the opposite direction. Come down from the mountain and go below sea level. There, you will find the complexity of a swampy port town. The *New Age* is over; we have outgrown it. Now is the time for *New Orleans*.

Like us, this port is decaying, making itself ready for the transformation of death into rebirth. There, the Rebirth Brass Band, among other brass bands that make their way to Donna's Bar and Grill on Rampart Street, celebrates the fact that soulful music arises out of a blues howl. In addition, New Orleaners have the *Alligator mississippiensis* as their mythical phoenix. Out of the swamp arises this living fossil that has survived for over two hundred million years. No matter how murky the water that covers it, it will surface over and over again to have another round in the sunshine. The Bushmen similarly know the *Crocodylus niloticus* that hangs out in its mud-lined deltas. Both the Kalahari and New Orleans know the old meat eaters, the spirited rhythms, and the importance of having their souls cooked by God.

Make Room for Spiritual Treasure

"Come on down, y'all. We've got some spirited gumbo almost close to a boil. We'd be more than happy to throw you into the pot. You been lookin' f'dat pot. Nothing less will get you cured, seasoned, and ready for spirit. Where y'at! It's time you served yourself—you are the meat in need of cooking. Dawlin', don't be bashful. Go ahead and embarrass yourself. It will help put your self in its rightful place. Make some room for your soul to get something extra, some spiritual lagniappe."

You can't get anywhere unless you move.
Shake your booty to find God's treasure.

Throwing yourself into the pot is a way of talking about the surrender to spiritual alchemy that has been around since the beginning of Kalahari spirituality. It's yet another invitation to be on the old ship Zion, always available for journeys into the spiritual lands.

The spirited shamanism of journeying is not done in stillness. You can't get anywhere unless you move. Shake your booty to find God's treasure; that's the pirate's call. I like to think of Bushmen as spiritual pirates, sailing across the sands of the Kalahari, always ready to seize some n|om gold. In fact, Johnny Depp brought Cap'n Jack Sparrow to life in cinematic splendor on the island of St. Vincent. Down here, we are all pirates aboard a mystical ship that takes us on voyages throughout the seas in search of spiritual gold.

New Orleans has a fascinating history of pirates, and not all of it has been heard and duly appreciated. General Andrew Jackson's defeat of the British Army in the Battle of New Orleans was due to Jean Lafitte, a flagless buccaneer often called the Gentleman Pirate and the Terror of the Gulf. He had an armada of fifty ships, spoke four languages, and looted the treasures of the rich. He was the one who prevented the British from capturing New Orleans on January 8, 1815.

Even today, New Orleans has its pirates. Every year it hosts PyrateCon, a weekend devoted to dressing up and talking like a pirate. We're not talking about having any positive regard for the modern day looters who attack ships. This celebration engages our mythopoetic imagination with those early swashbucklers who had some admirable traits. It is done in the spirit of fun like the doubloons of Mardi Gras, the silver coins minted every year for the various krewes to be thrown from their floats during parades. The sound of a doubloon hitting the cement can start a stampede. It inspires a crowd to shout, "Da-blooon! Da-blooon!"

Make room for some spiritual treasure to enter your heart. Ask the gods to throw you something. Listen to the sound of change that hits the ground with a percussive effect. There is a parade going by, and spiritual gifts are being thrown to you every moment. Wake up and see this marvelous party—this once-in-a-lifetime, never-ending, greatest show on Earth.

Has someone put a spell on you, making you afraid to be too happy, embarrassed to show too much joy, and timid about letting spirit have some fun with you? Then you need some gris-gris (pronounced "gree-gree"): some voodoo/hoodoo medicine that aims to ward off a problematic spell. There's a voodoo shop on Dumaine Street in the Quarter that will make you a gris-gris bag. Or you can make your own.

Look at the pinkie finger of your left hand. When is the last time you paid any serious attention to it? I bet that thumb or middle finger of yours gets more attention, doesn't it? Now we are going to change this situation. Take a black marking pen and write G-G (for gris-gris) on your left pinkie. Do you know why this finger is called a pinkie? It's because the Dutch word *pink* means "little finger." The same Dutch word inspired the term used to describe early Mediterranean merchant ships. They were called pink due to their narrow stern. Those ships carried the goods—the treasure and gold—of merchants.

Look at that pinkie of yours and know that its name is similar to the name of a ship filled with goods. Consider it the stern of your ship. In both a metaphorical and imaginary way, you are a pirate on a spiritual ship. Let us ritualistically declare the name of your ship as G-G. Consider the nail of your pinky as the ship flag. As long as you can see the letters G-G, know that you are sailing on spirit-filled waters. If the letters start to fade, write them again.

"Hoist the colors!" You are about to set sail with some new gris-gris. This flag will ward off any spells that want to deaden your imagination, stop you from ecstatically moving, and prevent the wind of spirit from blowing. Carry your flag with you at all times, for your tiniest fingernail carries a message, a declaration that there is gris-gris at hand.

Enter the water without fear and sail boldly ahead. "Batten down the hatches, mateys!" Become a spiritual pirate unafraid of anything or anyone who tries to keep you overly sedated and comatose. This is the only dose of protection you will ever need. Your pirate flag is to be worn with a smile and kept a secret from all, except for those potential mateys you are trying to recruit for another spirited armada.

In the Crack between Light and Dark

Back in the Kalahari sea of sand, Toma Dahm and I are holding one another during an inspired dance. We have danced throughout the night, and the sun will soon come up. That is when the n|om is strongest. As the sun first begins to appear on the edge of the horizon, its sliver of light injects every dancer with more intense feeling and inspiration. This is when you can pick someone up off the ground and hold him over your head—if you are one of the strongest n|om-kxaosi.

**This suspension of opposites, the line that separates
day from night, is the moment when n|om opens
the door to the world of the eternal.**

Toma and I are holding on to each other. The shaking vibrations of n|om are preparing us for entry into the sacred realms. Today we will go there together. The crack between the worlds only appears for a moment. It appears when the sun first marks the difference between night and day. It has its greatest power at that instant when neither night nor day has an advantage. It must be equally light and dark, hanging in the middle as an opening and departure for both. This suspension of opposites, the line that separates day from night, is the moment when n|om opens the door to the world of the eternal. Here, everything ever experienced—in the past, present, and future—is held simultaneously. This is the space of eternity. It is timeless and infinite. It is also an entrance to the library of all wisdom and spiritual know-how.

"Bo, we are one today," Toma feels. He is feeling this, not thinking it. When the vibration fully grabs hold of you, there is no consciousness that makes speech and thought. Only later can we use words to evoke what we were feeling.

"Yes, Toma, we are the ancestors." I feel this without thinking it. When I feel it without thought, there is no doubt, no arrogance, no humility, no knowing, and no commentary. There is simply the authenticity of raw, naked, unedited emotion, the language of the heart. This is our highest state of being. It is not quiet or still. This time is for making sound and movement.

"Bo, as you are on my back, I am on the back of my father, who is embracing his grandfather. Every ancestor is holding up the other."

"Yes, Toma, I feel my grandfather as well, and we are all holding one another. We are all becoming one thread, one line, one track."

"That's right," Toma responds in this communication that has no time and no logic with its immediacy and directness of heart-to-heart being. "This track is a rope coiled up inside your heart. When awakened, it will spring forth and lay itself before you. The track is inside you. It is held by all the ancestors, and all those who are bound together with love and longing."

The moment the rope is uncoiled and straight, we find ourselves moving on it; it happens the second it is opened. I am gliding along the route it has made. Into the so-called akashic record I go. I actually shouldn't use this name, for it is neither a library nor a record in the way that we think of those notions. It has nothing to do with book knowing. It is heart knowing; this is a library of feelings. It would be more accurate to call this place a sacred heart library of spirited feelings.

We could go on to say that this library is a part of the University of Sacred Hearts Divine. That's where the classrooms and wisdom traditions are held—they are inside God's heart. God's mind is a heart, and it feels. Thinking, as we habitually know it, is not necessary. Thinking, talking, and writing are instruments for play, not the luminous work of sacred transmission.

**We become the other—whether a friend,
butterfly, redwood forest, giraffe, or seahorse—
through our intensely felt union with it.**

When Bushmen say they own something, it means not only that they own the feeling for it but also that the feeling has transmitted its essence, its complex nexus of relationships, into their very being. We become the other—whether a friend, butterfly, redwood forest, giraffe, or seahorse—through our intensely felt union with it.

"You have to make love with God," Toma once told me. "The rest of the world seems to have had a marriage ceremony with God, but their marriage hasn't been consummated."

Years later, in a Louisiana swamp town, a former pastor confessed to me that after listening to my stories, he prayed to God requesting a more direct emotional experience with the divine. He had a dream that night in which God spoke to him: "You have married me, but we have not had sex."

"Awesome, Kevin," I replied. "You've had yourself a Bushman-like vision. What an extraordinary metaphor for intimacy. Yes, feeling God is akin to having sex or making love with God. It is a transmission and a reception of the highest and most powerful love."

Toma would be very happy to know that a man in Louisiana was learning how to be like a Bushman. If God is love and we get close to this big love, then how could it not be as amazing as the most intimate experiences of sexuality? The fact is that it goes way past human sexuality. It completely blows one's mind, heart, and soul. Literally, you may feel like your head is blown off your body and thrown into a rocket flight through outer space.

There are infinitudes of sacred experiences. This is what makes being human so open-ended and laden with the potential for surprise and never-before-imagined possibilities. However, let it be known that when we speak of encountering God's love, it is not something we can calmly receive while sitting still on the floor. It is more like receiving a trillion volts of electricity. Its power will make you move. It is a lightning bolt that cooks you to a crisp. A jolt from God, and the rapturous shaking brought about by it, feels awesome. It is not painful unless you fight it. Letting it come into your heart without resistance is the *piece de résistance* (main course) of life.

"Bo, you are becoming me as I am becoming you."

"Toma, we have become the ancestors and are moving toward the gods."

Quivering at such a high frequency, we have converged into a physical blur. We look like two intoxicated men with arms wrapped around each other, pulsing as if wires were attached to us, carrying electricity from a diesel generator placed in the Kalahari. Yes, Kalahari current—KC—is flowing through both of us.

We are singing, or rather n|om is zooming in, through, and out of us. Our bodies start to feel like they are stretching. I feel taller than a tree. I am becoming a thin line as I walk toward the streak of daybreak light in front of me. Into the heart of God I go, into the tender library that holds feelings that inspire words of wisdom readily available to heart-opened attendees. Entering the realm of the second mystery, there is music and rhythm present for its delivery. The drums are playing wildly while shrieks of joyous, wild delight intersperse the melodic lines that are ecstatically woven into the fabric of this Kalahari jazzfest.

Shake to make yourself clear.... Shake to become open to spirit. Shake because nothing else has sufficiently sustained itself and this is the opposite of everything else. Shake that booty because you simply feel like doing it no matter what anyone thinks.

In this crack of morning light, this dawn that mirrors evening twilight, is a holy passing. It reminds me of the resurrection in a St. Vincent mourning ceremony in which we lament the darkness in our lives, and when we fully and sincerely surrender to longing for any ray or sliver of transformative light, we find it comes and transforms our pain into heavenly joy, lifting any overbearing sorrow into unlimited bliss.

In the Kalahari, an all-night dance feels like it will kill you because the spirit refuses to say no, always moving you, and shaking you all night until you feel like it is impossible to keep going. Then, at the moment when you are passing into what seems like physical death, the straight and narrow line of morning light reveals a door that is slowly but surely opening—an escape route from the tiredness and overwhelming duty of being a human shell serving the play of the gods. At that moment, but only for a moment, you are instantly filled with the greatest strength and happiness possible. In the crack between light and dark is found the gate between life and death, and the crossing between human beings and the gods.

Get crazy for God, foolish for spirit, and wild for the holiness of all that is sacred.

Into the crack, the line of light, we fall and rise. Slowly revolving, becoming part of the luminous flux, sounding the melody of the turning—it has begun again. Inside a dynamo of creation, I merge with the oceanic waves of heart-centered emotion that teach us about the second mystery.

The Second Mystery

While natural movement helps light the spiritual fire and get things started, a full surrender to being used for the vibratory expression of the gods marks entry into the transitional realm of spirit. Here, we align ourselves with the spiritual fine line that announces each newborn day. This avenue of the dawning ray is the track for every sacred journey.

Wild movement always accompanies ecstatic joy. You will move when you truly have heightened joy. Being ecstatically happy triggers a natural body response to be in motion. This ecstatic movement is automatic. It requires no effort or learning; it just happens. It may include trembling, fluttering, quivering, shaking, quaking, rocking, bobbing, jumping, jolting, and even convulsing.

What is the sign that spirit is in your vicinity? You feel like something is taking over you—something other than the control exercised by habituated patterns that maintain membership in the status quo of normality. Instead, you get crazy for God, foolish for spirit, and wild for the holiness of all that is sacred.

We have been hexed to devalue, negatively connote, discredit, caution against, inhibit, prohibit, and even become scared and fearful of allowing spirit to express itself through our whole body, mind, heart, and soul. This is not the case with the Kalahari Bushmen and all those cultures that have not forgotten the original forms of a moving spirituality.

Imagine that long ago someone banned singing. Worse, consider if they had declared that song was dangerous, an unharnessed form of speech that acoustically shifted too much and led to the production of sound being too out of control, and possibly causing loss of speech and mind. In such an irrational climate of culturally prescribed meaning, if a song started to come out of your mouth, it would likely scare you. Fearful of the possibility that it might cause a pathological nosedive, you'd do everything you could to stop it and never permit it to happen again.

This is essentially what social control agents have instituted against ecstatic expression. You have been taught that it is unhealthy, even dangerous, to experience and express too much joy. The big prohibition was not about getting high on drugs but about getting high on God.

It is time for you to see that your spiritual expression has been frozen by a curse or cultural spell. It is time for you to snap out of your spiritual hibernation. Shake off the hex and go past illusions of sex—enter the course with the whole universe. Go for a whole-soul spiritual flight of ultimate delight. Say yes to the movements that awaken your deep-rooted desire to be fully and vibrantly alive.

Wake up and make yourself available to the movements that life throws to you, whether it's a slight wiggle of a finger or a whole-body roll upon the floor.

Shake your booty like your African ancestors did! You've spent enough time hearing about the offerings of both the Far East and the Far Out. Now keep circling the world and get to the mother continent, Africa. There, you will see how your ancestors never stopped shaking with joy. Their way was never far out. It was far inside the original way, the first home of spirituality.

Shake to make yourself clear. Shake away the nonsense, the talk, the meanings, and the never-ceasing inner and outer babble that thrive on the attentiveness of a stilled audience. Shake to become open to spirit. Shake because nothing else has sufficiently sustained you and this is the opposite of everything else. Shake that booty because you simply feel like doing it no matter what anyone thinks.

Yes, trauma and fear also make us shake, and that is part of the way the body protects and heals itself. But joy shakes you to send you on your way to the land of spiritual milk and honey. In the Kalahari, shaking is valued and promoted. People live to find n|om to experience the way it brings relationship and community, the matrix for optimal engagement with the mysteries of the spiritual universe.

Utilize the music and rhythms that inspire you to move. Do more than dance. Dance is too much an orchestrated means of maintaining a preconfigured way of control. It attempts to follow a pattern, a sequenced choreography of movement. Get out of the way, dance out of the way, and simply be shaken. What I am talking about is not making a movement. The second mystery concerns how you have a built-in mechanism that enables you to be moved by something outside your control. Find the switch labeled "Available for Wild Body Movement," and then let your mind-over-body take a hike.

Something is waiting to grab hold of you, to shake you up, and to prepare your heart for the highest vibrations. This is the stream you are trying to jump into. It's a river of energized waves of joy that are moving in many directions. When you get inside that stream, allow it to carry you somewhere. Not only will you travel, you will get what you need, whether it is healing, lessons, direction, or another good shaking.

The mystery of ecstatic shaking has been called shaking medicine. The Kalahari way of healing knows that being shaken by the spirits is the strongest medicine of them all. It tunes you, removes whatever is stagnant and dirty, refreshes your vitality, and prepares you for all the other mysteries.

When the gods shake you, only then may you say that you are being cooked; spiritual heat does that to you. It moves you about because it is getting inside you, stretching your heart, mind, body, and soul. Allow it to do its work. Ask it to do more than bump against you and knock on your door. Ask spirit to enter and live inside you. Be a home for spirit, and be at home with spirit.

When the spirit lives inside you, you become a spiritual jumping bean. Now you will tremble, vibrate, and shake whenever the spirit decides to move you. Don't worry about it getting into trouble because all *of this will become comfortably natural and you will be thrilled with its way of traversing everyday life. As you settle into being a shaker, the shaking will only come when it is appropriate. It will be as subtle or as explicitly expressive as it needs to be. Trust it.*

Your language-focused mind is an idiot; only spirit has wisdom. No matter how much book knowledge or street smarts you have, it won't help with spiritual affairs. Spiritual wisdom is only voiced by spirit. You may be its instrument, but you don't know jack squat. Get over yourself and allow spirit to take over. Easier said than done. And it's never done.

This is a daily invitation. We are addressing a recurrent twenty-four-hour revolution. You must awake each morning ready to start from a new beginning. Do not assume that you are any wiser the morning after a shaking encounter with God. Your mind is still there, up to all its old tricks. Give it just enough attention to help you giggle and enjoy the absurdities of how desperate it is to be in charge. The less mindfulness you are able to present on the center stage of your everyday life, the better for the whole of you and your interactions with others. Go for the awakened feelings. They carry old-school, finely seasoned wisdom.

Though many speak of the path of heart, few walk with heart. Words are tricky. Just because someone speaks about love, spirit, and heart does not mean that any of these things are embodied. You must care less about what you say or hear and be more concerned with what rhythms and music are present in your life. Spirit rides in on a rhythm, not a meaning. It truly doesn't mean a thing if it ain't got much swing, for it needs the ring-a-ding thing of more ecstatic swing.

The ancestors are asking you to navigate round and round the circle that is unbroken; this circle holds all the relationships of your life. Everything that has come to you, including both the good and the bad, the beautiful and the ugly, holds you in a unique orbit. No matter how much you try to break away from any part, your connection will remain intact. You can't ever leave home, even when you have packed your bags and started walking away. Home is where the relations hold and move you. The farther you try to move away, the closer you are to coming back. It's all a circle.

Stop fighting the circularities of life. Sure, there are parts that you prefer and other parts that you wish weren't present. That's the complexity of a rich life. Mojo, whether found in Louisiana or the Kalahari, utilizes the awareness of how everything is connected in a circular way. Start anywhere and keep moving; it's the motion that brings you home.

You want spirit in your life? Then get back into the swamp. That's where spirit lives. It doesn't want you to run away from complexity; it wants you to be shaken by it. Learn to live with the alligators and the snakes as well as with the birds and the butterflies. The light line between day and night is your lifeline.

It's spiritual roundup time! Move inside the sacred circle that sustains your life. The circle you have stepped into is the end of God's rope, a lasso dropped from heaven. Let the spiritual rodeo begin.

For the next event, you're on a bucking bull called Your Life. Do your best to ride the ups and downs of another bullish day. Avoid getting thrown off by staying in sync with the movements rather than opposing them. God has a bull ride for you, each and every day.

In the Kalahari, a rodeo awaits those who want to ride the n|om. Jump on it and let it take you away. Believe me, you will sometimes look like you are on a wild bull! As you master the art of n|om riding, each ride will be an unexpected adventure. Surrender to the experience for it is always perfectly designed for you, even when you don't have a clue as to what is going on. Whether you ride a bull or are roped in, know that you will be both lassoed and bucked in the Kalahari rodeo.

I feel the n|om taking me across a vast desert. Below me are all the animals with their African splendor. They, too, are lassoed, bucked, and taken on one journey after another. Like us, they are heading for God's pot, ready to be cooked and made into meat for the transformational show of Mother Nature. Ready yourself for being held between heaven and *earth so that the light and dark will toss you up and down, filling you with life, even though it appears to be taking your life. Surrender to the movement. Enter the crack between life and death.*

Now I come back to myself.

What Happens When You're Moved by Spirit

I am in a theater in San Francisco where a performance of shaking medicine has come to life. Spirit was called, and it has swept into the room like a hurricane of whirling and swirling emotion. We are in the Kalahari as well as in the French Quarter. We are everywhere, as the experiential locale changes at any moment.

A woman participant, a traditional holder of ancient Cheyenne medicine from Lame Deer, Montana, enters the dreamtime. Her grandfather comes to her in a vision, saying, "This holds even greater truth than what we taught you. Trust it."

Another person, from Phoenix, Arizona, steps into a transformation and is reborn with a mission to give rather than to receive. I ask our resident Jewish scholar to grant him a Hebrew name. The naming brings forth another visionary trip where he is danced and celebrated.

All of our errors, mistakes, sins, and faults
are shaken and cleansed in this quake
brought on by the mighty spirit.

Shape-shifting, time-shifting, and place-shifting: all are part of the wild, bucking n|om rodeo. Here, everything shifts, changes, and transforms while bringing a spiritual earthquake that runs along the fault line. All of our errors, mistakes, sins, and faults are shaken and cleansed in this quake brought on by the mighty spirit. In this groundbreaking movement, angst, guilt, and overbearing tension are sincerely uncovered and released. Here, we are resettled to return home born again, with new hope for being inside the circle of our life.

In these ecstatic performances, the Kalahari is reborn, brought to life anywhere at any time. We are all archetypal Bushmen unconsciously looking for the tracks that take us to God. We bring the dark with us, and it is one of our greatest resources. The light cannot be revealed unless there is darkness on which it can be seen. Our imperfection and human failings provide the stage for the gods to express their perfection. They need us as much as we need them. The sacred and profane, like night and day, are searching for the cracks in between. There, the Kalahari dances with the universe.

I come home from San Francisco with a buzz, an honest-to-God slam bam of spiritual intoxication. It's the same high that Louisiana members of sanctified church know about. When the spirit breaks free and whips everyone around, they say, "That was a good Holy Ghost party." They, too, go home high on God. That's what happens when you reach the highest spiritual bar: God becomes your bartender, and you get drunk on the spirit.

After getting the spirit in this old-school way, just like it happens in an all-night Kalahari Bushman dance, you can go to sleep filled with a vibration. After the performance, I arrive home with a vibrant, high-frequency pulse running from the top of my head to the bottom of my spine. Upon going to bed that night, I wonder whether I'll venture on a journey to the spiritual lands. Luck is with me, for I slip right into a visionary sanctified church. The singing is extraordinary. I hear familiar songs and original songs never heard before. Sometimes I wake up to write down these songs, but this night, I can't leave the service. It is too good to depart.

When I do wake up, I am still in this visionary state of spiritual mind and heart. I remain in that church. The music continues as I pulse and vibrate along with its soulful expression. This lasts for hours. I slip in and out of consciousness, but never out of church. I sing, pray, and even preach.

In one of my prayers, I begin with these words: "Let us pray inside the Lord. . . ." The words fall from my lips, and I am deeply moved. A few people are by my side at a college campus setting where the service has now place-shifted. More and more people come until there is a large crowd. The praying intensifies, and the emotions follow in kind. I begin to weep with joy. In this rapture, I wake myself up. Though the words of my prayer were understood in English when I was inside the dream—in the night of spirit—when I wake up, I am speaking in tongues, or what the Bushmen call n|om talk.

I immediately get out of bed and go to my computer. I enter some of the words of my prayer into a Google search. To my surprise, a PBS website pops up with a story and video clip about a "circuit rider," an old-fashioned itinerant preacher who travels from one small town to another, handling services at several churches each Sunday. These preachers keep the old-time religion alive for country parishioners in the South. This practice started in nineteenth-century America, when they rode on horseback rather than travelled by automobile.

The circuit rider in the story is Pastor Brown. He drives an old Chevy and pastors seven churches in Mississippi and Louisiana. He preaches with the words that were delivered in my visionary nighttime church: "I been sometimes up, sometimes down, sometimes right, sometimes wrong, but I go to somebody. He takes me in his arms. He rocks me when I'm weary. He tells me that I'm his own. Oh, he's all right. He's all right."

The circuit rider is a vanishing breed, and no one knows how many are still around. I continue reading the article. Pastor Brown barely makes enough money to pay his bills, but he keeps preaching: "I come to tell you that the world's greatest need is God. Not gold but God. Not silver but salvation. Not lumber but love. Not gas but grace."

I am shaking as I read his words. I heard them that same night and felt them come out of my mouth. Then I am jolted as I read the last paragraphs: Pastor Brown lives near me. He is a neighbor, and the churches he visits are in the same Mississippi Delta towns where I visit families in trouble as part of my work as the clinical director of a social service agency.

The next morning is my day to travel to Tallulah, a town close to the Mississippi River. Few people are home this morning. My colleague and I see a crowd gathering at a local church, so we go over to see what is going on. It is a funeral. I ask the first person I talk with whether he knows a Pastor David Brown. He replies, "I'm a musician for his services." He says Pastor Brown is out of town for a while.

When we finally arrive at the court-appointed session we are to conduct, we pull up to a housing project. Gang members of the Bloods are standing outside, displaying their colors. The leader comes close to our car but doesn't say anything. We go to the apartment we are to visit, and this young man follows us. Turns out, he is the brother of the woman we are to work with. He comes inside and stands in the living room so he can observe us.

Rather than starting a family therapy session, I speak without thinking, "I was up most of the night and am a bit tired today. I was in a Black Church in my dreams and kept hearing gospel music I had never heard before." I look at the young man and ask, "Do you know what I'm talking about?"

He pauses and answers, "Yes sir, I know about that church. I go there myself. It's where I get my songs."

Then the spirit gets a hold on me, and I go right over to him and speak from my heart, making room for n|om or the Holy Spirit to direct my conversation. "The Lord wants you to be a preacher. You are doing everything you can to run away from this. You think that you can hide in a gang, but you can never get away from this pulling. It's time for you to face what is happening."

Before I can go on, he interrupts and says, "That is exactly what Pastor Brown told me. You are saying his words."

It turns out that the young man is a member of Pastor David Brown's church. We are all struck speechless. There is little more that can be said. The mother and daughter weep, as we all know that something special has transpired. We have witnessed old-school spirituality. What took place in one of the poorest places in America is what also takes place in the poorest place in the world—the home of the Kalahari Bushmen. There, the spirit is rich and the gifts of its presence are bountiful.

This experience happened because of ecstatic shaking inspired by the unlimited generous spirituality of God's love. When we open our hearts to being moved by the power of spirit and n|om, anything can happen. And it does.

Shake as if Your Life Depends on It

Back in the Kalahari, I am watching a brilliant orange sunset with N!yae. "Tonight we will have a good *!aia*. Our *thara* will be strong," she tells me.

N!yae is saying that our strongest feelings will be awakened and we will be reborn. This is how the Bushmen define !aia. It is not simply a trance state as has been suggested by many anthropologists. It is waking up our feelings and being in a heightened state of emotions. Its purpose is to make you feel reborn. When you wake up, you tremble and shake, what they call thara.

"Yes, N!yae, I will give you the ||*auhsi* that you have been waiting for." I am speaking about giving her a needle or arrow of n|om. "*Koma hee-sha-ta*," I improvise as the n|om already starts to stir in me. I have already entered *qaqm*, which means "striking the match of n|om." My fire has begun, and N!yae and the other n|om-kxaosi recognize it.

So begins another firestorm in the Kalahari. One by one, every n|om-kxao is lit. We hold and touch each other, modulating and amplifying the vibrations that shoot n|om into us.

"*Hi-sha! Mo-no-ka-hi-sha*," the improvised n|om sounds pour forth. When n|om makes these sounds, it is called *n≠oahn*, and it is believed that the ancestors are using n|om to make strange sounds through us. The purpose of the sound is to awaken and to send arrows.

Tonight all the n|om-kxaosi are hungry for n|om. No one wastes any time getting into a huddle. We are shaking together and making the sounds of n|om. We are waking up the ropes coiled up inside our hearts. As they spring forth, we each know that other tracks to God are being displayed. Our heart must be pure so our track does not bend. It must be straight for us to have a good journey.

I happen to know that across the ocean in an Ivy League–sponsored workshop for wealthy business executives, a popular meditation leader is teaching how to reap the benefits from being still. The participants have each paid over five thousand dollars to spend a few days learning how not to move. I am remembering how sad the Bushmen elders were when I previously told them about this foreign situation. They weren't sad because each person paid more money than they would make in a lifetime. They were upset with what the teacher was advocating.

G|ao'o shook his head and spoke for all the Bushman community: "No wonder the ropes are being broken. It's no surprise that the tracks are being covered with dust. You have to shake in order to keep the ropes strong and the tracks within sight. Otherwise no one will know where to go. They will be tricked by talk that seems to explain everything but only in the moment of persuasion. When they go home, they will be as lost as they were before even though they try their best to believe that they are not mixed up."

Shake as if your life depends upon it. Shake as if the survival of the planet depends upon it. It does!

The Bushman elders have no doubt that we are lost and have forgotten how to keep the ropes and tracks strong. Worse, they believe that breaking the ropes is the same as ripping the fabric that binds together the ecological web of nature. We not only make ourselves spiritually lost and stupid we also damage the ecology and threaten to destroy it.

Shake as if your life depends upon it. Shake as if the survival of the planet depends upon it. It does! Whenever a teacher says to sit still, just say no and consider doing something spontaneously that shakes him. Whenever a spiritual leader sets forth a frame of meaning that demeans shaking and wild ecstatic movement, stand up and tell a joke. Here's one you can try:

> A man asks his neighbor, "Hi, how are you?"
> The neighbor replies, "I'm fine, thanks."
> "And how's your son? Is he still unemployed?"
> "Yes, he is. But he is meditating now."
> "Meditating? What's that?"
> "I don't know. But it's better than sitting around and doing nothing!"

When people laugh at the joke, ask your teacher if it is better to laugh with a vibratory movement or if the laughter would be better served if it were of the still variety. You are welcome to say that you said all this at the advice of an author who is advocating that spiritual teachers and their students be shaken equally.

The Oglala medicine man Black Elk once said that truth comes in two pure forms: through tears and through laughter. Both involve movement and can lead to convulsions. Both are medicines. We have lost access to the second mystery of ecstatic shaking because we have stopped the world. It has been stopped by words that make the case that our minds and bodies should be stilled and quieted.

That night in the Kalahari, after the shaking and dancing has subsided, N!yae asks me with grave concern, "Why would anyone think that God wants us to be still? We'd lose all the ropes, and there would be no tracks to God."

"God wants everyone else to be still so they can hear what the Bushmen have to say," I reply, trying to conceal my desire to tease.

But N!yae sees my intention before I display it. She quickly snaps back, "You need to bring a lion to those people who sit still. I'd like to see how long they avoid trembling when the Kalahari shows up."

We both start laughing, and imagine that her suggestion doesn't involve any lion but a shape-shifting Bushman who can turn himself into a lion. (Yes, there are Bushman lions, but we'll get to that later.)

I growl and pretend that I will turn into a lion. N!yae does her best to not shake, but she can't stop the oncoming wave of laughter. I can't make a serious growl anymore. We have been taken by the gods who want to shake us any way they can, including having a belly laugh over the futility and absurdity of teaching with words that are disconnected from spirit or n|om.

There once was a Bushman who became so hot during a scorching summer day that he dug himself a hole in the sand. He buried all of his body except for his head and was delighted to find that he successfully achieved a noticeable degree of comfort. He was so relaxed throughout the day that he decided to remain buried and still through the night. He continued this stillness for over a week.

On the thirteenth night, he had a vision and met the god of stillness. This god was neatly folded up and looked like a pretzel. The Bushman asked the pretzel god, "How long does a million years seem to you?" The god replied, "One second." Then the Bushman asked, "How long does it take for you to gather all the meat I could possibly eat?" The god again replied, "One second." The Bushman, who was now comfortably accustomed to not hunting or doing anything at all, asked the still god, "Please bring me all the meat I can eat." The god replied, "No problem. It will take me a second." The Bushman starved while waiting for his god to return.

Of course, we all know the health benefits of relaxation, meditation, and rest. But we know little about the value of its opposite: enhanced spontaneous motor activity, amplified ecstasy, and hyperarousal. It is time for us to rediscover the second mystery. We might find that rest is the prelude to the main show—the ecstatic awakening of our being. Or we might discover that shaking ecstasy is the prelude to the most profound benefits of relaxation. The Bushman view says that we need to be danced inside the interaction of both shaking and relaxation.

"Just tell them to get off their booty and shake it!" N!yae impatiently shouts, proud of the fact that she has remembered how we say booty.

"These folks are rather serious about sitting still," I respond. "They aren't used to anyone teasing or playing with their words and meanings."

N!yae continues: "Then they are truly sick. Every Bushman knows that we all need a healthy dose of teasing. It keeps us balanced. Watch out for the words that have spiritually stilled your people from both dancing and laughing at themselves. If this has been going on for a long time, then I fear whether the world can survive for much longer."

Let it be known that no one is spared from the teasing of the Kalahari. Neither the pope nor His Holiness the Dalai Lama would be safe from their arrows of humor. I can hear them now: "Why do these men wear those colorful robes? Do they think they are women?" Or "Why don't these spiritual leaders share their meat with us? We are starving. God wants us to share everything." That's Bushman talk, fully intended to immerse serious matters in absurdity and bring everyone down to the same level: grounded by the convulsions of giggling. Bottom line, the shake rules. Whether conveyed through longing, love, or humor, it has the final say.

If you listen closely to what the Kalahari are saying when they tease, you realize that it is another way to shake us up. The rhythms of their clapping and drumming as well as their outrageous teasing all serve the purpose of bringing on a shake. They want the same for you: to be shaken out of your slumber of ecstatic inactivity. The original ecstatic shakers of the Kalahari want you to shake your booty. It's the only way you'll find your way to the heart of God's love.

3

STAY TUNED

The Third Original Mystery

Something got a hold of me.

Traditional Gospel Song

"Most people who visit us, whether anthropologists or tourists, think that we go into a trance when we dance. They even call our holiest ceremony a trance dance and see us entering a kind of dreamscape. You must explain that we are not entering the dreams of sleep. We are doing the opposite: rather than going to sleep, we are awakening. We are waking up our feelings. Don't forget that our word for this experience is *!aia*, which means to wake up our strongest feelings. When we dance, we are trying to enter !aia and arouse the most powerful emotions of our heart."

With this explanation, Toma Dahm, one of the great Bushman n|om-kxaosi, wants the rest of the world to appreciate the truth about his spiritual universe, and to notice that it provides a very different way of knowing and being than that which most of us inherited from our own culture.

When Toma was young, he danced as strongly as his ancestors. He became an old-school Bushman doctor who brought an exhilarating joy and an openly shared, tender healing touch to the n|om dance. Now he is old and feeble after having suffered a stroke. Nonetheless, Toma says that he dances with me every night in the visionary villages. I remember our many years of dancing together in the communities sprinkled throughout what used to be called Bushmanland. I agree with Toma: today I continue to dance with him in the mystical Kalahari.

"Tell your people that they must learn to wake up their feelings. Their heart must arise from its sleep. It must rise and stand up. That's how you find the track to God."

Trance is a confusing word. Does it mean a hypnotic or cataleptic state? Is it detachment from your physical surroundings, as in a deep contemplation or a daydream? Is it a semiconscious daze that is halfway between sleeping and waking? Is it more like sleep than being awake? All these meanings have been associated with the notion of trance, a word etymologically rooted to the Middle English *traunce*, the Old French *transe*, and the Latin *transpire*, which refer to a passage or means of going over or across.

Where does trance carry you? Scholars say it is movement from a state of habituated pay-attention-and-be-aware-of-your-surroundings consciousness to a realm that holds reverie, semiconsciousness, absent-mindedness, bemusement, daydream, muse, a stunned condition, bewilderment, befuddlement, daze, discombobulation, muddle, fog, puzzlement, stupor, and mystification. Trance has been used to generally cover all fringe and out-of-the-box experiences, from possession to shamanism, divination, spiritualism, mysticism, and psychoanalysis.

The term loosely covers such a wide range of mental states that it even includes opposite ways of being. For example, trance supposedly explains both fear-based, cataleptic, frozen rigidity and delight-based, ecstatic, frenzied mobility. It seems to point to the entries to hell *and* to heaven. It is said to take you to both a deathlike coma *and* a lively rapture. It appears that trance does not make clear what it is and what it isn't.

The Buddhists, particularly as noted in the scriptures of the Pali Canon, propose eight states of trance that refer to different ways of being absorbed in experience. The first four absorption experiences, called rupa, involve a material orientation, whereas the last four, called

Arupa, are nonmaterial. All these absorption states are preparation for the so-called final saturation. For Buddhism, trance indicates a level of absorption, with the ultimate dissolve being the experience of oneness (along with its presumed nothingness) with the universe.

Sufism makes it simpler: Forget all the levels of trance and go straight for ecstasy, defined as the experiential union with Allah, or God. Like the Bushmen, they use body movement and music to reach the divine. Here, ecstatic trance is the ticket to getting admitted to the theater of God's merriment and joy.

Consider how *trance* is part of the word *entrance*, signifying an opening, conduit, portal, or channel. *Trance* is both noun and verb: "a bridge" and "to cross." For a Bushman, it is a track and it is movement along the path. The French *transir* means "to shiver." This reminds us that the track to the other realm, the home of the awakened sacred heart, brings forth an ecstatic tremble of excitement and delight.

The Great Awakener

Toma speaks to me in a vision: "No wonder people are stuck, and act like robots and zombies. They hold on to static words rather than ride moving emotions. Words get you stuck unless you play with them and move them around. How do you do that? By letting your heart awaken the words. You see, your mind puts words to sleep, and your heart brings them to life. Words can take you to death or to life. It's your choice."

To a Bushman, it is only possible to find your way when you are full of n|om. N|om takes you to the answers, directions, inspirations, and divine blessings you seek.

The world of vision, of which Toma is speaking, is different than a dream. Dreams have little importance to a Bushman. They are simply recycled autobiographical material—a daily reincarnation of your habitual way of being in the world. The question is how to get past the boring and lifeless reruns, and give birth to fresh, new episodes.

The soulful answers to your life cannot be solely voiced with words. They are carried in a form you can receive if and only if they are sent as n|om. To a Bushman, it is possible to find your way only when you are full of n|om. N|om takes you to the answers, directions, inspirations, and divine blessings you seek. It opens your eyes so you can see the tracks to God. It opens your ears so you can hear what the ancestors have to teach.

N|om is the great awakener. Its arrows are heart-seeking projectiles that aim to harpoon your truest center. When n|om gets a hold on you, you no longer have to look for the next step. Instead, you are pulled by n|om. It reels you in.

> **"The ultimate tracking is not achieved**
> **with the mind, but with the heart.**
> **The ancestors pull us, and God pulls us.**
> **This is our greatest teaching."**

The old men who grew up to become great Kalahari hunters explain this pulling: "The ancestors and God can attach a rope to you. When that happens, they are able to pull you to where you need to go; that's the secret behind our ability to track. A Bushman hunter feels something tapping on his arm when it is time to hunt. It is the ancestors pulling a rope that is attached to our arms. The other end is attached to the animal. We simply follow the pulling of the rope, and it takes us to a kudu, giraffe, eland, warthog, or gemsbok."

Toma has lived the old way of being a hunter-gatherer, and he is legendary among his people for being very brave. He not only was a skilled hunter, but he would take on the lions when they got too close to the village. He once ran out in the middle of the night to chase away a pride of lions. He has more to teach about the ropes that pull the Bushman hunter.

"The rope is our track. We feel it pulling us. When you wake up your heart and find yourself alive with good emotions, it not only makes you tremble, it also enables you to feel the pulling of the ropes. The ultimate tracking is not achieved with the mind but with the heart. The ancestors pull us, and God pulls us. This is our greatest teaching."

The Bushman trance is a feeling so strong that it is felt as a pulling. It is a rope, a bridge, a crossing, and a track that can take you anywhere. It can pull you to another village, help you find something that has been lost, assist you in locating an animal or medicinal plant, or bring you directly to God.

"Your feelings must be strong and pure in order for the rope to be straight. If they are not strong, the rope will bend and you will not get to where you need to go," Toma continues. "We help each other keep our ropes strong. That is why we enter thara, the shaking brought about by our love of one another and our love for all of God's creation."

Let the Rope Get a Hold on You

N!yae is on her way to greet us. She has spent the morning making ostrich egg beads for a necklace. As she walks, she is singing a song. She wants n|om. She always wants n|om and can never get enough. Toma is also that way, and I am the same. We live for n|om.

This hunger for n|om is no different from the cravings of the Shakers of St. Vincent who can't sing enough, shake enough, and love enough in order to feel more of God's grace and creative presence in their lives. The same goes for the Louisiana sanctified church members who would simply say, "We can't get enough of God. That's what it means when God has a hold on you." Once those ropes get hooked up, you'll be as intoxicated as Rumi, who couldn't say enough about the longing for love, which to the Bushmen is the pulling of love.

If you get a rope in the Kalahari, it will take you all over the spiritual world to be with others who know about the ropes. It will take you to Louisiana, to a church in the Lower Ninth Ward where folks gather on Sunday morning and sing:

Something got a hold of me
(Oh yes it did one day)
Something got a hold of me

I went to a meeting one night
When my heart wasn't right
Something got a hold of me

The Bushmen know exactly what these sanctified singers are talking about. God shoots an arrow of n|om (though arguably it is more like a harpoon because of the attached rope) and when your heart is soft, tender, and aching for something infinite that is missing, the point of that arrow can pierce you. When it hits, it may feel like lightning has struck. It has. This is n|om lightning.

"It's Holy Ghost lightning," our Louisiana brothers and sisters would echo.

When it comes through and hits the spiritual bull's-eye of your heart, God has got a hold of you. Yes, that's right. Would someone please say amen?

"Amen!" is the soul-based, heart-centered response. In the Kalahari, the singers are as spirited as the choir at First Thessalonians Missionary Baptist Church in the Lower Ninth Ward of New Orleans. There the Reverend Prevost is leading the singing with his son, Ed Prevost Jr., on the organ. Ed is my soul brother, and now that his dad has retired after Katrina destroyed his church building, Ed is my organist and music director when I take my ecstatic Life Force Theatre on the road.

The Kalahari choir makes improvised sounds around a general melodic line. Yes, it is jazz, and it is as syncopated and soulful as the gospel rhythms in the Black Church. One singer improvises off the chorus, like the Reverend Prevost and the Reverend James Cleveland are accustomed to doing in their spirited services.

It's the same spirit-filled world whether the words used are n|om or the Holy Ghost. It is music adorned and washed in the holiness of ecstatic love. It came from Africa, and it lifts anyone who is thrown into its bosom. The Bushmen *feel* its truth, and the old-school parishioners *feel* its truth. It's not about a theology of words. It's primarily a theology of being touched in such an authentic way that it brings on a spiritual earthquake. Your whole being is ripped wide open so that

God can pour infinite love into your deep valleys of longing, heartache, and sorrow.

> *I was at a revival*
> *On the mourners bench*
> *I was filled with misery*
> *The same God*
> *That touched my mother*
> *He laid His hands on me*
> *That's why I say . . .*

It is a relational thing. In this sacred circle, we feel our mothers and fathers, grandfathers and grandmothers, even if we did not know them and even if we didn't experience their love. We long for relationship with the ancestral archetypes. Longing is a feeling, and loving is a longing. The felt longing for love is the pulling of the ropes.

> *Something got a hold of me*
> *(Oh yes it did one day)*
> *Something got a hold of me*
> *I went to a meeting one night*
> *When my heart wasn't right*
> *Something got a hold of me*

Oh yes, it did, my brother. Yes, that's right, my sister. Something got a hold of you. It always has. Your mind has just been in the way of feeling it. Don't be embarrassed to feel what you long to experience with your mama and papa. Feel it for your grandparents as well. Feel it in a grand way.

Then go all the way. Get all the way down so you can feel it pulling all the way from above. I'm talking about—and I'm shouting about—the rope, the longing, and the pulling. Some folks like to say that it is going up the Highway to Heaven.

God wants you to know something. God wants you to know the divine through a special kind of feeling—feeling God's love with all your heart, mind, body, and soul. God wants you to passionately realize that the Holy of Holies has already got a hold of you.

They were singing
"Come Ye That Loves the Lord"
And I thought they were singing to me
Something hit me
Up over my head
And run right to my feet
I never shall forget it

Come on home to the rope. It's a straight line from above, and it is dangling right over your head. When it hits you, it will sizzle your mind and run all the way down to your feet. It will make you electrified with joy. It will move your feet to dance its glory on the streets of rapture. It's something you can never forget.

Come, all those who love to love with Rumi. Come, all you love hounds and love cats. Get ready for the n|om storm. The n|om is pouring. It is transforming into Holy Ghost rain, kundalini snow, and chi fog. Bring it on down; it's a spiritual thunderstorm. Stand under its shower of blessings.

Something got a hold of me
(Oh yes it did one day)
Something got a hold of me
I went to a meeting one night
When my heart wasn't right
Something got a hold of me

Welcome the spirited rain and all the blessings that pour forth. All this is yours for the asking—yours for the simple, innocent, and sincere opening of your heart. Get soft, make yourself vulnerable, stand out of the way, and let it rain, rain, rain! It's time for some Holy Ghost weather.

In the spiritual time zone of southern Africa, it's n|om time. It's the same weather across all the geographical time zones. Wherever you are, let it pour and drop you to the floor. Let it pour and make you rich in spirit. Let it pour and make you more than you are. Let it pour and free you to say there will be talk no more.

Now Brother Ed speeds up the music, and I shout out a line that the choir answers as a back-and-forth musical call. In this exchange, the music becomes a stronger rope, pulling us right inside its power:

> *It was the Holy Ghost (Holy Ghost)*
> *Yes (Holy Ghost)*
> *Yes (Holy Ghost)*
> *Holy Ghost (Holy Ghost)*
> *Yes*

I want you to experience the Kalahari, St. Vincent, and Louisiana. In every one of these places, you can step into the music that has been anointed and sanctified with n|om and Holy Ghost power. There, you can feel the pulling and have yourself pulled apart, opened, and made ready for a great softening, piercing, and filling of your heart.

In this way, you enter original spirituality; this is how it began with our Kalahari ancestors. Furthermore, this is how it spread throughout the globe, even when slaves had to spiritually free those who stole their lives. When your heart accepts this understanding, you too will be unable to stop your hands from clapping, your legs from jumping, and your voice from shouting as the whole of you dances down the aisle and circles the Kalahari sand.

I know you are capable of feeling all this because you are wired the same way as the Bushmen. You are a Bushman. The problem is that you have forgotten who you *are* and what you are meant to be. Now is the time for you to find yourself—to uncover your true self that is only at home inside the heart of God. There, all the spiritual rivers flow into the infinite ocean of love. This is where the rain waits to pour over anyone unashamed to show God the clouds of their blue sky.

The tempo gets even stronger and faster. Now's the time to let God really get a good hold of you. The spiritual harpoons are flying in every direction; let one of them pierce you. The Bushmen are shooting their arrows of n|om. Stand up so you can get hit. Jump high so your head is brushed and touched by the Sky God's rope. Wiggle and jiggle so every archer of Cupid's legion can take aim. Feel the line a-pulling. Get reeled in. Go ahead and lose your deadbeat mind as you soulfully shake that booty! Let the rain pour. Jump in and walk, run, dance on the spiritual waters.

Into the spiritual whirlpool you go, moved in every direction. Here and only here are you able to step into new spiritual seeing, hearing, tasting, smelling, and touching. This is the world of ecstatic spiritual living. Now you can walk right, talk right, sing right, pray right, and be saved from the hell of an out-of-control psychological mind. Forget self-esteem and get filled with spiritual steam. Its heat will cook you and make you ready for tracking God.

Listen again as the preacher and choir sing back and forth, pulling one another closer to the embodiment of the Holy:

Makes me walk right (Holy Ghost)
Makes me talk right (Holy Ghost)
Sing right (Holy Ghost)
Pray right (Holy Ghost)
It keeps me (Holy Ghost)
Saved me (Holy Ghost)

It's about the ropes that bring on the deepest pulling. It's entirely about something getting a hold of you. That something is God's love, a mystery that can never be understood. But it can be fully and wholly *felt*!

N!yae lets out a shriek, for she is feeling it right now. She is shaking and dancing in the Kalahari, and is in perfect sync with the swaying and rocking of the church choir in the physically faraway but spiritually inseparable Lower Ninth Ward of New Orleans. N|om is an arrow, a harpoon, a rope, a pulling, a longing, a loving, a sacred fire, a holy water, and a divine wind. It is conveyed, received, and shared by tender and awakened feelings, motions of emotion, wide-open inter-twined hearts, and spirited dancing on the King's Highway. The rope to God is the Highway to Heaven; it is right in front of you. Reach out and grab it. Get grabbed by it. Hold it. Let it get a hold of you. One more time:

Something got a hold of me
(Oh yes it did one day)
Something got a hold of me
I went to a meeting one night
When my heart wasn't right
Something got a hold of me

N!yae is singing and shouting at the top of her lungs. She is on fire with n|om, and I am right there in the pot with her. Together we compose a two-egg omelet for the spiritually hungry community. Toma is with us, as are |Kunta Boo and Ti!'ae. The meal is multiplying. It only takes a few n|om-kxaosi to feed a multitude.

We are holding on to one another, vibrating and singing together. N|om has got a hold of us. We feel the ropes. They are pulling us to the other people in the community gathering. Our hands are placed on others, brought there by the tugs of the invisible ropes. I say invisible because they wouldn't show up in a photograph. But for those of us who are fully cooked, we feel the ropes so strongly that we can see them with our eyes open or shut. Sometimes we even smell the ropes.

When in Tune, You'll Be Played by the Gods

To an untrained and uninitiated outside observer, questions arise: "Why would anyone shake like this, and become so wild and crazy? Is it simply a natural high to get spiritually intoxicated? What's the more profound significance of the Bushman way of spirituality?"

Yes, the original way of spirituality delivers an extreme high, a colossal hit of God. It unquestionably makes you drunk on spirit, but it's not the kind of inebriation produced by an alcohol still. This spirituality is, by its very nature, neither still nor subtle. It is uncorked spiritual white

lightning that startles and electrifies, as opposed to bottled white light-
ning that dulls the senses. A n|om high brings ecstatic delight, but there
is more to its presence than having supercharged fun.

**Like a musical instrument, we easily fall out of tune.
We then feel out of whack, out of sync,
and out of touch with spirit.**

Here are the million-dollar questions: What do we get out of sur-
rendering to original spirituality, the shaking way of the Kalahari?
Why is it so important? What does it bring that we can't already get
from other offerings in the spiritual marketplace?

The answer is simple but groundbreaking, and life altering. Like a
musical instrument, we easily fall out of tune. We then feel out of
whack, out of sync, and out of touch with spirit. And more knowing
about spirituality won't necessarily help. Unless we are *tuned*, none
of the mysteries and gifts of spirit can be received. Original spirituality, the Kalahari ecstatic work of the spirit, is the only way we can tune
our whole being. This primary means of tuning ourselves has been
missing in action in most of the world.

We are not without spirit; we are just out of tune with it. As an
out-of-tune instrument, we are unable to feel played by n|om, Holy
Spirit, or wisdom. Yet, in those times when we find ourselves acciden-
tally being in tune, all wisdom is able to naturally, effortlessly, and
spontaneously make music with every cell in our body.

We have forgotten that a human being is like a musical instrument
requiring constant adjustment. Although we are each a unique instrument, we all require tuning. You may be like a piano, whereas one of your
friends may be more guitar-like. Others are free to embody any of the
instruments composing the human orchestra. They may be wind instruments, have more brass, or be strongly rhythmic, among other varieties.

What is important to realize is that no matter how much knowledge
and skill you have, if the instrument is not tuned, the music will sound
terrible. When a breeze blows over the strings of a guitar or violin, the
musician must quickly retune it or face an annoying performance.

hit by spiritual lightning—openly available for inspiration, vitality, and creativity to fully surge through you.

When you are in tune and played by the gods, then and only then may it be said that you are spiritually awakened. In the Kalahari, you are a spiritually enlightened being, a healer, a teacher, and a wisdom keeper only in the moments when you are a tuned instrument for the gods to play. After each gig, you return to being a spiritual idiot; there is no such thing as a spiritual master. There are only moments in which idiots like us get masterfully played by the gods. But we can't perform unless we get ourselves in tune.

Saint Augustine, Abraham, and Sitting Bull were as ignorant as Larry, Curly, and Moe. They were stooges except for those moments when each was tuned. The same was true of the twelve disciples. Recall how little it took for those who were by the side of Jesus to get out of sync. One moment they were ambassadors of God, and in another, they were petty, scared, and lost.

The same is true of us, and you must get over it. There is no spiritual mastery, and serious efforts to attain it just throw you further out of tune. What you need is a good shake. It will tune you, and all will be good with the world until you fall out of tune again. Then you will need another good shake.

Tune In to the Mysteries with Spontaneous Movement

The first spiritual mystery presents the experience of being a tuning fork. I am referring to the natural body movements that vibrantly nurture a sense of vitality, the effortless flow of the universal life force, chi, kundalini, and n|om. These automatic movements are the vibrating tuning fork that allows us to hear the pitch we need to voice. These vibrations inspire health, creativity, and the enhancement of everyday life. With ecstatic spontaneous movement, the meaningful outcomes we aspire to achieve are facilitated and enhanced.

What is most important about this way-of-life tuning is that it requires spontaneous movements rather than consciously driven choreographies. The latter, exemplified by tai chi, qigong, or choreographed ecstatic dancing, may or may not tune you; it depends upon whether they are done naturally or forcefully. The original way is to ignore a scripted pattern and be spontaneously moved. It calls for improvised expression rather than memorized form. From the beginning of human culture, the Bushman dancers have encouraged the expression of body automatisms, particularly spirited trembling and shaking.

This spontaneous non-practice points the way to tuning our instrument; it is the first original mystery. It was carried to different parts of the world, with one of its most developed forms found in the almost forgotten Japanese practice of seiki jutsu. As we discussed in the last chapter, one of its greatest practitioners of the twentieth century was Ikuko Osumi, sensei from Tokyo. She was a master tuner. In her hands, you could be tuned and, more important, you could learn how to release the tuner that lies within.

Beginning with the first African Bushmen, the beneficial ways of natural body movements spread throughout the African diaspora from Africa to the Caribbean to the Americas. Here, the second mystery—getting into the river—was revealed. In a way, it is nothing more than an amplification of the first mystery. It calls for the big-time shaking of your booty for God, something ecstatically performed since the origin of human culture. In the spirited dance arenas of Africa, the second mystery proliferated and made the gods happily crazy with cosmic delight.

Whereas the Bushmen have the complete kinesthetic alphabet for fully embodied ecstatic expression, other cultures have held on to particular forms and their elaboration. However ecstatic expression is performed, its most enthusiastic performance spontaneously tunes and readies us to experience the divine and encounter the *mysterium tremendum*. Fully embodied ecstatic shaking has been well developed throughout the African diaspora, including the Kalahari Bushmen, Zulu, Himba, Ndebele, Shakers of St. Vincent and Trinidad, Umbanda and Candomblé traditions of Brazil, and the sanctified African American Church.

In addition to fully activated body shaking, the Bushmen teach us that we should also shake up our mind. This is the beginning of the third mystery: getting tuned and staying tuned to the mysteries.

Here, we can use words in a way that is different from what we learn at schools and universities. Rather than draw upon words to squelch the unknown and to eliminate mystery, we can use them to bring forth more unknowing. We can supercharge our talk with n|om, and allow it to spring forth as a different kind of arrow that disrupts and disengages overworn habits of thinking. By short-circuiting overly predictable outcomes, we make more room for surprise, creativity, and mystery.

Ecstatic Talk Tunes the Mind

N|om-charged words bring forth ecstatic talk, which often sounds like spirited shouting. Ecstatic talk cleans and sweeps away stuck ideas. More important, its resonance tunes the mind. Similarly, n|om texts may be created to shoot arrows toward the reader. It calls forth, evokes, and creates. The arrows of n|om constitute more than the life force; they are also the inspirational source of spiritual invention that enables us to create beauty, wonder, and enchantment in our world.

The Guarani Indians of the Lower Amazon Basin in Paraguay have a similar belief about the sacred use of words and talk. They say that "word souls"—the talk of someone ecstatically awakened—are able to tune, heal, and inspire. This ecstatically inspired communication, which I call ecstatic talk or n|om talk, shakes and tunes the mind, clearing it from distracting influences and opening a connection to spirited creative expression.

|Kunta Boo has the audience sitting on the edge of their seats even though there are few to no chairs in the Kalahari. He is telling a story about a hunter who is lazy:

> The hunter's wife, like all Bushman women, is always hungry for meat. She yells at him, "Grab your bow and arrows, and get out of here. Go and hunt me some meat. I'm not serving you anything else unless I get some meat!"
>
> The hunter carefully prepares his poison-tipped arrows and sets forth on an important hunt. He waits for the ancestors to

lead him to an eland, the kind of meat and fat that his wife sali-
vates over.

Lucky for him, the ancestors must have been in a good mood,
for the hunt is successful. He and his friends cut up the bounty
and prepare to bring it back to the village. They sing all the way
home as they imagine how happy their wives will be and what
treats they will be served late at night.

As the hunter with the hungry wife arrives at his hut, she lets
out a scream of delight. She runs toward her husband, rips off his
head, and completely devours him. She was too hungry to wait
any longer!

Full of her man, the satisfied wife falls asleep. In the morning
she relieves herself in the bush. To her surprise, her husband
drops out of her. He is angry and starved. Without delay and
before she knows what is happening, he eats her whole!

This is an example of a typical Bushman story. Emphasizing
surprise and transformation, the presentation is delivered with great
drama, and the punch lines are typically shouted with thundering fervor. As can be seen, the Bushmen are quite bawdy in their stories
about their bodies and sexuality. The women in their tales often trick
their husbands into eating the women's sexual parts, while the men
trick their wives into biting their testicles or anus. They also may make
love with their wives in the guise of dead meat.

The Bushmen are not perverts. They are masters at using words,
talk, and stories to evoke n|om. They know that change and unex-
pected moments of transformation are conveyors of n|om. When a
Bushman storyteller says that a wife ate her husband rather than the
meat he brought home, you are shocked and opened for an arrow of
n|om to enter. Laughter becomes the awesome vibrating life force.

With this understanding, it makes sense that the most valued ani-
mal part for a n|om-kxao to eat is the anus. No other organ holds as
much transformative power: it is the body part that marks the movement from input to output. It is the point in the body where there is

the most dramatic enactment of transformation—the alchemical transition from delicious food to stinking excrement.

"I hope this story shakes up some of your people. I am sure they will never expect it," |Kunta Boo announces, proud that he has done a good job of performing his story. And he does more than tell a story. He becomes the characters and uses his voice in multiple ways, as if it were an orchestra. One moment, he calmly delivers the words, but when an unexpected turn in the story is about to take place, he jumps in the air and shouts out the surprising part. That's when an arrow of n|om is shot from his story—when he has worked himself up enough to heat the story and have it be hot enough to cook the listener.

If this story about their stories shocks you, then you are ready this very moment for an arrow of absurd wordplay and story twisting that may just slip a trembling into your mind, loosening you enough to let go of some of the crap stuck between your ears. Please remember that a n|om story is all about shaking you up to help you let go of whatever your mind has become stuck in. It is the Kalahari means of achieving empty mind.

"Let's tell your people another story that will shake them up," |Kunta Boo adds. "Why don't you tell them about the husband who asked his wife to go to the library and bring him back an interesting book to read?"

"That's a good idea," I answer while pretending that all of this is serious business. It is, but it cannot feel serious. Otherwise, the n|om gets bored and refuses to drill a hole into your mind. I step onto the improvised Kalahari stage, which |Kunta Boo and I know is a pot for cooking someone who really listens but a pot that does so without too much seriousness.

A husband was bored with watching television and wanted a fresh idea to entertain him. Accordingly, his wife graciously went to the library and asked the librarian for a book her husband might enjoy. Together they decided she should bring home the book *The Life and Times of the Greatest Bushman Hunter*. She sang all the way home with excited anticipation, thinking how thrilled her husband would be with what she had found.

When she entered the village, her husband jumped out of a tree and wrestled the book away from her hands. He tore every single page out of the book. As he began to rip apart the cover, he turned to his wife and said, "Why would you ever think anyone else could hunt better than me? There isn't an animal alive that I can't rip apart with my bare hands. And that includes all the animals in this book."

His wife was so proud of her husband that she cooked all the pages that night and happily fed her husband the book.

|Kunta Boo and I throw ourselves to the ground, convulsing with laughter, unable to finish the story. We are already drunk with n|om and have no need to hear what happened next with the book.

"This should help someone receive an arrow of n|om," |Kunta Boo shouts out, barely able to get his words interspersed between the bursts of laughter.

"I hope they publish this," I add. "Otherwise we'll have to attach a tree to the book cover. Or some elephant dung shaped like a tree!" We die laughing all over again.

Welcome to original spirituality. It values sweet fruit as much as putrid meat, and gives as much importance to the ingestion of honey as to the passage of fecal matter. This is similar to the classic Zen understanding that it is potentially problematic to be sentimentally attached to the charismatic fruits and fauna—the pretty flowers and animals—at the cost of ignoring the most repellent forms of natural phenomena. Bashō's haiku expresses Bushman-like wisdom:

Fleas, lice
a horse pissing
near my pillow

A Kalahari Bushman might retell it, for in the Kalahari you can never retell a story in the same way. It must change or it will have no n|om. Here is the same tale told again, this time interwoven with the untold part of the other story about the husband:

Fleas, lice
a book shitting
near my sheet

"I want to tell you my most sacred *kabi*," |Kunta Boo told me before he passed on. A kabi is a vision or visitation with the ancestors and gods. It is not regarded as a dream but as an experiential encounter with the spiritual universe.

"I was in the bush and came across the most beautiful giraffe I had ever seen. It was not a giraffe to be eaten as meat; God set this one aside. As I admired its beauty, God picked me up and threw me up the ass of that giraffe. Once inside its intestines, I started dancing. The giraffe gave me strong n|om."

This is not meant to be a funny story. It is a personal account of a revered Bushman's intimate encounter with God. |Kunta Boo was more grateful for that vision than anything else in his life; it was his most valuable possession. He wouldn't give it away for all the money in a Swiss bank. This vision gave him ownership of giraffe n|om, which means that he owns a heart-to-heart connection—a soul rope—with the giraffe. From that day on, he was the strongest doctor in his village. The same n|om was later passed to his wife, N!yae.

"Your n|om is strong because I shot some of |Kunta Boo's arrows into you," N!yae pretends to boast. I know she is setting me up for a joke.

"When you feel strong in the dance tonight, know that it is because you received something from the ass of a giraffe!"

This time she gets me. I know the story of |Kunta Boo's kabi and she tells the truth, accentuating its power and importance but rendering it absurd by the words she uses to say it. The subsequent laughter makes me bounce up and down in search of comedic relief, but more important, it enhances the intensity of my n|om. She has given me another arrow.

"Tonight I will go up all the animals' asses and gather the largest arrows you have ever seen," I shout back to N!yae. "You have no idea what I am going to shoot at you. Get ready, because this n|om is going to sneak up on you from behind when you least expect it!"

This is Bushman absurd medicine, and it shows an instance where words can be used to muster up another kind of n|om. The transmission of laughter that makes you shake is as transformative as the music that lifts the heart. It, too, releases tiredness and helps renew your spirit. Above all, it prepares you to be cooked in a more combustible manner.

Activate N|om—and Get Tuned—with Absurdity

As absurd as the wordplay and meanings of the Kalahari can be, they have the paradoxical effect of enabling a deeper reach into the depths of spiritual transformation. The deeper into the absurd they go, the more prepared they are to be launched higher into the sacred atmosphere of serious ecstatic rapture. Other indigenous cultures have this same wisdom know-how regarding the relationship between utterly ridiculous absurdity and profound spirituality. The sacred clowns, heyókȟas, and holy fools also prepare the existential ground this way, clearing the path for an unobstructed journey into the extraordinary spiritual realms.

Kalahari days are filled with teasing and storytelling among the Bushmen. When it is time for an evening dance, they are well prepared to both give and receive arrows of n|om, for they have been emptied and cleared of all stuck cognitive attachments. Humor does that for you: it dethrones any emperors of the mind and sends them on their way. Being too serious about the ideas and beliefs you have become attached to cannot be helped by more serious concern. It is absurdity that makes overseriousness impotent.

Humor does that for you: it dethrones any emperors of the mind and sends them on their way.

The bawdy teasing continues right up to the dance. The mood changes only when someone's n|om gets activated—when feelings are lit in an inspired way. Then the people notice that the gods and ancestors are beginning to arrive. The dance, at that moment, becomes holy. This is the time when human beings move from tomfoolery to becoming sacred ecstatic technicians. It is typically a night job because the Bushmen are more likely to be spiritually awake during an evening dance. Then their hearts throw out the spiritual lifelines, the felt ropes that enable them to pull and be pulled by God.

"Bo, the women are going to send many arrows into you," Toma announces with a smile. "You'd better get ready because I am going to encourage them to fill you all the way up. I also have an arrow I have specially doctored and prepared for you."

"I'm happy you are going to shoot me," I answer back. "I need all the n|om I can get. Especially if I have to try to send one through your thick skin."

It has begun all over again, but it is always the first time. In this work, we remain spiritual virgins. Whatever has happened to us before does not matter. That was another lifetime. We come to the dance with a newborn beginning. We approach it as giggling children, excited, a bit nervous, and ready for anything. The less we care about what happens to us, the more we are able to care about authentically serving up n|om. We must stand in front of the Kalahari fire both not caring at all and caring with all our hearts. The difference between the extremes builds the tension necessary for being available for n|om work.

I sometimes say to myself, "God, please empty me and make me a vessel for your work." Then I say, "Whatever happens, happens." The place where I must find myself centered lies somewhere between these two utterances. Stated differently, "Take me, shake me, and bake me. I accept whatever you bring out of the oven." God only needs to hear that you are sincerely available for being cooked. The rest of the work is in God's hands. Your mission is to get out of the way and let all this happen without interference.

A vibratory gathering of whirling clouds is circling above. The n|om voiced by pulsing throats and the pulling associated with sanctified clapping hands has cleared the atmosphere for a colossal n|om storm. You can smell the holy rain coming. A clap of Bushman thunder penetrates the air, signaling that lightning has already struck. N|om has arrived, and it will circulate through each person. Though a few serve as lightning rods, the circulation of this electricity is shared with every member of the community.

I am feeling ready to enter the realm of vibratory wisdom. Tonight it comes quick and unannounced, and I can barely hold on to my conscious awareness. I no longer differentiate what is taking place; the whole world is spinning. I am inside a heavy though light-filled n|om storm. It is lifting me off the ground. The darkness is a mere periphery to this luminous core. I ascend into its column and find an evocation of unfiltered being. N|om finds a voice and speaks of the third mystery.

The Third Mystery

In the beginning, there were no words. The Bushmen called this world First Creation. Here, every living creature communicated with all the other creatures. Every living being was able to become the other creatures. In First Creation, I may look like a human being now, but in an instant, I could become a giraffe. As long as everything changed into any and everything else, there was no sickness or death. First Creation was a paradise of change and never-ending transformation.

Then the world stopped. It was brought to a stillness with the introduction of names and language. When a momentarily striped animal was called a zebra, it was tricked into believing it could only be one form, one thing. It no longer believed it could be a butterfly or a crocodile. This is when so-called problems and suffering began to appear. When life does not naturally and effortlessly change, it tries to do so in other ways. Sickness shows up. You get sick as an alternative means of changing you. Death comes knocking at the door. It suggests that there is another life after this stationary life.

Words brought an end to paradise and created another world, what the Bushmen call Second Creation. The creation of naming, explaining, and holding on to a rigid set of beliefs not only stopped the animals from changing, but it put an end to the ease through which life forms could change or shape-shift into one another. It also sent out word that it was better to sit still and rationally understand, rather than jump with motion and stand under the emotion of the divine heart's love supreme.

Whereas First Creation was the great dance, Second Creation became the great stillness. This is when the universe was turned upside-down, not by God but by trickster.

Who is trickster? Language invented trickster so it would have a new god. Trickster is sometimes called self, the inner mirage that thoroughly relishes seducing you to believe you are god. This god changes form but not in the manner of First Creation. It gives the appearance of change, as opposed to the essence of change. It is illusory. It is what Hinduism calls maya. It is the darkness of the shadows that cover the light.

Trickster talks all the time. It wants you to be owned by its inventions. It is confusing because it tells you to think in only one way, but then it is unsatisfied and asks for more of the same. It is never content, and when you listen to trickster, you cannot be satisfied. It is behind the contradiction of feeling lost, uncertain, and poor when you give the public appearance of being profound, certain, and rich. It is mind crap rather than the fruit of soul.

In trickster's world, you are told to be quiet and sit down to have a spiritual journey. You are warned about awakened feelings, ecstatic expression, and wild movement. Trickster wants you calmed down, settled down, and pinned down. Like a butterfly mounted on a naturalist's display, trickster is all about appearance. It wants you to be a dead model of life.

The shamans, healers, and wisdom keepers know that healing, growth, and transformation take place inside the kitchen of First Creation. That is where change is cooked and served. You must go on a pilgrimage to find this place, for there your life can be returned to vibrant living.

The Bushman n|om-kxaosi were the world's first doctors, therapists, healers, priestesses, shamans, and spiritual cooks. They say there is only one way to know that you have stepped into First Creation. You know you are there when your body begins to automatically tremble, shake, and quake. This is the sign of non-static ecstatic change. With shaking, changes are moving within you. In this original place of creative flow and movement, you step into the vibrant dynamic of being pulled by all the ropes and living creatures, and the whole diversity of life itself.

First Creation is beyond the chopped-up markings of time. Here, the past, present, and future are not separated. This is eternity, the holiness that exists before the names chopped it into illusory pieces. In First Creation is found all the ancestors, gods, helpers, protectors, guides, teachers, healers, inventors, creators, singers, drummers, and cosmic players. This is the action stage for whole-bodied original spirituality.

You must learn to find the crossing that opens to First Creation. Upon entry, the shaking will begin. Upon shaking, the entry will begin. Shake to find the door. Shake to open the door. Shake to walk through the door. Shake to keep changing, healing, growing, and transforming.

First you must undo the naming and the meanings that glue everything to a static place. Be gentle with your aim when you take on a name, for a meaning isn't trying to be mean. Loosen it with absurdity. Consider this the shaking of the mind and its habit of being over-attached to serious sense and strict reason. Now is the season for another kind of sense: the n|om-sense of First Creation.

How to begin? Stand up this very moment and turn around, all the way around. Do it three times. Stop and immediately puff out some air three times. Do not consider it breathing. Regard it as three puffs blown by someone who has been dragging though life. You have been huffing and puffing like a dragon who has lived alone in your cave, guarding the gold that is held deep inside its walls. You have yet to realize that the treasure you have been searching for lies within. The fire in the belly that you desire has been cooking inside. The idea that you need to find that which you don't already possess needs to be slain.

Lift your arm as if holding an ancient sword and proceed to flutter your eyelids as fast as you can, just like a butterfly's wings. Slowly turn around to face the opposite direction, and consider that you are facing the previous condition. This is where you were before things became coiled up within your hidden recess, staring at the boring daily cuisine of a 1-2-3 routine.

Now read these words out loud: "It is time for some unmeaning. I shall stop being mean and start being nice. The world needs less mean-ing and more nice-ing. I'm going to drop the letter n from the word nice because n reminds me of those *no* and *know* words. I will just say icing. The world needs less meaning and more icing."

Notice whether you habitually resist this directive. Is it because it sounds too illogical, nonsensical, or absurd? If so, then you really need to do it. Perhaps for the first time, you can pretend that you are saying the words aloud. Say them silently to yourself, but try voicing this silence as an inner shout. Make your mind talk louder!

This is how the mind can be shaken, its logical grip loosened, and its overblown seriousness deflated. Use your mind to trick itself—to out-trick trickster. When mind is free, heart has more room to expand. Shake your mind in order to shake your body! Shake your booty to disorder your stuck and imprisoning habits of mind.

You will soon begin playing with words and meanings, doing so to free things up for change. You will be spreading sweet icing over your everyday existence, making it a delightful dessert. Original spirituality does not send you into the desert to find God through starvation and pain. It asks that you spread some delicious icing over the ground of your being and turn life into a dessert. Forget any serious journey. Try a cakewalk.

The cakewalk was a dance performed by slaves in the Deep South, usually on Sundays. They would parody the prim and proper manner of their white owners, doing so with absurd play and fun. Rather than dance in a circle, they'd dance down a straight line, sometimes with a bucket of water on top of their head. The dance set them free in this Sunday prelude to each week. Seasoned with rhythm and liberating moves, the weak rode away on a mighty carriage, all the while dreaming of a new dawn.

The sweet madness of n|om talk is spiritually lubricating and awakening. It tunes you up, and enables you to smoothly voice and perform what otherwise would not flow. It is part of the great delivery, a freedom ride as well as a homecoming. It is the expression of the truest revolution—a walk along a straight line that ends up taking you full circle to your roots, our original ancestral home. Find the track to God and realize that its line is also a circle. Its meandering straightens everything out, and its absence of words is the spiritual sign perfectly designed to provide direction.

Now I come back to myself.

4

INSULTING THE MEAT

The Fourth Original Mystery

What we play is life.

LOUIS ARMSTRONG

Not only do you get teased in the Kalahari for having a successful hunt, but the bigger the animal you kill, the more you get teased. The custom of insulting the meat—mercilessly teasing the successful hunter—helps temper anyone in a Bushman community from getting too proud or arrogant. This way of regulating social relations has been duly noted by anthropologists. What has been less noticed by outside observers is how any opportunity to tease or stage comic absurdity will be brought to full fruition because it brings more shaking and n|om into their lives. Shaking things up facilitates vibratory experience and helps prevent n|om pathways from getting clogged. In the Kalahari, life means movement, change, and transformation. Ecstatic shaking keeps everything hopping rather than stopping.

In the Kalahari, life means movement, change, and transformation. Ecstatic shaking keeps everything hopping rather than stopping.

What does insulting the meat look like outside the Kalahari? Since we don't hunt for our daily meals, what areas of our life can be appropriately subjected to absurd ridicule and teasing? The answer: whatever we regard as important. Importance is what needs to be shaken down and brought back to its rightful place in the universe—to the holistic and ecological realization that all experiences are equally vital. Nothing needs to be elevated over anything else.

It is no more important to sing than to pass gas. Similarly, from the big-picture view, praying has the same importance as reading a comic book or drinking a milkshake. Said differently, prayer can be a milkshake and reading a comic can be prayer. We get ourselves into trouble whenever we implicitly or explicitly suggest a ranked list of expressive forms that reports some things as more important than others. This leads to setting up a social hierarchy followed by a proliferation of more distinctions of importance, then inequality spreads through the system like wildfire.

Consider that every human situation presents its own unique form of meat and potatoes, metaphors for the presumed primary and secondary aspects that are brought to the proverbial table. We know what it means to say, "Where's the beef?" Let's add, "Where're the potatoes?" Now we can underscore the importance of each—meat and potatoes together are more interesting than one course alone. When one item gets too much attention, the other item risks being forgotten, and then we set ourselves up to lose the whole combo.

Insulting the meat helps keep all the variety of courses on the table. This can be done by either lowering the importance of whatever is considered the meat or by deflating the boisterous claims of whoever brings home the bacon. It also can be achieved by boosting the status of the coexisting potatoes and praising whoever boils, bakes, or fries them. What is needed to keep things from turning less tasty is a means of bringing both meat and potatoes to the same level of importance. When we insult the meat, we preserve the relations of interaction, keeping intact the wholeness of diversity by not allowing any one item, part, course, or participant to hog the scene.

As another example, you may consider your salary as the meat of your job, whereas all other aspects of work, from health benefits to social relations, are considered secondary—the potatoes of your employment. If you think it is only about the money, you may overlook the whole of your employment situation. To keep your outlook balanced, practice insulting the meat. In private, make fun of your income. Call it the opposite name. Rather than saying, "income," try saying, "outgone." Continue thinking about this in a contrary way: the more money you make actually means the more money you have to see gone. Shake up the way you regard money by insulting its status as meat.

The goal is to come in touch with the absurdity of everything in your life so you are liberated from any attachment to limited preferences.

Be careful how you do this; insulting the meat is a skilled art. Do not harshly put down any aspect of your life through an overly serious critique. Instead, loosen up how you may be tempted to take it too seriously, and do so with the sweet medicine of absurdity. If it doesn't make you smile or laugh, then your bark has missed the mark. The goal is to come in touch with the absurdity of everything in your life so you are liberated from any attachment to limited preferences.

Catch a Wave of Absurdity to Arrive at Truth

Loving God means loving all manifestations of the universe, from seaweed to the Milky Way, and everything else, known or unknown, imagined or unimagined. Preference sorts things out, separating this as a beautiful flower and that as an ugly weed. God's love cares as much about the weed as the rose, and gives the same attention to the sparrow as the airline pilot. Absurdity is a healing balm that needs to be rubbed on all situations that have been stressed or disrupted by hierarchical tensions. This applies to the people in your life as well as the diverse parts of your own experience.

Make a list of the most important things you regard about yourself. (Don't worry whether others think they are important or trivial.) Write down at least six things that make you proud. Perhaps it is the way you can cook a pie, make yourself attractive, display cleverness at your job, perform funny lines with your friends, successfully parent, fix a tire, catch a fish, serve a table, sew a dress, or run a marathon. All that matters is that these are especially important to you.

Now consider insulting your meat: come up with an absurd thought and statement about each of these important aspects of your life. For cooking a pie, you could say that you enjoy enticing a bowl of fruit into a pan. For those of you delighted with your looks, choose one feature of your face, say your nose, and imagine seeing it from the perspective of a fly. From the fly-by perspective, your nose is a mountain, even a volcano that erupts from time to time. Mount Gesundheit might be the name found on the map of a fly.

"What are you doing with that stick?" one of the Bushmen women asks Ti!'ae, the oldest woman of the group. She's asking about the obvious—a digging stick used to find and extract plant roots. It's also a walking stick, a dance stick, and a stick for whatever other practical use can be found for it. But since a Bushman is asking, you can assume a tease is on the way.

Ti!'ae is skilled at insulting the meat and teasing whoever tries to tease her. She quickly snaps back, "What makes you think this is a stick? Last night I grew an extra finger, and now I have to carry it around. Be careful what you say to it because it may want to scratch your hide!"

The thought of that stick being a finger for the tiniest woman in the Kalahari is more than anyone can bear. The women not only giggle throughout the morning, they contemplate how grateful they are for this old woman and the many ways they have benefited from the n|om she delivers to the community. Though she has the smallest physical stature, she is one of the strongest healers they have experienced. Even the men n|om-kxaosi are scared of her power, and very few of them would ever dance with her. They are afraid her n|om might throw them to the ground.

She can look fierce in one moment and be laughing like a child in another. In her eighties, she is another woman that the community calls my n|om wife. She was the sister to N!xau, star of the film *The Gods Must Be Crazy*. What a commentary on the ignorance of the rest of the world that the movie depicted him as incapable of understanding the gods. Filmmakers had a chance to meaningfully portray the holders of original spirituality and their direct means of tracking God, but they chose to depict them as noble savages leading a simple, naive life. In the film, their life is turned upside-down when a Coca-Cola bottle is thrown out the window of a light airplane flying over the Kalahari Desert.

Critics did not know how to respond to the film. Though it grossed over one hundred million dollars worldwide (N!xau reportedly earned less than two thousand dollars for his starring role), some viewers thought it racist. The government of Trinidad and Tobago banned the film, and anthropologist Richard Lee declared that it was a "cruel caricature of reality." Fans of the film proposed that it was the opposite—an absurd condemnation of racism with the Bushman as a hero.

This is the thing about absurdity: it reveals truths that cannot be stated in any other way. These truths lie between the cracks of opposites. It is sort of true and kind of false.

What did the Bushmen think? They were shown the film and practically died from laughing. They chose to see absurdity and relish another version of insulting the meat, which of course, from an even more absurd perspective, is honoring the meat.

Ti!ae, sister to N!xau, is not only a great n|om-kxao, she is an extraordinary n|om traveler. She has the ability to catch a song and have it take her somewhere. While singing and playing music on her thumb piano, her mind can jump onto the waves of sound and be swept away into the n|om. It can carry her to another village or even to visit her brother, who now lives in the spiritual land of the ancestors.

Today Ti!'ae is going to use her stick to tease her friends, and she will be relentless. She will wave it over her head and say that a storm is coming. She will say that she was only teasing about it being a finger and then claim it is a large nail of n|om that she will put into someone at the next dance. When she says that, the women will act scared and pretend to run away. They'll know that she is kidding, but at the same time, they'll respect that there is some truth to it.

This is the thing about absurdity: it reveals truths that cannot be stated in any other way. These truths lie between the cracks of opposites. It is sort of true and kind of false. Paradoxical truth is something more complex than ambiguity. It is a clear truth but can't be transparently conveyed with words. It needs a wave to ride on (something like a giggle), an *aha* experience, or a rhythmic pairing of differences. In the same way that Ti!'ae is able to ride on a pulse of sound during her improvised music making, we need to catch a wave of absurdity in order to be carried to some of the more important truths about living.

The extent to which we are stretched between extreme absurdity and heightened spiritual exhilaration determines how far we will walk on our sacred pilgrimage.

How does insulting the meat, effective teasing, and absurd experience enter our everyday life? That's the problem. It usually doesn't. We are overfed with seriousness, whether in the classrooms, spiritual centers, spas, or playgrounds. We have lost touch with the medicinal value and spiritual contribution that comes from shaking our lives up in an absurd way. Without the sacred absurd, we have little chance of finding a track to God. The extent to which we are stretched between extreme absurdity and heightened spiritual exhilaration determines how far we will walk on our sacred pilgrimage.

The Significance of Changing and Sharing

I was fortunate to be inspired and encouraged by one of the foremost creative therapists of our time, Dr. Carl A. Whitaker. He was a professor of psychiatry at the University of Wisconsin and the first person who encouraged me to become a family therapist. Over the years, we held many discussions about the nature of human growth and transformation. He believed that psychiatry was toxic. As one of the founders of family therapy, he was regarded by Salvador Minuchin and other pioneer therapists as a genius. Whitaker was known for his ability to work with "crazy" people, purported schizophrenics. He actually saw every human being as crazy, the difference being that "some of us get paid for being nuts while others get in trouble."

What did he do differently? He insulted the meat, just like a Bushman does. If a family came to him complaining about a symptom, say Dad's depression, he would worry about Mom's perfectionism. If a particular child became identified as a troublemaker, he'd treat the sibling who never got in trouble. He brought everyone down to the same playing field. It was the whole system that mattered, not anyone's social rank or diagnostic label. As a result, he was able to facilitate healing and transformation. People's lives changed without being diagnosed or given meds. I have followed his example and integrated his methods into my own practice.

Is this hard to believe? Not if you're a Bushman. They know how everything is connected in circles, and how things get way out of kilter if you pull one person out of a system and elevate or lower them to a different plane than the others. Whitaker defined family health not as the absence of any problems, but as a system whose positive and negative expression constantly moved around all its members. He called this a rotating scapegoat system. Today, Johnny is in trouble, but tomorrow or next week the role will get passed to another child or to a parent. Change is what matters for healthy, vibrant living, not the absence of trouble.

Similarly, all family roles, functions, and forms of expression need to constantly change in relationship systems. Success and failure must be shared, as do other outcomes, experiences, and emotions. Like the weather, if it is raining in one part of the country and sunny in another, just wait. It will change. Our emotional climates are also change-based systems. Feeling cloudy and rainy? Just wait, and the sun will eventually shine again.

The problem arises when we rush in to fix a cloudy day. Leave it alone, and it will change—as long as everyone else in the system is also changing. Health is the constant movement of all things from emotional climate to physical condition. This is the systemic view of life that emphasizes the circular interconnections that link and sustainably regulate all members of a system.

In the beginning days of family therapy, therapists observed that if one member of a family improved, another member might start getting symptomatic. It was as if the whole social system, not an individual, held the symptom. This observation led to a distinctly different paradigm for mental health, one that sees the social system rather than the individual as the patient. With the systemic perspective, both psychology and psychiatry are instantly made obsolete, though they have yet to discern this assessment.

> **Bushmen value shaking things up so as to keep**
> **everything changing. When things aren't shaken,**
> **a life or relationship is at risk of getting stuck.**

Bushman culture maintains health and well-being by helping facilitate never-ceasing movement and change in life. Said differently, Bushmen value shaking things up so as to keep everything changing. When things aren't shaken, a life or relationship is at risk of getting stuck. It doesn't matter what kind of stuck state it is, or whether it is seen as positive or not. Being stuck as a perfect student is as troublesome as never passing a test. A healthy system must aim to share and pass everything around, from victories to defeats. If you show a failing student how successful he is in always frustrating his teacher and parents, the same skills can be used to create a different way of creating an even more satisfying outcome.

The Bushmen's reverence for change is intimately related to the value they place on sharing. In Bushman culture, stinginess is seen as a problem and one of the sources of disease. No one wishes to be a wealthy baron of the Kalahari sand. It makes no sense to hoard. For people who were once nomadic, having a lot of stuff is a pain because it is difficult to haul around. I'm teasing, but it is a fact that the average amount of stuff that a Bushman owns can be carried on a person's back at a moment's notice.

More seriously, a lack of sharing cultivates selfishness, and this causes conflict, bad will, and broken ropes of relationship. Insulting the meat not only brings people back to their humanness, it reminds everyone that it is community rather than individuality that holds their health and well-being. Similarly, family therapists know that a changing family system is the crucible for successful relational living. Helping a perfectionist have a successful taste of defeat is as good for the system as initiating a success for a failure-prone participant. This understanding comes from the same kind of thinking that values the Bushman way of both sharing and insulting the meat.

Experience Some Craziness in Order to Grow

"Tell them what needs to change," I hear Motaope say in one of the spiritual classrooms. "Tell them that all their goods, from meat to honey, as well as emotional ups and downs, must be passed around and shared for everyone to experience."

Motaope is from the village of Zutshwa in southwestern Botswana. Though blind, he can see with his second eyes—the eyes given to him by the gods. He always knows when I am coming to see him and announces my day of arrival weeks before I show up. Tonight he is talking about the importance of shaking everything up.

"When n|om shakes you, everything is cleaned in your mind and heart. Shaking makes you feel renewed. Similarly, your every day gets sorted out in unexpected ways. Don't forget that your daily course of action always needs a good shaking."

As the old man speaks, I am thinking of the time Carl Whitaker talked with me about the need for human beings to shake up their lives with wild creativity, or what he called craziness: "People need to experience their own craziness in order to grow. Without chaos and confusion, there can be no life, no learning, and no growth. Most people are like the walking dead. They haven't tapped into their unique craziness."

Your life cannot be awakened unless you develop a healthy relationship with your own unique kind of craziness.

You need to shake yourself up with absurdity and creativity. Your life cannot be awakened unless you develop a healthy relationship with your own unique kind of craziness. Begin by looking at your everyday habits. Though they provide an efficient means of helping you get things accomplished, you have to be careful that you don't become too mechanized and robotic with your routines. This applies to the whole range of your conduct, from how you get out of bed and prepare for work to the way you interact with your loved ones.

Without some spice, craziness, and chaotic shaking, there will be little to no life in your life. Forget creativity without these ingredients. You will be little more than a predictable automaton. Want to wake up those creative juices and get yourself on the road to transformative experience? Listen to your wisdom elders, whether they are the Bushman n|om-kxaosi or maverick therapists. They suggest that you sprinkle more absurdity into your life.

Read your newspaper in a different fashion, perhaps by first reading a random classified ad. Then turn to any page and read whatever story comes to you. Imagine that the previous classified ad is part of the story you are reading, but no mention has been made of it. Invent a connection and an elaboration of the news report. Consider telling someone your version of the news. Find more ways to bring additional meaning into your world by tapping into absurd ways of awakening your imagination.

Take three photographs of yourself, set up as follows: For the first photograph, sit in front of an empty dinner plate. Stare at the emptiness that has been served. Create an exaggerated lost-and-confused look. For the second photograph, place a piece of meat on the plate. Have a photograph taken of you insulting the meat. I will leave it to your imagination to come up with a way of enacting this scenario. It doesn't matter whether you give the meat a scolding, tickle it with a feather, or blow bubbles over its airspace.

The third course, the final image, will involve your trading places with the meat. Meet your meat in this totally absurd way. Have the meat insult you. This will require stretching your imagination. You may have to imagine someone else's imagination coming up with an idea for you. Come up with anything, even having the meat sit in your dining chair, held up by a fork and dressed as a face with olive eyes and a pepper mustache, while you sit below on a cut out piece of butcher paper that looks like a large plate.

Now you have a portfolio of images featuring you in different scenes that pertain to the theme of insulting the meat. Tape these three photographs to your bathroom mirror. Leave them there for three days. Then put them away in a safe and secure place. Repeat this every month. Know that there will be a triple threat coming to you each month. Three photographs will stare at you each morning when you arise and every night before you retire. Again, limit this to three days a month. The images will remind you of the importance of insulting your meat. (If you are a vegetarian, feel free to use a slice of tofu meatloaf. Also insult your vegetables by reminding them that you are a vegetable for not eating meat—you are what you eat.)

Why would you do such a crazy thing? Is it because you are low on absurd vitamins? Or do your other abs—your absurd muscles—require a workout? Yes, both of these are true as well as many other reasons, most of them too ridiculous for you to understand. If you want to see the light, you need to get a lighter spirit. Right now, all of us live in a non-Kalahari-like culture that weighs us down with over-seriousness. We can't get off the ground and sometimes find it difficult to get out of bed. Levity must first be mastered before heightened joy and spirited levitation is possible.

Flood your life with absurdity. Or at least hook yourself up to an absurd IV—an intra-*vain*-ous drip that treats your vanity. Even a boast about feeling you have nothing to be proud of needs some treatment drips. Drip drop, hippity hop, higglety pigglety, dickory dock, somebody needs to go to the barbershop. Shave off all those thoughts crowding your mind and make room for a Kalahari breeze. It will blow out your serious mind. It brings the defeat of meat and a meeting of dancing feet.

Albert Einstein once said, "Before God we are all equally wise—and equally foolish." He was insulting the meat.

He also said, "There are only two ways to live your life. One is as though nothing is a miracle. The other is as though everything is a miracle." Let's tease the brain that resided underneath that unkempt hair: "There are two ways to tease your meat. One is as though nothing is absurd. The other is as though everything is absurd."

"If a vegetarian eats vegetables, what does a humanitarian eat?" Yes, a comedian has insulted our meat.

"Let your karma insult your dogma." Neither karma nor dogma is your mama, so lighten up.

The gods of the Kalahari speak: "A world without religion doesn't have a prayer, but a world without absurdity is a joke. Furthermore, a world with absurdity is a better joke."

The career of piracy is called the sweet trade. It seeks the yo-ho-ho, and the spoils of land and sea. It isn't for the lily-livered or the faint o' heart. This work requires a strong heart brave enough to play and giggle like a child. Me hearty, my friend, we are looking for some sprogs, raw recruits for the swashbucklin' times ahead. Step right up and become a buccaneer of the absurd. It's the best way to see the sea and seize the breeze that promises to blow you straight to the dou-bloons of God.

When you do something absurd, you loosen the grip of a habit.

Every habit is like glue. The more you perform it, the stickier it gets until you finally can't separate yourself from it. You become your habit. That's when you feel motionless and unable to move; you're stuck on a habit—the habitat of the walking dead. To set yourself free, unglue the glue. Undo the habits in any way: mess with them; short-circuit, distract, immobilize their predictability; mobilize their strength; and utilize their potential for change. Rechannel yourself onto an alternative track, then follow the signs to the unknown.

When you do something absurd, you loosen the grip of a habit. Your logical, conscious mind doesn't know what to do. It is stunned and momentarily loses its control. Soon it will do its best to convince you that silly behavior is just that: silly and thereby unimportant because it isn't terribly serious or heavily rational. Don't listen to the intimidating voice of your conscious. Trust the deeper chorus of your unconscious, where your inner creativity is starving to have a go at your life. Be foolish, ridiculous, and absurd in spite of all those habitual reasons that say you shouldn't.

Embrace Your Inner Fool

Be serious about the performance of the absurd. This really plays a trick on your conscious mind because it is trying to convince you to be serious rather than playful. Your conscious mind doesn't know what to do if you are seriously absurd and absurdly serious. Try it, and feel the freedom it brings. You might even start believing that you have found a shortcut to activating previously hidden inner resources for humor, merriment, and creativity.

The Mardi Gras jester's hat is distinctive. It has three points (*liliripes*) with a jingle bell at each end. The points supposedly represent the two ears and the tail of a donkey that were originally worn by jesters of long ago. The importance of being crowned an ass with shaking bells on top of your head was known and respected in the

Middle Ages. There's nothing like the wisdom that comes from the middle.

During the Middle Ages, there were two kinds of fools. One was nitwitted and dismissed as moronic, while the other was revered and feared because he was licensed by the high court. It was assumed that official fools had been touched by God. They were entitled to not only be funny but to openly critique the rulers and their guests. Since they were divinely inspired, their outrageous words were accepted. They could say what no one else could get away with thinking let alone speaking.

However, there was a fine line defining what was holy and what was mad or bad. If a jester's criticism crossed that line, he could be thrown into unemployment or, worse, find himself without a head. To stay ahead of the guillotine, a jester needed the signs of divine inspiration.

A sanctified fool provided an important contribution to society. Fools were often the only person the king or queen could trust. Their wisdom was held in absurdity. In Shakespeare's *Twelfth Night*, Feste the jester is described as "wise enough to play the fool." King Lear's "all-licensed" fool had great privilege. The same is true for King James, whose jester, Archibald Armstrong, lived the good life until he lost his gig for crossing the line with too many nasty insults of influential people.

The profession of fool ended with the Puritans. They'd have none of those fripperies. At that time, the holy fool moved into the theater and has since remained a part of show business. Without the contributions of wise fools, a country might collapse. Sometimes a country is destroyed, or at least convulsed, because a comedian, whether George Carlin, Lenny Bruce, Wanda Sykes, Bill Maher, Lily Tomlin, Jon Stewart, or Stephen Colbert, says what needs to be voiced to keep things shaking with laughter and social change.

In the Kalahari, everyone is a holy fool and a sacred jester. I invite you to bring the same character into your life. Somewhere inside you is a Kalahari fool—a stand-up comedian who wants to make some clean and dirty fun about your life. It needs to express this jaded side of your being so as to keep your meat insulted. Without an unexpected trip, you can't fall into God's graceful catch. Let the games begin!

Illyria, the setting for Shakespeare's *Twelfth Night*, "is a country permeated with the spirit of the Feast of Fools, where identities are confused 'uncivil rule' applauded ... and 'no harm is done.'"[1] In Illyria, the fool is more than a critic. He is a merry compadre, a crazy wisdom ringleader, and a lord of wild misrule. Being equally welcome below, above, and left and right of the stairs, places a licensed fool in the position of being a most transformative character.

When Feste declares, "I wear not motley in my brain," he is saying that, although his clothes are made of motley or multicolored cloth, his outer appearance is not an indication of the wisdom he holds inside. Similarly, the foolish antics and sayings of a Kalahari n|om-kxao or a therapist of the absurd should not be lazily dismissed. They are hiding something within a clever Trojan horse that sneaks through the gate. They are delivering the much-needed wisdom tonic. The most important truths must hide and ride on the crack separating the extremes. The center point between wisdom and folly is the home of the great wisdom known as crazy.

Illyria was actually an ancient region on the eastern coast of the Adriatic Sea covering parts of modern Croatia, Montenegro, and Albania. Shakespeare also mentions it in *Henry VI* and notes its reputation for pirates. Today, we play with pirate talk and its mythical lore as a means of stepping into the important performance role of a buccaneering jester. Like the storytellers of the Kalahari, we delight in the release of exaggerated sounds and perform swaggering movements when we enact a story.

Bring the fool into your mind and home, disguised as either a pirate, an absurd therapist, or a postmodern Bushman. Blow the wind that shakes the sails of anything that is puffed up. Reveal the holes in what others proclaim as holy. Show them the Jolly Roger—the skull and crossbones—of your pirate flag.

As I construe these things in a place that is simultaneously the Kalahari, the Caribbean, and the blues backroads of Mississippi and Louisiana, all inseparable from the Shakespearean Globe, I fall like

1 Enid Welsford, *The Court Masque* (Cambridge University Press, 1927), 251.

Alice down a rabbit hole, maybe a porthole on a pirate's ship, or somewhere inside a classroom filled with spiritual gold.

The Fourth Mystery

Never reveal the secret of the Jolly Roger: the crossbones are the crossings—the lines that separate the contraries and opposites. In the crossings are found the tracks, the way to spiritual treasure. They bring life to the skeletons of death. They infuse spirit into flesh. In this you find ecstatic bliss, God's way of being jolly. Do you hear me? If so, say, "Roger."

All four of the beginning mysteries have prepared you to be ready to get on the holy tracks and begin a journey toward the mysterium tremendum. Entering the river of movement, ecstatic shaking of the mind, getting tuned, and the fourth mystery—insulting the meat—constitute four interconnected approaches to shaking the whole of you up. Being shaken is the preparation. It rids you of excess baggage, opens your eyes and ears, wakes up your heart, frees you from stuck habits, and sets you on an ecstatic, transformative course.

It is time for you to create a boarding pass. Go get a piece of paper and cut out a rectangle to create the ticket that enables you to get on board a train bound for Glory. Write these words on it, "This train is bound for Glory." Underneath those words, spell out your name.

Now for a surprise: cross out your ticket with a large X, just like the crossbones of Jolly Roger. As you cross out your ticket, say these seemingly contradictory words: "I don't need a ticket for the A train. I'm already on the choo-choo headed to Absurd Glory."

When you have completed making the ticket that you don't really need (though you need to make it anyway), carry it with you. It is good to carry it right next to your driver's license. From this day onward, make a semi-serious pledge to carry your boarding pass.

Look at it from time to time to remind yourself that there are spiritual travelers in the world, from the Kalahari to the Caribbean Islands, who know about this boarding pass. They know that they don't need a ticket that costs money. Their boarding pass is held in their heart and in the heart of absurdity.

With this ticket to ride, any experienced joy, small or large, is enough of a spark to ignite a spiritual fire. That fire can bring a pot to boiling. Soon the steam starts to rise, and we've got ourselves a Kalahari A train bound for Skydom. We've got a Caribbean steamship bound for the Spiritual Lands. Others might say, teasing us with crazy swamp mojo, that we have a Louisiana hot sauce bound for gumbo. Choo choo! Yum yum!

All aboard! This train's a-movin'. We don't want to leave without all the parts of you: the hope and the despair, the burdens and the gifts, the good and the bad, the beautiful and the ugly. Bring it all on board, for we are going to cook it in God's pot. We're going to make some spiritual gumbo with a little bit of dis and a little bit of dat. I hear the old spiritual, sung by the ancestors:

> *People get ready there's a train a-comin' . . .*
> *All you need is faith to hear that diesel hummin'*
> *Don't need no ticket, just thank the Lord*
> *There's a train comin', comin' down the track*
> *All the people who ain't ready better step on back . . .*
> *Don't need no ticket, you just get on board*

We're heading for the spiritual lands. There, we'll learn how to heal, receive the gifts of spirit, learn in the spiritual classrooms, and finally, to find our way to God.

All aboard! Get on board the A Train. It's a soul train. Just ask Duke Ellington: he took it and shook it. This train is bound for Soul and Glory! It starts at Kalahari Grand Central Station, and moves to St. Vincent and New Orleans, with stops everywhere in between. This includes the station where you are presently too stationary. Stand up, and get ready to move and shake. Prepare yourself because this train has some real startin' power. It has the kick to do the trick. It's going to get its hold on you and take you for a holy ride.

Now I come back to myself.

5

THE SPIRITUAL TRACKS

The Fifth Original Mystery

Without a song, the day would never end.
Without a song, the road would never bend.

VINCENT YOUMANS, BILLY ROSE, AND EDUARD ELISA

G od does not talk. A Bushman will tell you that anyone who says he had a conversation with God is deluded or hustling. At most, such a conversation is with trickster. God only makes music. The sacred universe of love is conveyed through feelings, and music is its voice. We get on the track to God through a song, not by concatenations of linguistic articulation. The greatest secret of the universe is that music is our link to God.

The greatest secret of the universe
is that music is our link to God.

Ask a whale. They communicate by songs as well. Their well-developed brains prefer a symphony to a wisecrack.

Second Creation, the Bushman name for the world of words that brought the end of paradise, is the mythological time of trickster. Its language games bend our minds in every imaginable direction. The only way to keep from getting lost in the cosmos is to have a song that fully awakens the heart to become your guide. In the early days of shamanism, before it became a weekend commodity, all you needed was a song from the spirits. Without a song, typically received in a vision fast, you not only had no right to call yourself a shaman, you had no entry to the spirit world. Authentic shamans have always been song catchers.

When your heart is full of longing, you desire a moonlight serenade for connection with the beloved. This auditory pulling of the ropes is capable of piercing and opening your reception to heartrending music. The great song catchers are shamans. They receive their music when God's ropes open the doors of their heart so that a holy song can enter.

"Have you told them that the ropes are the tracks?" N!yae asks me one evening. We are sitting under a canopy of stars, and the sky is so clear, it seems you can reach up and touch the falling stars that sail through it. We have been singing and embracing in the Kalahari way. She is determined to make sure that the rest of the world is taught the old way of tracking God.

I reply as I have before, "The difficulty, my dear friend, concerns how to say it. The rest of the world does not yet accept that a feeling is as real as a tree or a rock."

"Or a lion," she adds with the fiercest facial expression she can muster. She continues, "Are they emotionally blind? Do they keep bumping into feelings and emotions that they don't know what to do with? I bet they keep telling their hearts to go back to sleep."

She is getting at the core difference between the Bushmen and the rest of the world. For the old Bushman n|om-kxaosi, human beings are blind and sensory-deprived until we wake up our deepest emotions. Like opening our physical eyes when waking up from a night's sleep, we must go further to open our heart-eyes and feel the previously unfelt world.

"Tell them they need to wake up twice in the morning," N!yae continues.

This means you should first wake up in the morning and get out of bed. Then awaken your heart: walk out of the bedrock of objects and materialism and into a spiritual world guided by the felt lines of relationship that hold everything together. Now the ropes, rather than the objects they connect, are primary. They are the most important and the most real.

I answer N!yae, "Remember the zombies." I had previously tried to explain a zombie to her, saying they were like the walking dead. In this case, I am speaking of emotional zombies: people walking through their everyday lives without any heightened affect. Zombies get from one place to another by reading a map rather than feeling the ropes. They also talk too much and sing too little. They are as out of it—that is, out of touch with their ancestral way of feeling—as someone sleep-walking in the night.

"If you don't have a n|om song, you will never wake up twice. You will only be a half-awake and half-asleep zombie. You won't be able to get cooked by God. We won't be able to insult your meat; we'll have to insult your vegetables!"

I can hear N!yae appearing before the General Assembly of the United Nations and saying, "It's nice to meet the vegetable people. We are sorry to see that you have wilted. Would you like for us to cook your meat?"

I continue my daydream, seeing myself as her international interpreter, but I realize that it is impossible to interpret. N!yae is correct. What is most important to communicate cannot be written or spoken. It can only be felt. The hands must be clapped and the songs sung, with an invitation to feel what is held in the music—feel it so strongly that it wakes up an inner ecstatic joy that grows and grows until you feel released from the stasis that holds you too still. Then and only then can you feel what she is trying to express. (You can hear the Bushman songs for yourself at www.shakingmedicine.com.)

I recall the time I was in Santa Fe, New Mexico, teaching at an undergraduate arts college. The students were the fringe of their generation, complete with colored hair; tattoos; body piercings; edgy clothing; years of experimentation with drugs, sex, weirdness, and you name it. I had come to the college to teach ecstatic shamanism. On the first day of class, my students arrived to find a room filled with drums and musical instruments. There would be no lecture. Only music and wild drumming would emanate from this university class.

As I sat next to a drum and started a beat, I woke up my feelings and voiced sound improvisation. The atmosphere was suddenly charged with n|om. Without any verbal direction, the classroom turned into the Kalahari. The students felt the ropes and responded to them. They provided testimony to the fact that we are all wired the same as the Bushmen. One by one, the students woke up and found their Bushman bodies ready to shake and quake. All it takes is some spirited music to get things started. It only takes one person waking up, and then it can spread.

Songs Are Tracks to God

Pointer Warren of St. Vincent would not be surprised to hear how important music is in ecstatic realization and communication. He was one of the revered Shaker elders. Before he passed on, he rejoiced over how grateful he was to have found his rope, his track to God. He could never talk for long because his emotions would get so ignited that he had to break into a song. The love he felt for God could not be contained in talk. He needed music for its expression.

Pointer Warren would say, "You know when God has a hold on someone whenever that person can't stop singing. If God's child isn't singing on the outside, there will be music on the inside. You even dream of hearing songs of praise. When God gets you, the music is never far away." (A video of Pointer Warren and other St. Vincent Shakers can also be found on www.shakingmedicine.com.)

Pointer Warren is teaching a Kalahari lesson. God's nearness is presented as never-ceasing music. Whether in the Kalahari, St. Vincent, Louisiana, or other spiritual stops, I have found well-seasoned pilgrims of the spirit filled with music and rhythm. Some people may believe they find the holy through silence, but from the Kalahari perspective, the absence of music is an indication that you are nowhere near God's rock-and-roll club, the place where the heavenly band hangs out.

Many years ago, I was taken to meet the Guarani shamans of the Amazon. In Asunción, the capital city of Paraguay, the president of the Guarani drove me to a ceremony where, in the beginning, no one said a word. Standing in a circle covered with the paraphernalia of feathers, beads, rattles, special carvings, and indescribable bundles of mojo, they simply motioned for me to stand in the middle of the room.

My translator said they wanted to look at my heart. I was asked to sing. Reaching deep into my heart, I invited the n|om, Holy Spirit, and life force to take hold of my voice and bring forth spirited sound. It made me shake with joy. I was so absorbed in the singing that I closed my eyes and forgot where I was. When I opened my eyes, the shamans were weeping. They spoke, "We have seen your heart. We know who you are, and you are one of us. Let's go to the villages and share what we know."

Among shamans, mystics, and healers of the oldest traditions, there is no multiple-choice test that determines whether you are a licensed practitioner. It is a song that demonstrates your relationship with these matters. And not just any song but a song that awakens your heart to feel connected with the divine mysteries. It is not the perfected voice of a Grammy award–winning singer. It is spirited vibration—something that stirs the soul with its sincere longing for the heart ropes that bring us together in relationship.

N!yae is getting impatient. She wants to say something important, and she won't wait any longer: "It is time that everyone in the world knows that the songs are the tracks to God. When we say track, we mean a n|om song."

When we long for God's love and sincerely make ourselves available to receive it, it is akin to dialing a phone to the world of spirit.

The n|om songs are the sacred ropes; the Highway to Heaven; Jacob's ladder; and the lines that take you to people, villages, animals, plants, ancestors, and the gods. They are special songs that enable us to see the tracks. We are speaking of the holy songs—the ones delivered by God when someone longs for divine love. This longing is the pulling, and it is the sacred rope, the electrical power line, the telephone wire, and the channel of communication through which the original mysteries deliver their communication, inspiration, and teaching. When we long for God's love and sincerely make ourselves available to receive it, it is akin to dialing a phone to the world of spirit.

Hook Up to a Songline

Thinking about phoning spirit sets me on the spiritual road again, this time to St. Vincent. I am inside a spiritual vision, reliving the first night of one of my visits. Something seems to have a hold on me, and I am not being metaphorical. Someone is actually holding on to my two hands and pulling me up out of bed.

"I must be dreaming," I think to myself, but now I realize I am awake, with my arms are lifted toward the ceiling. And as impossible as it may sound, I am hanging in the air at a forty-five-degree angle because something has not only grabbed me but has lifted me in the air. I am so startled by this experience that a bolt of energy surges through my whole body. In an instant, I drop, and it isn't a subtle drop, and it is an immediate release, and I fall.

Without hesitation, I get on my knees and pray a simple and direct request, "Dear Lord, I know that you hold me. Please carry me on up. My heart wants to be taught. Thank you, thank you."

To my surprise, the excitement doesn't keep me awake. I must be exhausted from traveling all day to get to the island. Or the prayer relaxed me and handed me over to further doctoring by the spirit. Whatever the case, I go back into the world of mystery because I find myself inside a large room; a place that seems to be suspended above Earth, even beyond the sky. There I stand in front of a gigantic stairway covered in red carpet. I climb those stairs and, at the top, find a throne. It is also deep crimson red, and no one is sitting in it. As I approach it, I hear a voice say, "Archbishop Pompey has God's number." I hear it again, "Archbishop Pompey has God's number." This time, the voice wakes me up.

I ask myself, "Who in the world is Archbishop Pompey?" The next morning, I can barely wait to ask my guide and driver, Andrew, whether he is familiar with this name. He recognizes it.

"Archbishop Pompey is the head of all the spiritual shakers on this island. He lives on top of the island. I think you need to see him." Off we go on the narrow highway that winds up and down the hills and mountains next to the island's seashore. Almost two hours later, we arrive at the archbishop's home. He and his wife greet us, and following the introductions, the elder shaker says, "Let's go to the House of the Lord." He is referring to the small shack next to his residence, traditionally called a praise house, where ceremonies and worship take place.

We take off our shoes and enter the sanctuary. There is a pole in the middle with offerings at its base. I also notice an altar at the front covered with spiritual objects, including a huge brass bell. We sit down on a bench, and he directly poses his question: "What have you come here to ask?"

I tell him what happened to me during the evening. He listens carefully and stares as if examining my inside through some kind of X-ray view.

"Do you know what this kind of vision means?"

I reply, "No sir, I don't."

The archbishop chooses his words carefully: "You have been called to go to a mystery school—a spiritual place where things will be taught and revealed to you. You were brought to me, for I am to be your spiritual pointing father." He explains that a vision directs you to the person who will make the arrangements for you to enter the world of spirit, a classroom for instruction in the mysteries.

He then adds, "I do have God's number. It is a telephone number, and whenever I need to call Him, I dial His number."

I am stunned by the certainty of this man's reply. He is not being poetic, and he is not crazy. He speaks like he has God's phone number the way you and I have the numbers of our family members, friends, and colleagues. As he continues speaking, a song comes into my mind. For a moment, I am lost in the remembrance of some of the services I previously attended in the sanctified Black Churches of America. There, the two most popular gospel songs are "This Little Light of Mine" and "Jesus On the Main Line." I heard the latter song in nearly every Sunday morning church service. I assumed it was metaphorical, but now I am wondering whether they had the same spiritual information technology as the archbishop of St. Vincent. As the old man continues talking, I'm singing the song inside my mind and heart:

Jesus on the main line, tell Him what you want
Jesus on the main line, tell Him what you want
Jesus on the main line, tell Him what you want
You can call Him up and tell Him what you want

Yes, the song is talking about a phone line and a means of calling God. I continue to hear the choir sing in my imagination. The deacons are shouting it with great gusto:

You can call Him up, call Him up and tell Him what you want
You can call Him up, call Him up and tell Him what you want
Call Him up, call Him up and tell Him what you want
Go on, call Him up and tell Him what you want

I never thought that someone might have a spiritual telephone with a direct line to you-know-who. The song says you can call Him up and tell Him what you want. Here I am sitting in front of a white-haired elder of the St. Vincent Shakers, the spiritual authority for the practitioners of this faraway island, and he not only has a phone like this, he has God's personal number. I wonder what he talks to God about. The song answers back:

Hey, Jesus on the main line, tell Him what you want
Jesus on the main line, tell Him what you want
Jesus on the main line, tell Him what you want
Go on, call Him up and tell Him what you want

Fair enough, whatever I need to talk to God about seems appropriate. If I am lost, upset, or lonely, I can call God. If I need directions, I know whom to call. If I need a doctor, here's another place to call. The song confirms this:

Hey, if you're sick and you want to get well, tell Him what you want
Oh, if you're sick and you want to get well, tell Him what you want
Oh, if you're sick and you want to get well, tell Him what you want
Go on, call Him up and tell Him what you want

I am flooded with the realization that when you are in the middle of a spirited ecstatic morning service, and people are singing this song with all their heart and soul, you feel like you actually can call up God on a spiritual main line. The song creates the reality of this phone's presence. The song does not stop. It has me on hold:

Hey, Jesus on the main line, tell Him what you want
Jesus on the main line, tell Him what you want
Jesus on the main line, tell Him what you want
You can call Him up and tell Him what you want

God is surely a mighty God, and even the impossible is possible. What if everyone gave God a call?

His line ain't never busy, tell Him what you want
His line ain't never busy, tell Him what you want
His line ain't never busy, tell Him what you want
Go on, call Him up and tell Him what you want

I have heard the older Bushmen talk about this line to God, though they don't talk about a phone. They talk to the line, and it sends their words to their ancestors and God whenever the n|om is activated. They would fully understand this song:

Hey, Jesus on the main line, tell Him what you want
Jesus on the main line, tell Him what you want

Jesus on the main line, tell Him what you want
You can call Him up and tell Him what you want
You can call Him up and tell Him what you want

And then I come back to myself. The archbishop is looking at me. I think he understands that I am a traveler who is ready for him to supervise a journey to his spiritual lands. He gets very serious and goes straight to the point, "God is calling you to learn more about the spirit. Will you answer that call?"

"Yes, sir," I reply, as if I was in the army. I am ready for this recruitment to becoming a n|om soldier of the Lord, marching on the King's Highway. I await my orders.

Without a song,
there is no hookup, no connection
to the ancestors and the gods.

It is no accident that the Australian Aboriginal people speak of the songlines, for the Bushmen also say that their songs are the lines. They are the tracks that hook you up to the source. Now you can better appreciate and understand what it means to say that a shaman, mystic, or healer needs a song. Without a song, there is no hookup, no connection to the ancestors and the gods. Without a song, what you say about God is baloney.

Journey to the Crossroads

I live near a place in the southern United States where, legend has it, there are some crossroads where a person goes to become transformed into a spirited performer of the blues. Here, two roads cross with the center regarded as a place between the worlds. In the old Louisiana and Mississippi world of root doctoring, conjuring, and hoodoo, you must take your guitar to this spot at either midnight or just before dawn. There, you will meet a man of the dark who will give you the soulful spirit to play the blues. Some folks later went on to suggest that this spirit was the devil, but this is most likely a Christian reframing of an older truth, a case of mistaken spiritual identity.

I like to think that the man who shows up at the crossroads is a Bushman ancestor. He gives you some n|om. After all, the Bushmen were singing the blues a long time ago. Consider this lament, called "The Broken String," transcribed in the 1800s by Wilhelm Bleek and Lucy Lloyd. It is a blues song about the death of a Bushman's friend who had been a shaman and a rainmaker:

> *People were those who*
> *Broke for me the string.*
> *Therefore,*
> *The place became like this to me,*
> *On account of it,*
> *Because the string was that which broke for me.*
> *Therefore,*
> *The place does not feel to me,*
> *As the place used to feel to me,*
> *On account of it.*
> *For,*
> *The place feels as if it stood open before me,*
> *Because the string has broken for me.*
> *Therefore,*
> *The place does not feel pleasant to me,*
> *On account of it.*

The Kalahari strings must be unbroken and tuned in order for life to express its soul. When a string is broken, we long for the lost connection. In the Mississippi Delta, aspiring blues musicians bring their stringed instruments to the crossroads. They come with the deep longing to express what cannot be said through words alone. They need the musical sound that can deliver soul. There, at the middle of the crossroads, the strings can be tuned by stretching the lines that hold the midpoint between life and death, praise and lament, ecstasy and suffering—the originating passageway to the blues.

**You go to the crossroads to hitch a ride with spirit.
Its music rides through you and your instrument.**

Some say this place is located at the intersection of Highways 49 and 61 in Clarksdale, Mississippi, while others claim it is at Moorhead, Mississippi, and called "Where the Southern Crosses the Dog," referring to the trains of that region's railway. Wherever it is, many folks believe that the renowned 1930s bluesman Robert Johnson stood there with his guitar and later sung about it in his "Cross Road Blues."

*I went to the crossroad, fell down on my knees
I went to the crossroad, fell down on my knees
Asked the Lord above, "Have mercy, now save poor Bob,
if you please"*

It is more likely that the story about the crossroads ritual was first brought to the public's attention through a confession made by Robert's friend, Tommy Johnson, who was not related to him. Tommy suddenly started playing the guitar with great skill without extended practice and learning. His brother, LeDell Johnson, was interviewed by the blues scholar David Evans and admitted that Tommy had gone to the crossroads. Critics argue over whether Robert Johnson's "Cross Road Blues" is about the ritual to get his musical chops, as his friend Tommy did, or whether it is about hitchhiking. In the world of spirit, there is no difference. You go to the crossroads to hitch a ride with spirit. Its music rides through you and your instrument.

The old-time blues players who played during the 1930s sometimes said that the dark man at the crossroads takes your guitar and tunes it up. As one of them put it, "And he'll tune up your guitar an' hand it back to you, and you start to play." Some also say that it does not take place at midnight, but "'fore de sunup." They also say that the dark man can make you a dancer too. He'll "strike up a step." What seems most consistent is to "go to the forks of the road at about four a'clock, jis' commence dawnin' day, jis' about crack of day.... He'll tune it an' hand it back to you, and you start to play."

A few suggest that it is important to read the 136th Psalm while you stand there. When you read it at the crack of dawn, storms and high winds come upon you. Don't run away. "Yo'll meet what yo' didn't expect."

When I first moved to Louisiana, I looked up a retired anthropologist who had devoted himself to researching the juke joints and blues musicians of this area. I found Junior living in a shack in Tullos, Louisiana. He told me about all the great bluesmen he had known and about the shantytowns along the Mississippi River. He told me how to protect myself in those places, for my work was going to be with the families in the same towns he had visited over the years.

I then asked him about the crossroads. I did not have to ask whether it existed because without hesitation, he said, "It is real. They took me there. The old bluesmen drove me to the spot where two roads cross. I found a white stone waiting for me in the intersection." He reached over to a shelf and grabbed the rock, rubbing it a while as he continued telling me stories about what had happened to people who went to that spot at the right time. Then he placed the stone in my hand and commented, "It's now yours. It is your time for the journey. Someday I'll take you to the crossroads myself."

I built an altar for that stone. It sits beside a thumb piano, or *mbira*, I received in the Kalahari. The white stone reminds me that the crossroads is the place and time when our feelings come to life. It is not a medieval philosopher's stone. It is a Kalahari musician's stone of pure heart alchemy. With it, the emotions within us are turned on, amplified, and converted into a luminous rope that connects us to the original mysteries. When stretched out and filled with even more stress and tension, soul is felt, plucked, and heard in song. When we enter its midpoint, we are danced, transformed, and brought into First Creation, where life improvises the ever-moving music of creation.

To understand the origin of the crossroads, we have to go all the way back to Africa. In the voodoo tradition, Papa Legba is the *Iwa* (spirit) of the crossroads. He is a gatekeeper who determines who can speak with the sprits. He opens and closes the doorway to spiritual connection, and he holds the rope enabling the gods to make their hookup with you.

**When we enter its midpoint, we are danced, transformed,
and brought into First Creation, where life improvises
the ever-moving music of creation.**

Papa Legba is also the master of language and the trickster. Just as in Bushman belief, language and trickery go hand in hand. In ceremony, he appears as an old man with a cane, wearing a broad-brimmed straw hat, and is typically smoking a pipe and sprinkling water on others. He is sometimes identified with Saint Peter, who holds the same role in the Christian tradition. In Haiti he is also depicted as Saint Lazarus or Saint Anthony. If you visit Benin and Nigeria, you'll see that he is characterized as virile with horns and phallus.

Over twenty-five years ago, I made my first trip to Brazil. I was invited to give a lecture on psychotherapy at a university in São Paulo, but I arrived a day early in order to be introduced to the leader of an Umbanda spirit house. We drove outside the city to a poor area where the woman lived. She was an African woman in her late sixties. Over the years, West African spiritual leaders of the Yoruba faith had come to her for spiritual guidance. She had great respect among those who practiced the ecstatic ways of African-bred spirituality. I shall never forget our first meeting, and I see it now in my mind's eye:

It is a sunny hot day, and I approach her house. The moment I knock on her door, the sky changes and hail starts falling. Ice the size of a baseball is pitched down from the sky. When her door opens, we take refuge while hail flies through all the open windows. We run to the center of the room and watch Mother Nature's extraordinary display. When the hail stops, we meet. I can feel her truth and strength. After we talk and share stories, she invites me to her ceremonial space. There, I fall into a crack, a crossing, and find entry into a different identity—a form of spirited expression I have not met before. I become the embodiment of Papa Legba, the old man who stands at the crossroads.

I am falling into the ground through the Earth, seeing and feeling the traveled ways. Moving from Nigeria to Brazil, Cuba, Haiti, Brooklyn, and São Paulo, I see the sign of the crossing. Enter the ways of the Kingdom of Kongo, now occupied by the countries of Angola,

Cabinda, the Republic of the Congo, and the western portion of the Democratic Republic of the Congo.

One line indicates the boundary that separates all the important yin/yang relations, while the other line is ambivalently both the horizontal road that traverses the boundary and the vertical road linking the above and the below.

In the Kongo, a ritual space is created when you mark the symbol of a Greek cross [+] on the ground. One line indicates the boundary that separates all the important yin/yang relations, while the other line is ambivalently both the horizontal road that traverses the boundary and the vertical road linking the above and the below. It is the crossroads between the living and the dead, the old country road to the ancestors. It is the nodal point, the crack of dawn that separates your life from death. Invoking the circular motion of human souls whirling around the intersecting lines, this space invites and holds the wind of Holy Spirit. Welcome to another entry into the Kalahari's original spirituality, the vortex of a life and death dance. It is where the old one voices a teaching about the fifth mystery.

The Fifth Mystery

The sacred cross is the intersection of the cracks of daybreak and nightfall. It is the whirling logs of the Diné, or Navajo, deities, the symbol of the origin of life. It first moved across the Kalahari sand and reemerged throughout the diaspora, including the Mississippi Delta, all the while giving voice to chant ways and blues ways. Whether a Navajo land hogan or the Delta House of Blues, the Kalahari sand reveals one universe after another in its shape-shifting grains.

Know that the lines of the cross are not the geometry of the seen scene. They are physically unseen, though spiritually realized, ropes of the heart. These lines are the tracks and highways to God. What is a spiritual track? It is a soundtrack from God. The old ways call the holy songs tracks, lines, ropes, roads, and highways. God's music is the music of the spheres. Its geometry is felt rather than measured. Its measures are to be sung.

Now is the time for you to mark your entry through the spirited gate. You need to find your crossroads, the gateway that can take you anywhere in this world or in any other worlds. Take a piece of chalk and make a cross on your bed sheet. It doesn't matter whether the mark is seen. Call this your crossroads. Before you go to sleep, stand on your bed, directly in the middle of the crossroads.

Imagine yourself standing on the actual crossing of the blues roads in the delta country. Know that others have stood there and had their instruments tuned; that's how they made themselves ready to be played by the gods. Visualize and feel yourself standing there, and continue to consider how the sign of the crossing was carried across the ocean, moving from Africa to the Americas.

Now imagine yourself standing in New Orleans at the historical site of Congo Square. There, the slaves were first permitted to openly express their spirituality with rhythm, music, and dancing movement. Think of how many crosses have been on the ground of Congo Square. The Kongo was brought to Congo Square. It opened the door so the soul of our ancestors could come through the gate.

The ropes from the Kalahari were first stretched across the African continent and then across the Atlantic Ocean. When they arrived in Congo Square, the ropes were carried farther up the Mississippi River, like a great snake of kundalini, stopping to pour n|om and soul into the music of all its port stations. From Congo Square in New Orleans, it traveled to Beale Street in Memphis and on up to St. Louis, Chicago, Kansas City, New York City, Detroit, San Francisco, and then the rest of the world. Soul got into our water. We drank it, and the new world came alive again as it had been in the beginning.

As you think of how the ropes moved everywhere and brought spirited music with each stretching and pulling, select a song that has soul for you. It doesn't matter what genre of music you regard as soulful. Sing it out loud or croon it softly to yourself. You can even choose to play your stereo as you carry out this ritual. Allow the music to make you bounce on top of your bed. Up and down you go on your own crossroads. As you stand and move at the gate, invite a song to soulfully pour into your whole consciousness.

Music brings life to the lines. It makes them move and whirl. As they move, you move as well. Go to sleep imagining that the crossing is a whirling wind above you. It wants to lift you and carry you somewhere, and it needs music to fuel its movement. It brings music to inspire your movement. Pray for a song. For the rest of your life, stop praying for things and ideas. Only pray for the music, for it is the sacred track to the mysteries. It will lead you to whatever you need.

The songs that come from God may be recognizable music or tunes never before heard. It doesn't matter. When it comes from God, it becomes your song. Such a song is your lifeline to the holy. Now that you know what it is you are looking for, start asking for it and expecting it.

Now I come back to myself.

A Song Gets You Moving in the Spirit

George Gershwin was one of the great song catchers in the history of American songwriting, but he was cut down in his prime due to an inoperable brain tumor. The last song he wrote was "Our Love Is Here to Stay." His brother, Ira, wrote lyrics for George's music. They were very close, and it has been proposed that their last song expressed their longing for their brotherhood prior to George's passing on. In their last song, love is presented as the bridge of eternity. It never ends and is very clear that it is here to stay—"not for a year, but ever and a day."

Music brings life to the lines.
It makes them move and whirl.
As they move, you move as well.

Was Gershwin a shaman? Yes, he was an ecstatic Broadway mystic and a Tin Pan Alley shaman during those moments when his heart opened and threw out a rope that lassoed a song, a tune holding the heightened longings of love. But, like a Bushman, he was only a shaman when he was receiving and performing his song, allowing it to pull the ropes inside our hearts. Shamanism and mysticism bring on the soul train of music when someone truly feels the passion churned by a moving song.

What is your song? This is the question that needs to inspire your life. Find the song that opens and pours the magic potion of love into your heart. All lovers know that a romantic melody instantly pours their love into one another. The same is true for the heart-opening songs that access our intimacy with the gods. Somewhere out there is a sacred song for you that provides connection and relationship with the divine. One of the biggest secrets about spirituality is that all medicine people were strong spiritual healers and leaders because they had a sacred song that hooked them up to the Creator.

A song from God is a rope. It's all you need to make a connection with the holy. If you are lucky enough to have more than one song, you are overflowing with ropes, and this constitutes great spiritual wealth. One of the names an Amazonian Guarani Indian elder gave me was He Who Catches the Songs because my heart has been able to catch more than a few sacred tunes. Some are original melodies, others are simple improvisations, and a few are recognizable songs supercharged with n|om. They are my link to the divine heart.

A song from God is a rope. It's all you need
to make a connection with the holy.

The original teachers of spirituality ask us to live as if getting a song will be the answer to all our questions and the fulfillment of all our desire. Like lovers who ask a band to play their song, we each need a love song with the divine so we can ask the orchestra inside our heart to play it whenever we need a closer connection to the main source. A sacred song is the track that will lead us to whatever we are looking for in our life's mission.

Do you whistle while you work? If not, then start doing so. Hum, croon, or sing if you prefer. There is no better seed for happiness than making music. If you feel down, express a sad song. It will pick up your emotions and carry you somewhere. Feeling happy? Then put on a happy face and sing about it.

Get yourself a new address book. It doesn't matter what size it is. Fill the book with as many names of songs that you know. Every time you hear a new song that you like, add its name. Carry this address book with you. Whenever you catch yourself stuck in a feeling that needs to change, get out your address book and dial a song. Sing it to yourself. Know the Bushmen's secret that passionately singing a song can build a road if you sing it with all your heart and soul. Each song leads to an address, and at the end of its road is a place of transformation, unique and perfect for the situation in which you sing it.

Songs are lines because they connect your heart with the beloved, whether it is your spouse, child, ancestor, or God. You sing to make your relationships strong. Without a song, you aren't going to have strong ropes, and you won't get anywhere without them. Try playing a musical instrument—even the comb or kazoo—in order to build yourself another Highway to Heaven.

A sacred song is the track that will lead us to whatever we are looking for in our life's mission.

Without exception, you cannot significantly heal any human being, including yourself, unless you have a song in your heart. As Lorenz Hart and Richard Rodgers proposed, "But I always knew I would live life through with a song in my heart for you." With a song in your heart, you feel the touch of your beloved. With a sacred song in your heart, you feel touched by God. This is how the world of soul was designed and built.

When we started prioritizing thoughts over feelings and serious-ness over play, our emotions became ignored. We forgot what was possible if we kept our good feelings well fed. This is how we lost hold of the ropes. Fortunately, they never went away. They are sleeping in our hearts, waiting for a song to wake them up.

Never stop serenading the one you love. String titles of songs together if you can't remember the lyrics of a particular song. Sing a bit of a melody and splice it with other melodic excerpts. For example, you can sing this string: "For once in my life, I love every breath you take. Fools fall in love, because they want someone to watch over me and be close to you. Embraceable you, I can't stop loving you, which is why I just called to say I love you. What the world needs now is love, sweet love—love makes the world go 'round."

God also wants to be serenaded, so get on your knees and sing about your love for God in whatever cultural mode and genre touches your heart most deeply. Make another string, your own rope of melodic strands: "Precious Lord, take my hand, for nobody knows the trouble I've seen. This little light of mine wants everybody to know that Jesus loves you, this I know. Something got a hold of me because He's got the whole world in his hands. It's amazing grace when you have a closer walk with thee. When his eye is on the sparrow, it brings a blessed assurance and the sweet bye and bye."

Do you want to feel all the mysteries? Then start singing and dancing. You can't move the way you need to move unless there is a concert in your soul. Consider purchasing a drum. Any kind of drum will work. Go to a music store and select the percussion instrument that tugs at you. Maybe you can start by simply purchasing a pair of drumsticks or brushes. Bring it home and treat it like a sacred object. Consider that a single instrument that makes rhythm or music is probably holier than all the sacred symbols and holy trinkets that are so seriously sought and collected.

Replace your crystal with a kazoo, trade in your feather for a pair of bongos, and substitute a CD of soulful music for a religious book. Call your altar, if you have one, a concert hall. If you are altar-less, then clear a space in your home to honor music. Maybe you need a shrine for your stereo. Replace images of holy people with photos of musicians. Swap a yoga image for a photo of Ray Charles. Do whatever it takes to make you more mindful of the sacred importance of music. Can you draw a highway and add some images of musical notes on it? Take note: you need more melodic scales swimming up and down your spiritual stream.

Pirates also have their songs and shanties. They sang while they worked and when they played. There was a song for good times and bad times. They even sang when they were knocking each other down to the ground: *Please pay attention and listen to me. Give me some time to blow the man down.*

Without a song, you ain't goin' anywhere, mate. You can't get down or be lifted up without a tune. Even a loony tune is better than no music at all. The St. Vincent Shakers also call sacred songs the lines, tracks, and roads to the spiritual lands. They go on to propose that a song is a ship, which is to say that it enables your heart to set sail across the ecstatic ocean of emotions with its longed-for horizon, ever so close but so far away.

As the old spiritual put it:
'Tis the old ship of Zion, 'tis the ol' ship of Zion
'Tis the old ship of Zion, git on board, git on board

It has landed many a thousand
It was good for my dear Mother
It will take you home to glory

A song is what gets you moving in the spirit. It doesn't matter whether you walk or run, or whether you travel by land, sea, or air with a horse, train, ship, or plane. Every song provides a unique way of carrying you across the gulf that divides. It gets you on board the line of relationship. There, you feel one with the other.

In relationship is found union and eternity. It is outside the reach of historical time. We all desperately want to enter spiritual time, the syncopated jazz of being in the enlivened moment. As Diana Ross sings, "In time the Rockies may crumble, Gibraltar may tumble. They're only made of clay." But in the universe of spirit, "our love is here to stay."

6

THE ECSTATIC PUMP:
THE ORIGINAL MEANS OF HEALING

The Sixth Original Mystery

It is the shaking that heals.... When you touch someone with this shaking,
the power of spirit flows into them. This is the secret of healing.

MOTAOPE SABOABUE

No one has any business trying to heal unless they have received a song from God. That's old school. Whether you are a Native American medicine person, a Hawaiian kahuna, or a Kalahari Bushman, a sacred song is the line that connects you to the divine and enables the medicine to come forth, whether by direct infusion or recommended prescription. Sanctified healing takes place when music moved by the love of God anoints our doctoring.

The musical expression of the Bushmen in their ecstatic dances involves soulful singing, strong hand clapping, and the percussive sound of cocoon rattles that are wrapped around the legs of the male dancers. The women's dance adds a drum, sometimes in the form of a large empty fuel container. The performance of each song is delivered in a unique fashion involving spontaneous embellishment of the tune and polyrhythmic hand clapping. As n|om fills their hearts, the clapping turns to a crisp cracking sound, and the singing of some of the best improvisers gives way to a kind of free-form, yodel-like scat singing that soars above the melodic line. Kalahari jazz is all about holding on to a basic melody and then awakening your heart to be wild with embellishing its performance.

A sacred song is the line that connects you to the divine and enables the medicine to come forth, whether by direct infusion or recommended prescription.

When the community gathers for a men's dance, music is sung by a tightly woven circle of women, their legs and knees loosely brushing against one another. They clap rhythms that are complexly syncopated, singing various strands of undulating melodies. Dancing men move around the feminine circle of singing women. The women's clapping and singing constitute the medium through which arrows of n|om are shot outwards. The men emotionally soften their feelings as they dance around the women, allowing the heart-inspired music to pierce their hearts.

In the women's dance (see www.shakingmedicine.com for a film clip of the women's dance), the women move inside their circle while most of the men sit outside the dance perimeter. Most men are afraid of the strongest women, believing their n|om is so strong that it may knock them out. It is not surprising to see the mightiest hunter teased because he fears getting too close to a granny whose n|om may track him down and result in an arrow that slices through any pretentiousness he might carry.

Whenever the men or women n|om-kxaosi start to feel cooked by the n|om music, they step inside the inner circle and come near the fire. There, their arms reach out to the evening air to catch the ecstatic offerings of the cosmos. All the energies of life flow through those who are open to its many forms—undercurrents of earth and overcurrents of sky, bioelectric fields of plants and animals, magnetically charged attractions of intimacy and relationship, and even the danced opposites of the sacred and profane. This is a genuine awakening of life that is set on fire by the heart-struck match of spirited music.

The sun has just gone down, and darkness is settling in for the evening. Two old women start a small fire. They sit near it, and start clapping and singing. Soon more women step out of the darkness. Children are giggling and playing nearby. You wouldn't be able to predict how things will soon change. It begins as fun and merriment. The women gather to become a singing group sitting in a circle, protecting a fire. A few of them start clapping a different beat than the others, making exhilarating rhythmic patterns. Children continue to play around them. The dance is preparing itself for the night.

Without announcement, the men dance themselves onto the fire-set stage. The darkness was their curtain, and they have made their first appearance to the women. They look serious and ready to initiate a new act in the evening drama. They wear ankle rattles of dry cocoons that shush softly with their carefully orchestrated movement; they know this is serious business. They come to the dance to help the community and to keep each other strong. They also arrive to enjoy themselves and to open their hearts in an extreme way that few cultures have ever known. They begin their flight into ecstasy with the performance of tiny dance steps that are stamped hard on the accented beat. All the while, the women continue clapping with their fingers spread stiff.

The men dance with more determination and certitude. The dance is taking over; they are being danced. The women are being clapped and sung. Everyone is made available for the gods to have an evening that embodies flesh and fire. Sweat and dust join in, and the stars glimmer from above. The dance gets more and more intense, and some bodies start standing erect and falling like trees struck by lightning. Screams are heard. Kalahari transformation has begun.

The people help each other go in and out of other worlds of experience. Some sing, clap, and dance while others go to places no words can describe. They are the holders of the Kalahari mysteries. They stamp the hardest. They sing with the most fervor. They enter the wild gracefully. They become the gracious gift of the wild.

Old men and women with wrinkled skin and failing sight get reborn by the flames of this awakened night. Here, the cough of a

127

hunting lion may enter a man, and the mighty leap of a beautiful kudu may possess a woman. All this is orchestrated far above the Kalahari Desert, far above the great southern sky, far above the ever-turning Earth, far above the twinkling stars where the Bushmen believe all great dancers eventually find their original home. The journey of the Kalahari dance begins with music and ends in the stars where it all began. This is the Bushman circle of life, created by the songs that express the longings for original love-inspired spirituality.

The Guarani Indians of South America teach that a sacred song not only awakens your heart, it provides a channel for what they call the word souls to be carried and delivered to the community. The word souls are the songs and messages their shamans deliver while under the influence of divine inspiration. When a sick person asks for help, healing takes place through this straightforward sequence: a shaman sings a sacred song, a divine connection is made, and the word souls express the balm.

The particular form of tonic administered may be rhythm, music, lyrics, movement, touch, a specified direction to take a plant, some form of action, or a poetic rendering of meaning. Whatever the divine brings forth through the word souls is the medicine the clinic in the sky has cooked up for you. Without a song, there will be no clean connection, and the consciously prescribed recommendations will come from the mind of trickster rather than the divine nurses and doctors.

Calling on the Doctor Within for Healing

Albert Schweitzer proposed that each person has a doctor inside, and all that healers and medical doctors do is knock on the inner doctor's door to request care of the patient. Whether you take a sugar pill, a pharmacological substance, or a prayer, the bottom line may well be that all these agents perform the same role of ringing the doorbell of an inner doctor.

Who is that inner doctor? It is the whole living system that holds the self-regulating processes inherent within the organization of your biological being. In other words, you are built to be self-regulating and self-healing. When you need to heal or self-correct, somebody needs to wake up your inner doctor. From this perspective, the rituals of the Kalahari and the Mayo Clinic are the same. They are wake-up calls.

Each person has a doctor inside, and all that healers and medical doctors do is knock on the inner doctor's door to request care of the patient.

I met an extraordinary folk healer in Brazil named João de Carvalho. When he was an adolescent, he would wake up in the middle of the night and experience a vibrant green light in his room. Other family members watched him communicate with this luminous presence, and these mystical experiences ultimately made him a healer.

In the early days of his practice, João would pray for the sick. Saying his prayers with a deeply felt cadence—an inner voice assumed to be associated with the luminosity that always guided him—he would announce a medical prescription. He would write down the recipe for the medicine, and the local pharmacist would make it. Before long, hundreds of sick people lined the streets of his town every morning before he woke up. He never charged anything for his practice because he felt it was a gift from God, something he never earned and that should be shared freely with the sick and needy.

Before long, the powerful pharmacological corporations from the United States and Europe heard about some of his new remedies. They wanted the recipes so their profits could increase. João refused to cooperate. They offered him a large fortune, and when he refused to go along, they had government officials charge him with unlawfully practicing medicine. He went into exile, hiding in one village after another. Wherever he went, the people lined up to see him. Word always got out. Through his prayers, João was told that he didn't need to give anyone a chemical mixture. The same medicinal effect took place if he prayed over a glass of water. The people continued to be healed, but this time they only needed to drink a glass of blessed water.

João also found that he could effectively write out a prescription of scripture. Like a doctor writing out the medicine needed for treatment, he would write out a verse of scripture to be taken in by the patient. This, too, was healing. Modern science would say that all these results take place due to the placebo effect: if you believe you have received medicine, then it is medicine. Dr. Schweitzer would say that each treatment is a message sent to the patient's inner doctor: "Wake up. Please come out of your room and heal me."

Arrows of Healing and Arrows of Harm

What do the world's first healers and doctors have to say about healing sickness? Having over sixty thousand years of practice to empirically inform their culture, they have had the time to get some basic things worked out. First, the Bushmen understand the psychosomatic nature of our human condition. Second, they do not split the mind and body but conduct holistic medical practice.

In the Kalahari, a group of n|om-kxaosi has gathered to talk with me about their healing way. "What make you sick are dirty arrows," Toma explains. "Either your own arrows or those that someone else shot into you can get dirty and make you ill."

An arrow may be partly regarded as a Bushman metaphor for the vehicle that carries medicine, whether it is good or bad. A clean arrow brings health and revitalization, whereas a dirty arrow brings sickness and tiredness. Arrows that carry n|om are called *tchisi*. Sometimes the Bushmen refer to needles rather than arrows that transport the n|om. The ||auhsi are needles charged with n|om, and are usually assumed to be more directly dispensed by the Sky God rather than mediated through other living beings.

"The main culprit for making your arrows dirty is anger."

"What makes an arrow dirty?" I ask the group, and they all start speaking at the same time. Though articulated by several individuals, they generally bring the same message: "The main culprit for making your arrows dirty is anger. The same is true for needles, thorns, and nails."

Since anything sharp and pointed may pierce and cross the boundary of your skin, all these names of physical objects are used to refer to that which delivers either sickness or medicine. In the old days, the elders spoke of thorns, whereas today's Bushman doctors speak of nails and arrows.

They continue, "Anger makes your arrows dirty. The other two toxins that make them dirty are jealousy and selfishness. Be careful when you lose your temper, for it shoots a dirty arrow that can make someone sick. The same thing happens when you lose control of your jealousy or forget to share your wealth with others. All these things make people sick."

When a feeling is intensified to such an extent that it feels real and solid, then it has become an arrow.

The arrows and nails are amplified feelings. When a feeling is intensified to such an extent that it feels real and solid, then it has become an arrow. It is as experientially real as an arrow made of stick and bone. Once you pass a certain emotional threshold, a feeling has the same relational impact as any physical object that makes contact with you.

"You might as well tell them everything," Twa shouts out. As the chief's wife in the village of Chokwe, she is respected as a holder of the women's way of healing. She believes that human beings are destroying the world and the old ways must be made available before it is all over. When she says, "Tell them everything," I feel her rope pulling on me. She is going to pull the words out of me.

I have learned many things from diverse shamans and healers throughout the world. As you delve deep into their spiritual knowledge, they teach you both sides—what the Balinese call the left and right ways of practice. The left signifies dark sorcery, whereas the right indicates positive light, the domain of healing. If you want to put a spell on someone, make an appointment with a practitioner of the left. If you want to be healed from sickness, seek a person of the right. To be a master of the medicine and an elder of the whole nature of spirituality, you must understand the ways of both. Otherwise, how could you possibly handle situations that come at you from the dark side?

The secret to both light and dark doctoring involves the ability to escalate your inner feelings, doing so in a way that concentrates rather than disperses the energy of the emotion. Most people can't amplify a feeling without quickly short-circuiting it. They either switch tracks to become too cognitively aware of the situation or they start worrying about losing control of their consciousness. When you are able to amplify a feeling without interference from the trickster commentary and the influence of your conscious mind, you enter the alchemical work of the shamans, healers, and mystical doctors.

Practitioners of the right side only amplify feelings of love. Those on the left side accentuate anger, hate, jealousy, and selfishness. Both practitioners know that there is a ricochet, or boomerang, effect associated with their work. What is shot out may come back and hit you. If you shoot arrows of love, affection will come back to you. The cost of shooting dirty arrows is that you or someone close to you may get sick as well. It's a tricky business.

A wise shaman never shoots an arrow of harm unless he or she feels there is no other choice. When someone crosses the line and threatens to harm your family, it is very difficult to resist fighting the aggressor. All shamans are human beings and have been tested in ways that go far beyond what most people are challenged with. They learn what the consequences are for using the left side. With wisdom, they learn to never indulge in overprotection or retribution. They also learn to not indulge on either side. Too much light, after all, can draw in and highlight the dark.

Healing through Pulling

Toma is getting ready to shoot an arrow into me. I can see him concentrating. Something has taken control of him, and he is staring at me. A ripple of energy travels up his chest like waves of an ocean in fast motion. N|om is boiling in his belly. Now he is wrapping his emotion into a fluidic, almost taffy-like ball the size of a fist. His lower belly is tight with this ball, ready to be thrown at me. In a moment, a threshold will be reached, and he'll release the n|om ball without effort. It will be smeared on the tip of an arrow and shot out of his belly, traveling along the rope attached to both of us. It travels inside the hollow tube of the rope and hits me straight on. I jump as if startled, even though I have watched it coming. It hits me like an ecstatic lightning bolt. I have received an arrow.

I know what he is doing because I have done the same to him and other Bushmen for many years. For over twenty-five years, I have been shooting arrows like this. (You can see a young Kalahari woman receive an arrow from an elder woman n|om-kxao on the Bushman video clip posted on www.shakingmedicine.com.) What a strange thing to confess: yes, I, a university professor, admit to shooting arrows into people. Sometimes it takes only a second or two to shoot one, while at other times, it takes a little longer. Once you feel an arrow needs to be shot, the process kicks into motion without any effort.

**Bushman healing involves both shooting arrows of pure
n|om into another person and cleaning dirty arrows.**

I am looking at Twa, another of my n|om wives. She always wants the arrows and nails of n|om; I feel it coming. There is a tightness and immediate wiggle in the muscles of my hip. The vibration takes place in a second and pulses around five times before the release. There is a sound, a kind of shout associated with its release, particularly if it is carrying plenty of n|om.

Bushman healing involves both shooting arrows of pure n|om into another person and cleaning dirty arrows. You clean the dirty arrows inside another person by removing those arrows or by sending so much clean n|om into them that it blows out the dirt. Or you do both at the same time.

When you pull out sickness, you must pull with enough strength so that the other person's sickness doesn't get stuck in you. You must pull it out of them and out of you. Strong healers never—I repeat: never—get sick, weary, or exhausted after doctoring another person.

They feel revived and invigorated after healing others because the process has also healed them.

"Many Bushmen become n|om-kxaosi, owners of n|om," Twa makes clear. "They own the feeling for n|om, the energetic force associated with the love of God. But few of us become healers because our n|om must be strong enough to pull the sickness. We use the word ≠hoe to refer to pulling out the sickness with your hands."

Pulling requires the ability to boil the n|om, amplifying your good ecstatic feelings, without falling over. Most people can't hold on to n|om for very long. When you first experience it, you may get frightened because it feels like something has taken over you or that it will kill you. You do not feel in control of yourself, and that is what many of us fear most. If you get past the fear and allow it to grab you, it will bring such an intense rush of energy that few can stay with it for long. An infant with n|om usually falls over or faints. When you go to a Pentecostal church service and watch folks "slain in the spirit," you see that they fall to the ground when the preacher touches them. They are infants in n|om. They do not know how to stand, walk, let alone dance with the Holy Ghost n|om power.

It takes a lifetime of devotion to n|om to find your place in its current. You must learn not only how to jump into its stream, but how to float, splash, and swim inside it. Some Bushmen sit at its periphery, feeling it charge them up in an invigorating way as they remain on the outside of the dance. This is no small outcome. Being on the edge of a n|om river of fire will heat up your life and bring you more positive benefits than any spa, spiritual practice, or renowned healer can offer. This in itself is a remarkable mystery and gift.

Over time, you become a n|om being, a spirit-filled person. This is when you live for n|om, the ecstatic love that permeates your whole being.

You also can choose to reach out and touch the n|om, getting a direct hit from it. Its electricity will enter you and work on you. If you do this often enough, n|om will rewire your insides and turn you into a different kind of human being. You will learn to drink, breathe, and travel in it. Over time, you become a n|om being, a spirit-filled person. This is when you live for n|om, the ecstatic love that permeates your whole being. A person who catches a love for n|om is a n|om-kxao.

Whether you get rewired enough to activate ≠hoe, or the pulling, is a matter that is entirely between you and God. No human being can determine this for you. You simply can't decide that you want to be a healer because it sounds like a nice thing to do for others. You can't enroll yourself in a healing school or weekend workshop to learn to heal. It's not a human choice; you and God have to work this one out. If you are chosen to become a healer, then you will find that when you spontaneously heat your n|om to a required extent, the pulling, the ≠hoe, will be switched on. You just have to find your way to the on switch. It has less to do with learning and more to do with turning it on.

Pulling is not a simulated action of grabbing something off another's body and throwing it away. If you wonder whether you have ever pulled, then you haven't. Pulling is an experience you will never forget. Though invisible to an outsider's eye, you will feel pulled by something so strong that it will shock you to the core. It will feel like an actual rope is attached inside of you, and yanked back and forth.

Experience a Kalahari Musical Within

Tonight, tonight—it's not just any night. It's n|om night in the Kalahari. I've danced most of the evening, and my n|om wives, Twa, N!yae, and Ti!ae, are surrounding me. We are pulling the ropes. There is a tightened knot inside my belly that has become as hard as steel, but it pulses like a piston. I am pumping n|om and sending it up my spine. But there is more to it than that. It also is pulling a rope that is going to the bellies of these three Bushman women. We are pulling one another. It is far more intense than the in-and-out movement of sexual intercourse. As wonderful and strong as that can be, it is an entirely different experiential universe to have your ropes pulled.

A Kalahari n|om dance is as thrilling as a Broadway musical. On this night, there is passion, music, and heavenly love. I want to sing along with Tony and Maria from *West Side Story*, though tonight it's *Kalahari Story*, and the lyrics are felt and changing all the time:

Tonight, tonight, it all began tonight,
I felt you and the world flew away.

Yes, in the midst of a n|om dance, the world of heavy problems and burdens vanishes. It is a new world tonight, bathed in love and intimate rejuvenation with the whole universe as we dance together under the glittering lights of a Kalahari sky.

Tonight, tonight,
There's only n|om tonight,
How you are, how you move, how you sing.

The women n|om-kxaosi answer me as a chorus:

Today, all day, I had the feeling the ropes would take us flying.
I know now I was right,
For here you are and what was just our world is a star tonight!

Like Broadway, we all sing together now:

Tonight, tonight,
The village is all light,
With stars and moons all over the sky.
Tonight, tonight, the world is wild and bright,
Singing n|om, shooting sparks into you.
Today,
The world was just a village,
A place for me to walk in,
No stronger than all might,
But here you are,
And what was just a world is a star.
Tonight . . .

The ancestors and the stars sing back to us:

Goodnight, goodnight,
Sleep well and when you dream,
Dream of us
Tonight.

Back and forth, like mighty engines, our pumping, singing, and dancing falls into sync. The ropes make us feel closer. They blur the boundaries of our skin. As we do this, the rope gets thicker and stronger. Twa knows that she has pulled away the materiality of my body. My whole chest is wide open and empty, as are the sky and the universe.

The women then place their hands inside of me. Yes, it feels like all their hands have entered. They are holding my organs and pulling them, removing them, making room for the dance to expand. There is no longer a rope as there was before. Their hands and arms are now the rope, and it has grabbed me from the inside. We have gone past the limitations of skin, organs, and materiality. We are soulfully inside one another.

This experience is not worrisome. It is the delight of a Broadway musical multiplied by infinity. This Kalahari deep cleaning, ecstatic inner massage, profound loving, intercourse of n|om is a mystery seldom imagined by those outside this distant desert venue. It is a peak performance of a n|om-way musical that deserves to win every Tony Award. This is a show that swings and rocks. It sings and delivers a home for every Maria. Its somewhere takes you everywhere. Tonight's Times Square has become Kalahari Circle.

You must hand over your voice to the gods.
They must sing through you. N|om sings you.

There is absolutely no possibility for this kind of ecstatic experience to take place while being still or silent. You have to be moving, pulsing, vibrating, and most important, singing with all your being.

You must hand over your voice to the gods. They must sing through you. N|om sings you. This n|om-sanctified Broadway singing of joy is what triggers the pulling. I will say it once again: there is no show, no pulling forth the magic of transformative theater, without n|om surging through you as a feature song you'll never forget. You will hum it to yourself for the rest of your life.

"I love to hear you sing like my grandmother," Ti!ae says after we have fallen to the ground. The oldest way of singing pours through my vocal chords, sometimes sounding like scat yodeling when the pulling is strongest. I don't know whether it is the vibrations from the n|om singing that does the pulling or if it is the other way around. Does the pulling in my belly bring out the music? It doesn't matter. Does the Bushman audience pull a great performance out of the doctoring actors on stage? What is important to know is that there is no pulling in a Kalahari show without vibrant sound making. When this takes place, the night becomes a life-changing musical under the open canopy of the Kalahari starlight theater.

Sometimes the sounds go past being a recognized form of human music. They may sound more like a Bobby McFerrin–type improvised voice drum, or they may involve shrill shrieking sounds like those made by excited African birds. However n|om finds its voice, rest assured that you have no control of it. The singing of n|om is outside the range of conscious mind. Your well-rehearsed mental tricks and treats have no influence on the aesthetic choices regarding a n|om performance. When n|om cooks you, the deeper parts of you wake up and come onstage. You will feel things and do things you never knew existed. Welcome to the greater mysteries of original spirituality.

Holy Pulling Activates the Ecstatic Pump

A Bushman healer is another kind of n|om-kxaosi. The Ju|'hoan Bushman word for those who can pull out the sickness with trembling hands is !aaiha. An !aaiha's n|om can pull another person's strings. When the pulling is strongest, you feel like your torso has a pump inside it. It bends you over and is accompanied by the extraordinary vocalizations of n|om. This is what the Bushmen call the ecstatic pump. There can be no pulling of the sickness, no healing, no cleanup job, no grand performance of n|om without this pump operating at full steam.

There are ancient images of Bushman rock art showing dance scenes in which a n|om-kxao is bent over, with arms and hands held stiffly behind his or her back. That is a depiction of the pump in operation. It does that to you automatically. All Bushmen recognize when someone is ready to heal others because they see that the body pump has started doing its thing.

When you get a song from God, it links you to the holy pulling, which in turn activates the pump. A n|om song brings its own powerful vibration and a motion that is like pulling the cord of a lawn mower to get the motor started. Once the motor is running, the whole of you sings and moves, and makes the spiritual landscape trim and beautiful again.

There is a natural healing process within us that is activated by the ecstatic pumping movements of the abdominal area. This is the spirited means by which sickness is pulled out of others and oneself. Surprisingly few healing traditions know about this ecstatic body pump. The Bushmen's ancient knowledge about these matters calls for an immediate reconsideration of our understanding and practice of healing.

Bushman elders believe it is dangerous to attempt healing without mastery of this experiential ecstatic pump. The pump not only helps pull the sickness out of the patient, it pulls sickness and tiredness out of the healer. Without this pump, you risk taking in the other person's sickness. A healer should feel rejuvenated and healed after a healing; this is the indication that one is ready to heal others as a master.

In the middle of a hot Kalahari day, Toma stands underneath a camelthorn tree, the only place in the village where there is any shade. His pump is rippling contractions up and down his abdomen at a pulse of approximately one pumping movement per second. As he is naturally pumped this way, he performs a gutteral sound with intermingled singing. His hands are fluttering as he touches Twa's head. He gently trembles them, and his fingers vibrate her scalp. Soon he carefully holds the sides of her head, and I can see the vibration transfer to her. Her head appears to be vibrating Toma's hands rather than the other way around. Their vibration is the same, and they have both submitted to its harmonic interaction.

As Toma holds on to Twa, his singing gets louder, and I can see his whole body pump the sickness out of her. He is cleaning her. She isn't sick, but like every human being, she needs regular tune-ups and inner cleanings. This is a Bushman gas station. Hook yourself up to a human n|om-kxao pump and get filled with n|om. You also get a free Bushman car wash because your insides get cleaned and vacuumed in the process.

When you observe the doctoring of healers from other indigenous cultures, pay attention to how the song they sing carries a pulse. Note how it embodies a pumping—a lifting with its rhythmic pulse and its tonal ups and downs. All healing began with pumping, triggered automatically by n|om. The pump remained alive in traditions of the African diaspora, but too often faded away in other cultures where ecstatic expression was toned down by institutionalized rituals and their more cognitively oriented means of constraint. However, whenever healing is present, no matter where in the world it is taking place, the pumping is present in some way. It may be hidden inside the music and the rhythmic movements that help the healing action pull. When the music and drums stop playing, there is no healing, only ritualistic role-playing that simulates and pretends to remove sickness.

This is not to say that quiet means of healing are a waste of time; they are simply something other than pulling out sickness. They surely comfort, relax, even inspire, but without the pump, it is something other than healing, from the perspective of Bushman spirituality. Worse, if you try to calmly remove sickness with your conscious mind, then you risk bringing it into yourself. Compassion and intent to heal another without an ecstatic pump is naive. Your conscious mind doesn't belong in the spiritual operating room and neither does your conscious heart. The skilled doctors come from your unconscious, and they don't take their orders from your will power. They are not influenced by your textbook knowledge.

The only sure way to clear away the nonsensical mind that leads us down the wrong road is to enter into the purest heart of love.

Your conscious mind has no wisdom. The latter resides in the deeper parts of you. It is so deep that it reaches all the way down to your heart. It is heart-and-soul mind, and it holds the ropes. All the mental trickery of the language games spun by conscious mind is noise when compared to the felt relations and complexity of your unconscious process. The masters of therapy and the global healing maestros have learned how to enter its realm and to mobilize it into action. The art of healing is distracting your conscious full-of-itself mind so that your deeper mind, your heart-and-soul mind, can awaken and spring to action. It is where your inner doctor has its office.

The only sure way to clear away the nonsensical mind that leads us down the wrong road is to enter into the purest heart of love. When you unreservedly feel the love of your loved one, you are able to heal them. Pour your love into this person with a song. Allow the longing for this love to pull out everything that stands in the way of love's natural movement. This is healing. Learn to love and you will heal those whom you love. The art of healing those you don't know is to participate in God's loving them so that a greater love embraces the longing and the pulling forth of well-being.

Feel the Spirit of Congo Square

Congo Square in New Orleans is the site of an old-age (rather than a new age) vortex. Located near the end of Orleans Street in the French Quarter, it stands in opposition to the other end of the street, an area called Jackson Square. Whereas the slaves were allowed to assemble in the open field at the crossing of Rampart Street and Orleans Street, they were hanged for disobedience at Jackson Square, also called Place d'Armes, site of the two structures that administered social control—the Catholic St. Louis Cathedral and the old city hall called the Cabildo.

Before the African slave trade arrived, Congo Square was the former sacred ground of the Houma Indians where the annual corn harvest was ceremonially celebrated. By the 1740s, it had become internationally famous as a free gathering place for people of African origin to drum, dance, sing, and express their spiritual lives. As many as six hundred people gathered there on Sunday afternoons when the Bamboula, Calinda, and Congo dances were often performed.

Feeling the spirit of the sacred Indian ground, some of the dancing Africans began wearing feathers and the attire of the former Indians who previously worshipped there. This gave birth to the Mardi Gras Indians. The dances on Congo Square became the Second Line, the dancing of the common folk who follow the band and parade organizers (the First Line) in a parade. They move with a beat, sometimes twirling a parasol or a handkerchief in the air, what Nick Spitzer called "the quintessential New Orleans art form—a jazz funeral without a body." Finally, Congo Square, with its African drumming and spirited singing, planted the seeds for what would later become New Orleans jazz, rhythm, and blues.

When the Louisiana Purchase was signed at the Cabildo, slaves were given Sunday off. Nineteenth-century Congo Square was filled with African spiritual expression. In addition to drums, there were gourds, banjo-like instruments, and quill pipes made from reeds strapped together like panpipes. There were also marimbas, triangles, tambourines, and European instruments that included violins. No historian will decisively admit that voodoo rituals took place, but let it be noted that the drums were free to call whatever spirited form of expression the people wanted.

Sunday was Africa in Congo Square. There was freedom until 9 PM, when the evening cannon would be fired from the other end of Orleans Street to signal an end of the week's ecstatic flight. Then the world was handed over to lawyers, business proprietors, and military officers. A week later, however, the heavens were opened again. "On sabbath evening," recorded the writer H. C. Knight on visiting the city in 1819, "the African slaves meet on the green, by the swamp, and rock the city with their Congo dances." Ned Sublette, in his book *The World that Made New Orleans*, proposes that Knight's description involved the first use of the word *rock* as both a metaphor and a verb. This subsequently led to the later use of the word to indicate the hot, hip, and cool idioms of pop music and youth culture throughout the world.

Whereas Congo Square rocked and infused soul into the sweaty bodies that came every Sunday afternoon, Jackson Square squelched the human spirit and sometimes took away the life of our ancestral people. On the straight line called Orleans Street, New Orleans held a pulsing tension between freedom and slavery, spirituality and materiality, life and death. In this juxtaposition of opposites, the first slaves from Benin, the Ardra people, brought their Foddun spiritual practices that became the core of Louisiana voodoo. The Wolof and Bamara people from the Senegal River delivered the melismatic singing and stringed instrumentation that led to the banjo and the blues. The central African forest culture of the Kongo brought the polyrhythms that later underscored dance rhythms from Harlem to Havana, Rio, and Trinidad.

Walk that line on Orleans Street today and feel the skeletal tension that holds the flesh and blood of being a soulfully awakened human being. On the one side of our existential condition is the conscious control and documentation of material possession. Its obsession with ownership paradoxically leads to an imprisonment of our individual and collective soul. Walk on over to the other side, Congo Square, and meet the deeper unconscious impression of vibrant rhythm with its invitation to spiritual possession that paradoxically liberates ecstatic forms of soulful expression.

Don't try to avoid either endpoint of Orleans Street by standing still in the middle. If that's what you choose, then make sure you notice where you have landed: it's Bourbon Street, home of the wildest party in America. There, it floods every night, washing away all those who unwisely give in to the wrong spirit in this crossroads between monotone Christianity and African polyphony.

Go ahead and walk back and forth along Orleans Street, and feel the tug between the day and the night. Allow it to become a dynamic dilemma, a kinetic dialogue pushing you back and forth. Surrender to its locomotion and awaken the African healer within. The holy water of St. Louis Cathedral, the liquor on Bourbon Street, and the sweat of Congo Square are not separate. One flows into the other, making a continuous river of transformation. Each has its own unique high, from High Mass to the intoxication of spirit and drum.

**When you feel a pumping within your body,
you'll feel the line that announces the vertical dimension
of ecstatic spirituality. It is the rope to the gods
with all their mysteries.**

Go deeper into your walk and experience a bimodal tidal movement, flowing first in one direction and then another. This movement is an ancient teaching regarding how healing works. It visits the highest ground and the lowest valley. It goes back and forth with a rocking action. Be careful about settling in. What looks like pure, uncontaminated holy water may only be the whitewashing of an arm that dictates human cruelty and covers it up with mindlessly thrown platitudes. On the other side, what looks like frenzied insanity and dirty fun can be the pathway to a life force carnival, an old-fashioned Holy Ghost party. Again, be careful not to settle for any lazy midpoint between the two extremes. There is always a bar waiting to serve you a drink that makes you spiritually paralyzed and disconnected from the trying, though exhilarating, back-and-forth motion between the magnetic poles of good and evil.

When you feel a pumping within your body, you'll feel the line that announces the vertical dimension of ecstatic spirituality. It is the rope to the gods with all their mysteries. Take a pilgrimage to one of the crossroads that truly matters—Orleans Street in the French Quarter, New Orleans. Walk and move on it in order to get caught by an African pulling. Let its extremes pull you back and forth while your heart gives birth to a vertical rope to the sky. This place is one of the oldest crossroads to transformation. Enter it and find yourself cured by African emotion. Its motion will carry you to the oldest healing ground in the Kalahari.

"Aye, healing is a Jolly Roger thing. If you want to avoid Davy Jones's locker, then I advise you to walk the plank, but don't go too far out on it. The plank I'm talkin' about hangs between life and death. Some jacks call it a rope rather than a plank, but it's also like a cutlass, a blade heavier than a saber. With only one cutting edge, you'd better be careful where you step. Off with you now! Fair winds."

Find your line, whether it is Orleans Street or the edge of a pirate's plank or sword. Move as if your life depended on it. Now turn around and move the other way as if your death depended on it. Back and forth is the motion that keeps you on the line, on the track to soul liberation. If you stand still and fixate on what it all means, you'll fall into a Dead Sea scroll—endless words that cover up what needs to be felt and put in motion. Try standing still in a canoe and rest assured that you will fall. Rock the canoe, moving back and forth. Do it just right and you'll find yourself balanced by the ever-changing movement.

The moment the rocking just manages to keep you out of the grip of either extreme is when another line springs forth. It brings an invitation to ecstatically dance along another street, the spiritual road to God. Don't head for the cathedral in order to escape the wild call of the drums. And don't run too mindlessly toward Congo Square and jump anywhere into the jazz. (You may be beaten to death by a never-tiring beat.) Too much purpose to arrive at either end, whether fueled by fear or desire, may result in falling off a teeter that totters on the wrong edge.

You should never set out to destroy the left or right, or conquer evil or good, because it will make you hallucinate delusions of self-importance. You might think you are the defender of the good. Or you might think you are the feared and almighty evil one. As different as these two positions sound, to any old-school wisdom keeper they are the same thing—affirmations of false pride. It doesn't matter whether you are for one end or the other; each end is an ass. Either way, you end up at the end, and that's the end of your dance. Move back and forth, and become a dynamic pump pulled by the tension of all imaginable opposites. This is the motion, not the stasis, of kundalini, Holy Spirit, chi, and n|om. It is the oldest secret behind all the original mysteries.

Live Your Life in the Second Line

In New Orleans, as I've said, the band with the principal members of the organization that authorized the parade makes up the First Line. Behind the main performers is the Second Line, the common folk who come to have fun and enjoy the festivities. The gods should be the First Line of our lives while we make up the Second Line. Enjoy the music and motion they make, but stay on track. And keep marching with the band. Its motion will go forward and then backward, but all in all, if you keep in the parade, your life will march forward. The heart and soul of New Orleans jazz is the Second Line jazz played in the streets. The same should hold true for you. Your heart and soul comes from being in the Second Line, right behind the music, dance, and spirited play of the gods.

One of the main songs of a New Orleans parade, besides "When the Saints Go Marching In," is "Oh, Didn't He Ramble." Louis Armstrong often sang it, beginning with the verse:

His feet was in the marketplace,
His head was in the street.
Lady pass him by said,
"Look at the market meat."

You're here for a while, ramblin' in the streets. But the gods know you're just a piece of meat and you need to get cooked, cooked in God's frying pan. That will give you some old-fashioned soul and make you ready to dance. Then it's time to live full-steam ahead, rambling on and on, dancing in the street. Now we come to the chorus:

Didn't he ramble, he rambled,
Rambled all around, in and out of town,
Didn't he ramble, didn't he ramble,
He rambled till the butcher cut him down.

This is the story of your life: You ramble until the butchers cut you down. Then it's over. As Porky Pig used to say, "That's all, folks." So get on with some spirited rambling. Do it as a member of a Second Line. That way you'll enjoy yourself.

Healing is all about getting you some music and motion for rambling. You need some doctoring whenever your life comes to a halt. Medicine provides some inspiration and choreography for the next steps. Whatever it takes to get you moving again is healing. Then you keep on rambling until the butcher finds his meat. However, death is no problem in New Orleans, where even the casket is rocked to the cheers of a Second Line. Keep on rambling all the way up the highway until you find your next Second Line.

I am in New Orleans, on Orleans Street, and I am feeling the pushing and the pulling. The vibe of this place easily gets a hold on you and pulls you in for more. It's a real complex place, however, and you will also see the dirt and garbage, along with all the disgusting elements that belong to its swamp, from crime to house-destroying termites, city-destroying hurricanes, and the blown deals of corrupt politicians. Its dark side pushes you away. But how can you leave that music, food, and soul? Back to the table you come for more. This is how New Orleans dances and pulls you in and out with its Second Line.

Once you've been thrown into this marching party, you never want to be too far away. Put a smile on your face because this is the vortex of King Rex, ruler of Mardi Gras. Here, the echoes of suffering and joy reverberate from the early days of Congo Square. Everything is stirring inside this spiritual gumbo. Throw yourself into the pot of New Orleans, the new world gateway to African spirituality. Absorb its spirited emotions, for there is something more to be said about the healing nature of the sixth mystery.

The Sixth Mystery

Welcome to the Second Line. Right this very moment, there is a n|om rope hovering above your head. It wants to enter your crown and travel all the way down to the bottom of your spine. This is your personalized rope, your main line to God. It brings on the pulling behind the ecstatic pump.

This rope can pull out the dirty-dirty. I'm talking about sucking out the real mud, not just the surface dust. The dirty-dirty refers to all the word games that entice people to esteem themselves. It inspires you to say, "Be nice to me and make me feel special or else I will leave." Self-esteem is the dirty-dirty. It makes you stop and watch yourself in the mirror, or obsess over the reruns and previews of your social cameo appearances.

Don't idly stand by and watch the parade of life pass. Get in with the main line and celebrate with a Second Line. I'm telling you something, so listen up.

Look up. There's that line hanging over your head. It's come to put a noose around your ego head. It wants you to dangle for the gods. Off with your head! Bring up another head, one full of heart-steam rather than ego-dream. Allow it to bob up and down. It has soul and moves to a beat.

Move ahead with a Second Line head. It will pay attention to the movements from above to below. It will lead you on the street and provide a band of angels. Gabriel's trumpet, Michael's tuba, Uriel's clarinet, and Raphael's drum are in this parade. They are the First Line. Get in line right behind them. They'll show you how to utilize death as a party, how to transform suffering into ecstasy, and how to bridge a blues lament into a Dixieland celebration.

The Kalahari gave birth to syncopation and improvisation. It is the medicine of original healing. It wants to rock you as it did those who needed healing at Congo Square. It wants to shake you like it did to the Shakers from coast to coast—from the Indian Shakers of the Pacific Northwest to those of New England. The medicine that heals must be pumped into the whole of you, from top to bottom. It will fill you with the Holy Spirit, the life force, and the n|om of God's care as it dares you to be more alive.

Imagine yourself as a well, a borehole in the desert. Your arms are the pumps. Pump them up and down as you listen to music that has real soul. See this as priming your pump to bring up the holy water, the swamp oil, and the creative juice of everyday jazz. Circulate all the tonics from every direction as you step into the crossing that channels the movement between all that is sacred and profane. Let it pour throughout you. Let it become you.

See each movement as both a bigger breath and a more important beat that pushes you between the ends of the crossroads going to heaven and hell. Get pulled by both the angels and the demons. Move toward God's Preservation Hall where the life jazz is played. Think about why its New Orleans address is St. Peter Street.

Pump those arms up and down, doing so with ecstatic fervor. Up it comes; down it goes. Up and down. An invisible current has grabbed you and thrown you into the rapids. It will pull you under so it can spit you out. It will lift you off the ground so it can blow you down again. Up and down.

May I introduce you to Alice, Wonder of the Kongo? She's always on the go. She'll show you the rock that wants to be cracked so it can expose the hip-hop of every hare that dare enter the center of the flow. She's ready to hold your hand and spin you around, making sure you're unsure about your direction, for it really never matters whether up is down or left is right, does it now? It is the pulling between the differences, not the static separation firmly erected on the ends of a street.

We are talking about whirling directions, whirling logs, whirling lines, and whirling streets. This spinning makes a mighty wind, a vertical current intersecting the flowing Mississippi down below. Is it a river or is it now a swamp? Did the current change course again? Did you miss a sip of the river? One line changes into another, and then one body of water transforms into a secondary steam, all while the first breeze becomes another final hurricane. The Kongo River is on the go. It brings a flow you have been waiting to know.

Draw a horizontal line on the palm of one hand, whichever one you want to begin with. Now draw a vertical line on the other palm. Hold them up, drop them by your side, and move them all about. If you must, do the hokey pokey. Experience how the lines transform, sometimes this way and then another, directions changing direction in their irregular movement.

Clap your hands so that the vertical and horizontal cannot run away from one another. Notice how the clapping is a pump. The hands come together, and then they fly apart. Use this motion to get your middle body circulating. Add your voice to the mix. You have to sing with a vibration. When the voice is shaking enough, it will cause a wiggle down your spine or in your belly, or both.

This is how it all starts, your healing and the healing of others. When it kicks into place, know that healing is a ride. You are riding the pump. You might get lucky and realize it isn't a pump at all. It's a pony ride, perhaps a horse ride. Who is the horse? Is it you or the movement? Let that answer pump back and forth as well. While on this ride, everything is going to dance and breathe while carrying a beat. Insult your meat with this beat. Any and every thought must swing as well. Now it's true; now it's false. It matters; no, it doesn't matter. I'm living; I'm dying. I'm bringing sickness; I'm delivering wellness. I am sick; I am well. I am lost; I am found.

Every distinction now rides the horse of Haiti. Now ride the horses of the Kalahari—jump on the giraffes, the eland, and even the birds, your fair-feathered friends of de-flight. They, too, invite you for a ride, a n|om ride that begins where it ends and ends where it begins.

All aboard! The Kalahari express has pulled up to your station. Wildlife is getting off the railcars. "The animals are coming, the animals are coming!" They are moving toward you. Hop on top and be ridden into ecstatic health. Do some rambling in the Second Line. Do not stop until the butcher comes to get you.

Now I come back to myself.

7

TRANSMITTING N|OM TO OTHERS

The Seventh Original Mystery

When you transmit n|om, you hold the other person very tight.
It is like electricity, and it goes straight into the other person.
Then they start to shake.

XIXAE DXAO

"You must first establish a skinship with another person before you can give them seiki," Ikuko Osumi once told me. The Bushmen would agree. Ikuko Osumi is old-school samurai. She places her hands on people. They are not held at a distance from the skin like so many energy healers do today.

In the Kalahari, Toma shakes his head in disbelief over how anyone could claim to heal without touching. "If they call their healing subtle energy work, then tell them that we call ours non-subtle healing," he says. I have told him about the way other energy practitioners conduct their work.

"Trickster really has done his job. These 'healers' have everything mixed up. Without touch, there is no feeling and no rope. There is nothing. Tell these healers to stop healing the air. It's the people who need healing." Everyone starts laughing at the thought of a hands-off healer being an air healer. Here, as much body contact is made as is felt necessary, with healers often stacking on top of each other.

Toma won't stop. His funny bone has been awakened. "Do they touch their food, or do they eat the air in front of it? Do they have sex while floating in the air?" By now everyone is on the ground. It is simply too much for them to imagine being inspired by n|om and not hugging and touching another human being. It is probably the most absurd thing they have ever heard. The reason you touch another person is that it makes the n|om stronger and enables the ropes to be pulled. It is also pleasurable—it feels good to touch. More important, we need touch as part of our daily existential diet.

We are in desperate need of being touched by n|om and by hands capable of giving us n|om.

The Bushmen see the rest of the world as dehydrated for touch. It shows in the tired drought lines of our faces and in the uninspired, nonfluidic postures of our bodies. When they hear that we seek spirit while avoiding touch, their diagnosis is immediate: we have become caught in the traps of trickster. We have been convinced that the world is a frozen thought rather than a dynamic feeling. We are in desperate need of being touched by n|om and by hands capable of giving us n|om.

Owners of n|om thoroughly enjoy their experiences with n|om. This is true for the !aaiha, the pulling doctors who help keep the community well. There is a stronger type of n|om-kxao who enjoys n|om even more. This is the person who can give arrows and nails of n|om to others, helping them come into a relationship with n|om. These ecstatic shakers transmit n|om. They are called the *tco-kxao*. They are the strongest healers, but they also are able to help the gods create a new doctor.

Xixae was a n|om-kxao ever since he was a child. His work with n|om is effortless and natural; it is a habit. He is a tco-kxao.

"N|om is from God. It may come directly from God or through the ancestors. It can even come from the animals that love us. When it is inside you, it shows you a string or rope of light. This light tells you where to go, whom to touch, and where on the person's body your hands and body should shake. The light is n|om."

Xixae is teaching about the transmission of n|om. He knows all too well how people are easily scared of n|om because they haven't yet formed a close relationship with it. But once it comes inside you, you can't get enough of it.

"If my heart is open to you and your heart is open to me, then when I hug you and shake you, the n|om will come inside you."

"I love to give people n|om. I wish people knew there was nothing to be scared of when you receive n|om. It is the greatest gift in the world. If my heart is open to you and your heart is open to me, then when I hug you and shake you, the n|om will come inside you. It will settle into your body, ready to be awakened whenever the n|om songs are sung. When you receive n|om, you will shake. The shaking makes you feel energized and pleased. It makes your heart very happy. I want everyone to know about n|om. It doesn't belong to any culture but is in the air, free for everyone. Ask for the n|om, and it will come. Ask for me, and I will transmit it to you. N|om will awaken your relationship with God."

The Key to Receiving Is Softening

The phone rings in my home. It is a long-distance call from Japan. An interpreter speaks for Ikuko Osumi. "She is on her way to visit you. She will give your son seiki. Please empty all the furniture out of your living room. We will be there in a couple of days."

When she arrives, she announces, "You will help me give your son seiki." She knows I have prepared my twelve-year-old over the months before her arrival. Though I have not told her how I have given him the vibrations, she knows. She always knows.

A year earlier, my son developed serious bronchitis. A phone call from Japan came in during that time, and Ikuko Osumi's interpreter said, "She wants you to heal your son. His lungs need for you to give them seiki." This is one of the ways she taught me. I learned that it is

153

possible to know things about people and situations without being with them on the physical plane. There are invisible phone lines that can carry our communication in other ways. Ikuko Osumi had a rope connected to me, and this hookup enabled her to feel the reality and relationships of my life all the way across the ocean.

The ancient art of seiki jutsu prepares a person to receive seiki. A skinship must be created so that a trusting relationship of tactile contact is set in place. It is the bridge, the rope, the path through which seiki, or the life force, will be transmitted.

When I told Toma about seiki jutsu, he replied, "It is the same with n|om healers. We must first make a person soft. Their g||abesi must be soft."

A person's feelings must be tender and open to receiving the love-tipped arrows of n|om.

As the Bushmen say, g||abesi soan, which translates to "the g||abesi is soft." The Bushmen refer to the lower part of the abdomen as the g||abesi. They believe this is where the arrows and nails of n|om reside once they enter the body. Getting soft means being pulled and less resistant. It also refers to a softening of the heart and spirit. A person's feelings must be tender and open to receiving the love-tipped arrows of n|om.

You can't go up to anyone and give a zap of n|om. It will bounce off of them, or it will be too much and knock them out. In either case, the n|om doesn't find a home to reside within. Both the Bushmen and the tradition of seiki jutsu prepare a person to receive the life force. To an untrained eye, this preparation looks no different than someone receiving a hands-on healing.

To a n|om-kxao, people in need of softening are immediately recognizable when you touch them. They feel stiff and hard. There is little or no vibration, or there are forced vibrations that feel out of whack. These folks need to grow more accustomed to touch, vibration, movement, and n|om. There is no particular protocol for softening them up. They just need to be around n|om and to be touched in whatever ways spontaneously come forth from a n|om-kxao. This softening is needed for recipients of both seiki and n|om.

Whether in Japan or the Kalahari, it is the same thing that is being transmitted—the universal life force. Though it may be called by different names, it is essentially the same. We should never forget this as we place-shift from one cultural tradition to another. Each culture will ascribe different meanings to the life force, and this creates different ways of relating to it. But the life force is the same. What we do with it is what varies across the world. Some fear it, and others love it. Some ignore it, and others master it.

How Do You Come to Own N | om?

I am recognized by every Bushman elder I have met as a n|om-kxao (an owner of n|om), !aaiha (a pulling doctor), and tco-kxao (an ecstatic shaker who transmits n|om to others). I heal people in the old Kalahari way, and I transmit n|om into the other doctors to help them get stronger. I also help other Bushmen become n|om-kxaosi. My colleagues and I have traveled all over Botswana and Namibia, and almost every Bushman we have met knows about the big doctor. Stories about my adventures over the last decades have spread to the extent that people recognize us from the descriptions given in anecdotes. Even a national border guard in Botswana asked if I was the big doctor because I looked like what he imagined from the stories he had heard. I hope he wasn't talking about my waistline!

I recognize that although this testimony may sound weird, it is the most unique truth about my life. I became a Bushman doctor who embodies their oldest ways of working with n|om. The Bushmen tease me, saying that the gods are having fun—that a non-Bushman Bushman provides a big joke that makes the gods laugh. They also sincerely plead for me to live with them so that their doctors can be kept strong. My n|om wives say I am the strongest doctor in the Kalahari, but wives always lie like that. I am sufficiently strong, and I do things the old way.

When Ikuko Osumi entrusted me to carry on her tradition, I thought of how the Bushmen would tease me about it. I could imagine them saying, "Congratulations, we can't wait to see you wearing a kimono and sharpening a samurai sword with your n|om. Please, please, give some seiki to the animals. We know they would love to have you give them some Japanese love." They would be relentless, as I have learned to be with them and myself.

Several wealthy Americans actually visited Ikuko Osumi over a decade ago and asked her what was special about my experience. Why did she pass on her tradition to me? Osumi, sensei, did not hesitate to reply, "It is his destiny. This is who he is." When her daughter told me this story, it freed me from asking why I am a master of seiki jutsu and an owner of n|om. It certainly has nothing to do with earning or learning it. I didn't have enough money to buy it, and I wasn't clever enough to steal it.

I heard a similar story from the Bushmen. A well-known physician who has written several popular spiritual books visited them and asked how it was that I had become a traditional healer and elder of their way. Twa answered for the villages, "He is a big doctor because God loves him." I think this is getting closer to what is essential regarding the ownership of n|om.

God loves those who love to love. I think this is the secret, and I speak as someone who has deep experience with loving love and handling n|om. I am a love dog belonging to the same mosque as Rumi. I am a missionary of the amplified, extreme love, freely available to everyone, from your goofy neighbor to the bumblebee in my backyard. My heart is the owner of my mind, not the other way around. This is embodied by the way I utilize whatever life brings to the table. This is expressed in every vibration my body performs when inspired by soul. This is what it means to be a player of life. Life is jazz, and its music awakens the sharing of n|om, the creative life force that is trying to dance us along the road to ecstatic glory.

Be Danced by the Tension between Opposites

The Bushmen believe that healing is facilitated by playing with extremes. You may have heard the Japanese proverb that the opposite of any great truth is also a truth. If there is day, then there must be night. This further means that if it's good to dance with the gods, it's also good to dance with the devils. If it's wise to be healthy, it's also wise to get sick from time to time. If it's smart to be right, it's as smart to be wrong.

> **It is the *relationship* between God and trickster (also called the devil, as in deviled egg) that brings forth the sacred dance—the movement of seiki, n|om, and the Holy Spirit.**

Now brace yourself for what I am going to propose: God is not the whole enchilada. It is the *relationship* between God and trickster (also called the devil, as in deviled egg) that brings forth the sacred dance—the movement of seiki, n|om, and the Holy Spirit. The Bushmen teach that God has two forms. One is the stable Sky God, who never changes. This God is pure love and is infinite in its oneness. The other form of God is trickster, and it is the changing side of God. You can never depend on it because it can change its presence, intention, and impact at a second's notice. Trickster came into being in Second Creation, the Bushman name for the world left over from paradise. Language is trickster's voice, while the Sky God is about the steady flow of love, conveyed through music and rhythm.

Trickster turns everything upside-down. It chops and dices. It tells us to go the opposite direction from what we seek. We live in Second Creation, and our gods are the talking gods—the tricksters who have brought on a lot of trouble. The Bushman name for Second Creation is *G!xoa*, which means "now there is speech." Talking trickster is found in every faith and religion. He convinces you that war is holy and that material wealth is a manifestation of successful spirituality. The tricks of trickster talk are also known as con jobs and all center upon disqualifying one side of a relationship. Its trick is to get you to hold on to only one side of a distinction, one end of a street, one half of a whole.

Trickster says honor God and destroy the devil. It then says it is God, when in fact it is a deviled trickster. The Zulu and practically all the African wisdom traditions didn't fall for this prank. They say we should neither surrender to one extreme or the other, but choose to be danced by the tension, the energy, that exists between them. This is the wisdom behind absurdity. It teaches the value of the displaced and disqualified other side. It belittles the revered, and celebrates any and all irrational means of bringing opposites back in line with one another.

Give your emotions more importance than your thoughts.

Owners of n|om and seiki do not call for crusades or war. They ask us to be open to the pulling of opposites. As I mentioned earlier, getting soft means being pulled. Every part of your experience needs to be pulled. Your funny bone and your serious bone need to meet one another. That will get a laugh. Your reverence for certain things and irreverence for other things need to exchange places. Give your emotions more importance than your thoughts. Trade some nonsense for that bulwark of rationality. Dance for a demon and insult God. That will shake you up. I guarantee it!

All this will soften your g||abesi, making you less rigid about anything. The softer you are, the less judgmental of others and yourself you will become. More important, it will open you to receiving a transmission of the life force. You might even get lucky and get nailed by n|om.

The softer you are, the less judgmental of others and yourself you will become.

When a television evangelist gets worked up and strikes out against what he thinks is sin, he is hardening his heart and soul, making it less likely that God's arrows of n|om can get inside him. He is falling away from God by the very way he thinks he is bringing others to God. His god is trickster, the god of words who can twist any scripture to mean anything, including justifying meanness to others.

The Sky God is the god of love. This god is not one god but a family of gods. Yes, some Bushmen say that there is a Father God

(*Mban!a'an*, "Sky God"), Mother God (|*Aqn-*|*aqnce*, "Mother of Bees"), and God's children, among other relatives. Why not? If God loves to love, he or she sure the heck isn't going to live alone as a hermit. God isn't an idiot. God wants other gods to love.

Does this kind of playful God talk make you tense and upset, or does it inspire you to smile and giggle? This is a test to see how soft you are. You must become tickled by all meanings and mysteries, rational and irrational ideas, sane and insane action, or your thoughts and words won't get soft enough for an arrow of n|om to pass through. Lighten up and get soft as butter. Tell those rigid ideas and beliefs to butt out.

Give God a different name each week. The Bushmen do. Once, after a thunderous Kalahari rainstorm, the frogs made a lot of music. The next day they called God "frog." If you enjoyed that chocolate cake you had last night, call God "chocolate" for a week. Had the best sex of your life last night? If so, call God "sex" for a week. God is everything, and that means all things. God is honored by the names that are associated with what you love. God wants you to play, so go right ahead and soften your theology. It is the only way you'll ever have a chance of getting a personalized direct line to the Operator in the sky.

When you get soft enough, an arrow of n|om can be shot inside you. If it finds itself at home, it will be there to move you whenever you knock on its door.

"Everything we do to one another, from teasing to dancing, is how we soften each other's g||abesi," |Kunta Boo pipes in. All the original mysteries we have been discussing are about getting you soft. Tuning is softening. Whether it is physically moving naturally and ecstatically, insulting your meat, teasing every aspect of your thinking, rendering your habits absurd, or healing you, all of this helps make you soft. When you get soft enough, an arrow of n|om can be shot inside you. If it finds itself at home, it will be there to move you whenever you knock on its door.

Let the Life Force Rock You Every Day

Ikuko Osumi told me about the first time she gave a transmission of seiki to a non-Japanese person. She gave it to Professor Burton Foreman, who taught English at a Japanese women's university in Setagaya, the same institution that hosted my speech to a Japanese professional psychotherapy conference. Osumi, sensei, thought that an American might be too hardheaded for seiki to enter, so she went overboard in softening him up. The day she chose to transmit seiki, she asked two helpers to join her. They supercharged themselves with seiki and proceeded to send a lightning bolt into the top of his head. To everyone's surprise, Professor Foreman was vigorously thrown backward off the wooden bench. His head nearly touched the floor, and then he was propelled forward with the same thrust. He looked like a superhero in a comic book as he performed a movement that appeared to be physically impossible. As transmission of amplified life force, or seiki, can be an extraordinary event outside of any conventional category of explanation.

I recall the first time I gave a public demonstration of instilling seiki. It was in Belo Horizonte, Brazil, in a workshop conducted with Dr. Ernest Rossi, the renowned author, hypnotist, and psychotherapist from Los Angeles. I asked for a volunteer, and a woman psychotherapist came forward and sat on a chair. As I explained seiki to the audience, I patted her back and shoulders, and began establishing a skinship with her.

Soon I felt the seiki in the atmosphere. My hands reached into the air over her head, and I kneaded the seiki that was hanging there. It felt like the seiki that I had helped instill in my son years ago in our home when he was suffering from bronchitis. It felt like taffy. As I prepared the seiki for transmission, the moment came when her head felt like a magnet pulling my seiki-filled hand to it. My hands went to the crown of her head, and the seiki immediately entered her. It went from the top of her head to the bottom of her spine. She began to automatically rock. She had received seiki. From the Bushman way of looking at this, she had received her rope.

To my surprise, more seiki had been stirred in the room because several audience members in the first rows reported having spontaneous orgasms. I certainly had not intended that, nor did I think that others in the room would feel the presence of seiki. Seiki and n|om are like that. You can simply be around it and get an unexpected dose of its vibrant impact. How it touches you is between you and seiki; the transmitter only arranges the electrical connection, hooking up the wire to the outlet.

My son also sat on a seiki bench as Ikuko Osumi and I brought the seiki into him. His rocking motion was simple and sweet. There was no huge drama surrounding its impact. He rocked like a baby being held in a rocking chair. Osumi, sensei, taught him, like she does everyone who receives seiki, that he should allow seiki to rock and move him every day. It is what she regards as the most important secret in the universe.

Become a Willing Target

"I'm going to send you an arrow of n|om right now," N!yae shouted at me. She was across the village and running toward where I sat. Her arrows were already flying before she could get a hand on me. Yes, you can shoot n|om without touching skin, but only to someone who is extremely soft and open. The strongest n|om-kxaosi enjoy shooting each other at a distance. I receive arrows from the Kalahari that travel all around the planet. I shoot them back in return.

Few people can receive a transmission that way; this is why the Bushmen laugh at subtle energy practitioners. Their clients are in great need of being softened, and that requires touch. Being made soft is the same as getting cooked. You are cooked so you can be made soft.

The strongest n|om-kxaosi, the few who others say are fully cooked, are softer than butter. When they are hot with n|om, they feel like they are a cloud without a body.

Everything tco-kxaosi, transmitters of n|om, do before transmission is about making you soft. When they talk, listen, look, touch, shake, tease, and even write a book—all of it is about softening you so that you are made ready to receive an arrow of n|om. In fact, you are being softened as you read this book.

I can tell how soft people are the second I touch them. If they are soft enough and ready for n|om, I can send an arrow into them within seconds, even while talking to an audience or telling a joke. It happens effortlessly. If people aren't soft, there is nothing any n|om-kxao can do to send them an arrow. They need more experience that will soften them.

Most likely they need their meat insulted and their trickster carpet pulled out from under their feet. Trickster must be defeated for the meat to get cooked. But this victory can only last for a moment because trickster is also part of God. Its constant tricking must be utilized to help shake things up. The problem arises when you don't let trickster do its job. You settle for one of trickster's outcomes rather than letting the show go on.

You must change to find your truest self.
And keep changing.

The paradox is that you need trickster's changing forms to liberate you from any particular form in order to move toward God's love. You must change to find your truest self. And keep changing. The false idol is any form that hangs around too long and gets fossilized. It's worth considering the idea that if your ideas about God don't change, then your ideas are dead. God isn't dead. God simply went elsewhere because you were too boring. God is the God of Creation, and if you aren't being creative, it's adios for the Sky Dude.

Love supreme is the same: it must be allowed to dream you with its imagination. This spawns unpredictable and extraordinary creative encounters. Otherwise, it's bye-bye love and bye-bye happiness. You're going to cry if you lose the love mojo that trickster offers. Let change spice up your love life and add some hot sauce to your dream life. The two go hand in hand, marching down the wedding aisle: "I, trickster, take you to be my wife and husband, to have and to hold from this day forward, for better or for worse, for richer, for poorer, in sickness and in health, to love and to cherish from this day forward until death do us part."

**If you desire to be full of spirit, soul, and God's love,
getting nailed by n|om is what you are looking for.**

Don't fight trickster. Marry that shape-shifting multi-gendered sucker who really is a sucker for love. You need all the wit, charm, and cleverness that trickster can bring to your table and bed. You do want some lovin', don't you? Then go to dinner with trickster and maybe tonight you'll get lucky.

If you desire to be full of spirit, soul, and God's love, getting nailed by n|om is what you are looking for. Why not draw an archery target over your heart and ask the gods to shoot an arrow of n|om into its bull's-eye? If you want to get hit with n|om, then make yourself a target. Show the gods that you are soft, willing, and able. Do not resist the advances of God's love; reach out and hug God. Do it now. Open your arms and imagine that you are hugging God. God is a sensual experience that the mystics grooved on getting high with. They were turned on by God's love. Flirt with God and open your heart so you can feel the same.

Transmissions from Others—Even Direct from God

What's the difference between healing and transmitting? They are very similar, but healing involves more pulling out, whereas shooting an arrow of n|om feels more like a pushing in. Both use the pump, and both require spirited singing. The n|om-kxaosi draw upon a variety of ways to transmit n|om. In general, they like getting as much tactile contact as possible. Here, you can hug another person and send a pulse or vibration into his body.

Xixae likes to talk about giving n|om to others. He is wise enough to know that the way he talks about this is itself another pathway of transmission. "I hold someone like they were my child and as if it is the last time I will ever see them. My heart breaks open, and the rope shoots out. My rope grabs the heart of the one I see as a spiritual son or daughter; it makes me long for their being with me forever. My emotions are so strong that my heart rises, and the rope above my head pumps me up and down. As I hold on to my spiritual son or daughter, I carry them up the rope as well. Somewhere in that traveling on the rope, I'll get hit by a huge bolt of n|om lightning. It will go right through me and enter straight into my child. We are both taken inside the n|om, and my child holds on to me as I swim for both of us. Into the n|om you are taken while carried on the back of a n|om-kxao."

Before I knew that Ikuko Osumi would come give transmission to my son, I had prayed that spirit would reveal itself to him. One night after his mom and I sang his night-night songs, I prayed silently, "Dear God, please show your presence to Scott. He is so immersed in the world of Nike shoes and video games that I want him to know you are there. Let him know about the Great Mystery." No one knew what I had prayed, not even my wife.

We all went to bed, and then six hours later, we were awakened by some shouting from Scott's room. "Dad, Dad, get in here! Get in here. I think someone has broken into the house."

Alarmed, I ran to his room to find him sitting up in bed in a state of shock.

"What happened, sweetie?" his mom asked.

"I am not sure. It was like a dream except it was real. I was running down a street, and I think I was shot. Then I saw a rope hanging from the sky. I floated all the way to heaven and met God. God told me how everything works."

We were blown away. God had answered my prayer. Be careful what you ask for because I would have been happy if Scott had simply felt the loving presence of a guardian angel. What I didn't know at the time was that he had experienced the holiest voyage any human being can know. He found the rope to God and followed it all the way.

I told him that there was nothing to be scared about. He replied, "I'm not scared. I'm tired now." I went on to say that this was a big gift from God and that he was very lucky.

I knew I shouldn't ask him what God said, but I couldn't help myself. I asked anyway. Scott replied, "I'm too tired to talk now. I want to go back to sleep."

We never talked about it the next day; this experience was not for words. It doesn't matter if Scott remembers any of it with language or with his mind. The experience is in his heart, and he has a rope to God.

Scott was very lucky. Only the strongest n|om-kxaosi are given a direct transmission from God. I was also lucky like that, as were many of my spiritual teachers in the Kalahari. The elders I was led to in visions had received their n|om directly from God.

Sometimes God uses another human being, a tco-kxao, to shoot the n|om into another person. It is still from God; it just goes through a lightning rod. There's really no difference. Lightning is lightning, and it will fry you whether it hits you directly under the sky or it is deflected off a metal pole.

I remember the time I gave an arrow of n|om to a young man in the Kalahari. He was an adolescent who made everyone laugh. He acted like a clown, and could make funny noises and faces. He was also a great dancer. Like the other young people, he was scared of n|om, and the elders teased all of them about getting nailed at each dance. That night, I felt a rope bring me to him. I held on to him and shot an arrow into his body. He felt it and shouted out as if he was actually pierced by a real hunter's arrow tip.

Later that night, something happened to him. When the dance was over and he fell asleep, he had himself a kabi, a visitation from the ancestors. He experienced them attaching ropes to his body. They hooked up his shoulders, arms, legs, abdomen, and head; he got himself some ropes. That can happen when a strong arrow of n|om gets inside you: it starts the process of making you a n|om-kxao.

I have witnessed other people receiving their ropes after being nailed with n|om. A professor of nursing from Minneapolis got her ropes when she visited the Bushmen with me. Several of the young art students from Santa Fe got their ropes, as have hundreds of folks who have shaken with me in ecstatic gatherings throughout the world. The ropes are right here, hanging above our heads. You just have to get soft and allow your heart to rise up and grab on to them.

When a !aaiha pulls the sickness out of someone, a loud sound is voiced that helps release it. The sickness exits out of a spot on the back of the neck, the !ain-!'u. The sound made by a !aaiha when sickness is pulled is called a kau-hariri. However, when you give an arrow of n|om, the act of giving is called |'ua-n|om. If the arrow is received, the person's body shakes. This shaking, called thara, is evidence that the n|om is inside that person's body. Every Bushman dance is about this kind of pulling and shooting, removing dirty arrows and sending in clean arrows of n|om.

When I give a public talk about ecstatic spirituality, I often ask people to come forward and stand by me as I speak. One by one, I place my hands on them and see if they are soft enough to receive an arrow of n|om. I have found that many folks are. Others are ready to be softened. When I shoot an arrow into people, they feel it enter and spread throughout their body. It might start as a trembling, a quaking, a shaking, a sudden rush of heat or cold, or even a visionary experience. All the experiences reported about a kundalini awakening or a Holy Ghost zapping are also true for n|om. It is the same. What differs is the context that holds it.

Plug into the Wild, Giggly Network of Ecstatic Shakers

The Kalahari, like New Orleans, suggests that n|om brings a party and is fun, fully democratic, and freely available for all soft-hearted folks. Though n|om is a serious thing, our preparation for receiving it cannot be too serious. Quite the contrary, playful insults and bawdy teasing help soften the target. You can receive an arrow even if you are laughing. But be careful about being silly because the arrow of n|om might catch the giggles also. Then be prepared for complete insanity: when your laughter is amplified by n|om, you will think that it is impossible to stop.

This spontaneous outburst of wild laughter has been named Holy Ghost laughter or holy laughter by charismatic Christians. It was reported at a revival meeting held in 1994 at the Toronto Airport Vineyard, near Pearson International Airport. Christians feeling the Holy Spirit ignited an epidemic of uncontrollable laughter that spread quickly from one church group to another. When the purported blessing hit the parishioners, they became so tickled that they wept with convulsions, fell to the floor in an ecstatic state, and made animal sounds like barking dogs and roaring lions.

Though this same phenomenon was previously reported as taking place among Christians attending the Cane Ridge Revival held in Bourbon County, Kentucky, back in 1801, its reappearance in Toronto is marked as evidence of a new outpouring of the Holy Spirit. Super charismatic leaders from Oral Roberts to Kenneth Copeland, Marilyn Hickey, and Benny Hinn have celebrated its authenticity.

The modern appearance of holy giggling can be traced to Rodney Howard-Browne, a Pentecostal South African evangelist. In 1979, he prayed for hours and challenged God, "Come down here and touch me, or I am going to come up there and touch You." As he described it, his whole body immediately felt like it was on fire, and he began to laugh uncontrollably. As he wrote, "I was plugged in to heaven's electric supply" and "since then my desire has been to go and plug other people in." Though he got the ball rolling for a new wave of holy rollers, the mecca for its expression became Toronto. There, services often lasted until 3 AM, and resulted in people wildly shaking as they made sounds that were like something that came from a "cross between a jungle and a farmyard," as one reporter described it.

None of this is new to the Bushmen. They've been laughing like that for over sixty thousand years. They call it g||auan-n|hai, meaning "the laughing caused by the ancestors." It is n|om laughter, the same as holy laughter.

|Kunta Boo explains it to me: "The ancestors like to come inside us. There, they can feel the world of flesh again. Sometimes they use us

to experience laughing. It is very wild, and it will make you drunk with n|om."

Many of my ecstatic performances are visited by the n|om giggles. Someone usually gets tickled and, without warning, her hee-haw gets supercharged with n|om. Then it spreads, and some of the folks laugh themselves into heaven's comedy club. It's all part of the n|om show, the Life Force Theatre that softens us in any way it can, including through laughter, so that we may be made available for receiving seiki, n|om, and the Holy Spirit.

It is also possible to receive a very tiny arrow of n|om that barely makes you rock or wiggle, but it is still an arrow. Consider it a n|om seed. It can grow and bring forth a strong vibration in your future. Other people get hit with an arrow the size of a lightning bolt. It turns them into a superhero n|om character. They can leap over the pews in a church, like some parishioners have done, or they can be filled with enough n|om to stand upside-down in a fire. Of course, all that is silly and deserves some good old-fashioned n|om giggling, but it again makes the point that n|om is rarely subtle.

When I am giving n|om to the n|om-kxaosi of the Kalahari, my ropes are pulling me along. It is more than giving medicine; it is entering into the medicine and the wisdom it holds. It is another trip to the crossroads. It sometimes brings you to the voice that holds the deeply felt wisdom.

I can feel my n|om friends in the Kalahari. They are linked to my shaking colleagues in St. Vincent and my Holy Ghost congregations in Louisiana. All of us form a Second Line that includes the ancestors from Congo Square and the newcomers in a Life Force Theatre held in Rio, Toronto, New York City, New Orleans, and San Francisco. When we shake, the arrows of n|om are sent to all the shakers. It's a circulatory system, this network of ecstatic shakers that extends across oceans, from one land to another. It is available in dance and in ecstatic vision.

I am feeling it now as it pulses through each of us, making us an ecstatic community—a tribe called to wake up the world so the original mysteries may take charge of the planet, diminishing the control of trickster's greed and eco-wrecking manipulations. There is an earthquake coming, and its tremors will be felt around the globe. Its vibrations will make a new sound, something that needs to be said in a n|om kind of way so it can be both felt and heard.

The Seventh Mystery

N|om is looking for you. It is tracking you as you track it. An arrow has been shot at you this very instant. Jump out of your seat before it throws you out. Shout before it takes over your voice. Shake with excited antici-pation before it shakes you up. The n|om has come back. It has returned. Don't fight it; go on a flight with it. Don't forsake this moment; shake with it.

Don't stop now; keep on moving. Do so knowing that you are already there. It's the ropes that need to be attached. Pinch your belly and your arms, hands, and ass. Then flick the crown of your head. Prepare the way for the arrows to enter by pointing to where they must hit. If you point, they will strike.

There's not just one arrow but a train of arrows. This train, seen from far away, looks like a rope, but it is a locomotive motivated to pick you up and pull you to the sky. All aboard! There's a n|om train bound for glory. Its tracks lie everywhere. Its tracks are ropes, and its ropes have a spear on the end. These arrow-rope-spear-tracks want to tie you up, put you on board, and pull your behind—the hind of your being—across the sky.

Surrender to your rope. It is a rope especially made for you by God, and it has always been there. God is shouting something to you, "Come on up and pay me a visit, you hear? Come and stay a while."

Tell that puny little pipsqueak of your ego self to get lost because you have just been found. Get on board the heavenly express, the elevator ride to God.

God is shooting his arrows, throwing his spears and harpoons, and sending down a train, a lifeboat, a ship, a horse, even a mule, and all the angels and ancestors are helping. Even a few demons are trying to get you on foot and on board. Stop talking and stop thinking. Just do it. Shake that booty and get kicked all the way up the rope.

You need to get yourself a shiny nail. If you'd like, you can go get an arrow, but a nail will work as well. Tie a string to the nail's head so it makes a necklace to put around your neck. Wear this nail, and as you feel it brush along your skin, contemplate how there are thousands of nails and arrows coming at you every day, but your spiritual skin is too thick to feel them hitting you. Soften yourself so you can get pricked and feel it. You don't need a pierced ear or any kind of body piercing as much as you need some spiritual piercing.

From time to time, take that nail of yours and gently prick yourself. Be as gentle as you can so as to make it barely perceptible. See this absurd task as a softening. Do it with music. Do it while feeling love. Realize that you are one prick away from being nailed by God. One of those pricks may be all it takes to help God's nail slide on through.

You've heard of those folks in India who sleep on a bed of nails. Now you know why. After the first people left the Kalahari, they started talking too much. By the time they got to India, their words had mixed everything up, and instead of awakening themselves with God's nails, they tried to go to sleep on metal nails. You, too, have been sleeping on the wrong kind of nails. You need to be pierced and awakened by God's nails.

God has a fingernail that is reaching down to scratch your spiritual itch. The finger of God is the main rope. It has a nail for you. It will surprise you. It isn't what you expect. How could it be? This is God's infinite divine play. It is beyond understanding because it is raw, unknowable— though feel-able—mystery.

Get cooked. Get nailed. Be a fool. Shake everything up. Get down to get that God high. Meet your soul meat. These are the beginning scriptures for your new holy book. Write these words out, one page for each sentence. *Make sure you add something new—change it a bit—so there will be more n|om in your book:*

Verse 1: Get cooked.
Verse 2: Get nailed.
Verse 3: Be a fool.
Verse 4: Shake everything up.
Verse 5: Get down to get that God high.
Verse 6: Meet your soul meat.
Verse 7: Mix all the above to make yourself a gumbo. Here we go with the first stirring: Cook a nail so you can fool yourself. Shake when you're done. This is how you find your self and change where it's at. . . .

Find a way to bind these seven pages together. Add a title page that says, N|om Holy Book. Punch out holes in the cover and the inner pages. Give more importance to the holes than the words in the book. Leave this Holy Book in hotel rooms for lost travelers. Attach a note that says: "This is not from a Gideon. It is from a n|omster who wants to simply say with all the joy that is possible, 'Git it on!'"

Now I come back to myself.

8

THE SPIRITUAL CLASSROOMS: WHERE THE MYSTICS AND SHAMANS GO TO SCHOOL

The Eighth Original Mystery

If you dance and see this rope, you don't have to grab or touch it. You just float away with that rope. That line just takes you. You become so light that you simply fly away.... You have no control over where you will go.... The rope can take you to your ancestors. It is our link with them. They tell us what to do. The rope takes you to the house where the ancestors live.

Motaope Saboabue

All the previous mysteries have prepared you for what is forthcoming. At this stage of your journey, you will meet the most amazing experiences that are possible for a human being. There is more to knowledge than what colleges and universities teach, including the college of hard knocks and street smarts. There are virtual classrooms in the world of spirit, outside the range of radar and scientific measurement, where the most transformative teachings are dispersed. When you are on the track to God, you are led to these extraordinary ethereal classrooms. Here, the Bushmen learn songs, dances, various ways of healing, where to find plants and animals, and even instruction for the design of art and fashion. In the Kalahari, the libraries, classrooms, lecture halls, laboratories, training grounds, workshops, initiation chambers, design studios, and performance stages are found in the visionary world of mystery.

Bushman healers and ecstatic teachers experience visionary travel to what they call the classrooms where they receive specific guidance and instruction. The visionary classrooms can be described as cities, underground places, mountain and sky regions, as well as unexpected encounters with a wide variety of idiosyncratic mystical presences. Throughout the African diaspora, including Brazil and the Caribbean, and in other ancient cultures where the oldest ways remain alive, the mystics and shamans go to the spiritual classrooms.

The most authentic spiritual teachers can only shake you up and help make you soft. After that, they can do little more than point you toward the spiritual classrooms.

The most authentic spiritual teachers can only shake you up and help make you soft. After that, they can do little more than point you toward the spiritual classrooms. Human beings are not the ones who teach you the most important lessons about spirit. It is spirit itself that does the teaching and the anointing. In the classrooms, you find your mission and role in life. There, you will receive spiritual know-how and, more important, be infused with pure n|om.

When you spiritually visit your ancestors, the experience is called a kabi, but if you are lucky enough to have an encounter with God, your classroom time is called a *cunkuri*. The most extraordinary original mysteries are revealed to you in the spiritual worlds. But be very careful, for you must go past the world of mere dream, where trickster plays mind games with you.

Wash Away the Dirt to Reveal What's Real

The oldest spiritual cultures make sure their elders are available to hear about the assumed spiritual experiences of its community members. When you consider that a single visit to a classroom can change your life, provide you with the spiritual education you need to help others, and give you a lifetime shot of n|om, you can appreciate that having a kabi or cunkuri is a very special gift. It doesn't happen daily. I mention this because I have met spiritual seekers and enthusiasts who claim to have multiple visions every night. They have no elders to tell them that they are having dream fantasies. When the primary desire is to own spiritual gifts and inherit spiritual importance, the lures of spiritual materialism lead them to trickster's spiritual comic book extravaganza.

The Kalahari elders, as well as those from St. Vincent, and the old-time sanctified Louisiana church deacons and spiritual mothers, can discern whether your experience has been a trip to a spiritual classroom. In general, dreams inflate you. You are supposedly given superpowers and experience yourself as a superhero. They make you feel important and instill you with power. When your experience is solely about power, you can rest assured that it was brought to you by Trickster Productions, Inc.

The sign of an authentic vision—a spiritual entry into the class-rooms that matter—is that it deeply touches and pierces your heart. Here, you often wake up weeping with love and longing, especially for the loved ones in your family. When you get the most important lessons, you wake up vibrating, shaking, and singing. These are indications that you have met the ancestors and the gods.

When you get soft enough for the arrows of n|om to pierce you, the insides of your body enter thara, the ecstatic shaking that accompanies being filled with spirit. Again, this is good for you—a better treatment than any spa or health club can provide. The more n|om shakes everything up (your body, mind, heart, and soul), the more you get cooked.

"Come on into the pot tonight," G|ao'o teases the young men who will dance tonight. "God wants to burn off that dirt and make your meat real clean, tender, and tasty."

G|ao'o is the elder n|om-kxao at the village of ||Nhoq'ma. He knows everything there is to know about Bushman spirituality and healing. He is teaching that n|om can burn off and clean out the inner dirt of ego-self so that trickster can't get a hold of your dreaming. It is your heart—the spiritual meat—that the ancestors and gods want to make a connection with. This is the part of you that must be tender and soft for them to enjoy interacting with you. Your encounters with n|om cook you for the gods. The more cooked you are, the more likely they will visit you and become a part of you.

If you aren't cooked, ego-self—or more accurately, trickster-self—shows up on center stage. It becomes inspired to feed you more of itself. It will use every opportunity it gets to trick you into believing that you have been empowered to make it king or queen of your inner world. Trickster-self will do anything to keep itself in charge.

This is why so many indigenous cultures propose that no one attempt to take a journey to the spirit lands without first being purified and made ready. Even ancient Greece with its dream incuba-tion temples would not admit someone who merely desired to have a vision. In ancient times, you had to have a dream that told you to go to a temple to get a sacred dream before you could enter the holy ground. Similarly, the old timers among the St. Vincent Shakers required that a dream bring you to a spiritual pointer before you could be prepared to go into a ceremony meant to send you to the spiritual classrooms.

My experiences with the Lakota, Ojibwa, Cree, Crow, Cheyenne, and Micmac medicine traditions taught that you must sincerely pray and often fast before knowing whether you should seek a vision. This helps make the desire-oriented self disappear from the spiritual scene. You don't show up at a motel in Lame Deer, Montana, or a tepee lodge in Pine Ridge, South Dakota, pay an admission fee, and then expect an easy-to-purchase visionary journey during the weekend. Instead, there is typically an ordeal that helps minimize the presence of trickster-self. These wisdom traditions knew that something needed to be done to keep trickster from short-circuiting or wiretapping your communication line with the holy.

Old-school shamanism would see trickster working this way: Trickster would first convince you that it is not important to love God, let alone exercise belief. It would first try to knock out your main line hookup. Having dispensed with your communication with God, trick-ster would say that what exists is a multitude of spirits, living in a three-story brokerage house, that hang out to negotiate power with you. Of course, all these spirits are the many forms of trickster. He has many tricks up his sleeves, and some of them convince you that his magic is in this house. This is how trickster attracts your curiosity and places you in the palm of his hand.

In trickster shamanism, anything that could inspire you to feel the presence of God is eliminated. You will be asked to sit still, not get excited, and not sing with a vibratory ecstatic voice. You might even be taught that there is a simple trick to getting to the spirits. The shortcut may be setting yourself up for a trance by entrainment with a metronome-like pitter-patter of a tom-tom drum. Simply follow the voice of trickster as it guides you to have a convenient journey.

This marketing campaign makes many spiritual consumers, both the naive and the less naive, quite relieved and happy. There will be no pain, only gain, perhaps fame. Sit down and listen to the drum. It will take you into the other worlds, make all the introductions to spirit, provide all the underground and over-ground networking you need, and promise that this is the path to spiritual enrichment. Trickster will sell this experience and say that it is the foundation for being a shaman. Believe me, trickster shamanism is out there, not only packaged as shamanism, but as prosperity Christianity, and all the other scams that carry people more deeply into their trickster-selves rather than into the heart of hearts named God.

Love God and all else will follow.
Love God and the rope will pull you to the classrooms.
There, you get whatever you need...

God's shamanism has no empty core; it has a full heart. It is the shamanism practiced by Rumi. Love God and all else will follow. Love God and the rope will pull you to the classrooms. There, you get whatever you need, with or without a drum, with or without a spirit helper, with or without understanding, with or without a certificate saying you had a spiritual experience. Love God and that love will be reciprocated, lifting you into the eternal wisdom that you most deeply desire.

The timeless Bushman prophets may meet you on your journey. They will warn you against the charlatans, the vendors who talk about love and healing but smell of dirty power games. There will be too many attempts to exercise control, both of you and of the spirits. There will be no insulting of the meat. No shaking or absurd medicine will be allowed. They will reek of overseriousness and be starved for play.

The bottom line is that trickster has infiltrated all the holy systems and made them stink like rotten meat. No one is getting cooked, and the teachers have not heard God's call; they do not know how to swim in the ecstatic currents of n|om. The ceremonial grounds, churches, temples, ashrams, and sacred grounds have become public toilets over-flowing with zebra dung. The hucksters are painting the world in black and white dualities. All of this is due to trickster.

What can you do about it? Insult its meat. Laugh your posterior off and leave it far behind. Get yourself cleansed by the shaking and quaking of some old-fashioned belly laughter. As you get softer, find your rope to God. Allow your heart to ready you for the crossing.

Do not give in to the temptation to become angry at the attrac-tive-on-the-outside-but-rotten-on-the-inside fruit trickster has served. Overly cultivated bad feelings will make you hard and move you farther away from God's love. Laugh it away, for trickster's offering is so ridiculous that only morons, and that easily includes both you and me, could fall for it. It's a pratfall, and that can be a good thing if it brings a laugh and an unexpected trip into the world of good-spirited fun. Sound the horn and stop the harnessed dead-end trips. Take off the copyrighted reigns and let God's free-falling rain pour. It alone will wash away the dirt, so ask God to make it rain. The lightning shall commence, and it will fry any remaining filth. The spiritual floods are coming. There's a storm brewing in the Kala-hari sky.

Long ago, the Bushmen found the most natural way of handling trickster. In the Kalahari, trickster is teased to death—its importance is slain through ridicule and insult, both done with a good heart and spirit. Above all, n|om is infused to such an extent that trickster realizes it has met its match and leaves the premises for a vacation. You are shaken by n|om in order to make yourself ready for a visit to the classroom. N|om shakes trickster into a stupor. It can't keep up with all the movement and is knocked out. While trickster is asleep, the gods and ancestors slip by and make a house call.

Turning Away from Power, the Heart Rises

Knocking out trickster is just what we are doing tonight in the Kalahari, where I am dancing with the old blind man, Motaope. We are healing the people together. When the n|om fully cooks you, there is no need to keep your eyes open. Mine are closed so I can join the old man in the world of spiritual vision. "Ah ee aye, ah ee," we sing together. "Ta, ta, ta, ta, ta, ta, ta," we proclaim with a n|om staccato. "Ah eeeee!" the old man shrieks a n|om scream, letting go of what needs to be released in this ecstatic wild work.

We hold one another, each sending n|om into the other. This is what doctors do. They send each other arrows and nails. A n|om-kxao can't wait to meet up with another strong n|om-kxao because it means they will each get stronger. In sharing, we each get more n|om.

All night, we send the arrows of n|om, singing as we work. We are participating in the grand work and play of the ancestors, inspired by the love of our Creator. To send an arrow, you must have gone past the station of power—the place where trickster tempts you with whatever he thinks you might desire. In the Kalahari, like the biblical desert, you will feel the fire make you strong. You may want to test the power of n|om, seeing if you can turn stone into meat; or become the honcho of all the tribes in the world; or dare death to take your life. These tests are not about introducing doubt but are ways of trapping you in the carnival of tricks that can be achieved by power. You have to walk away from the seduction of power.

The final battle is between love and power.

"Your heart must rise," Twa said earlier that afternoon while resting underneath a baobab tree with Toma, |Kunta Boo, other n|om-kxaosi, and me. "Go past the station of power and move to the station of your heart. There, the ropes will pull you. Hand over power and will power to the effortless availability of an open heart that is ready to be pulled by God."

The final battle is between love and power, and love wins by not engaging in a single blow. Love conquers all because its pulling takes you to the highest height where, as Rumi said, love can turn a thorn into a flower. Heart alchemy takes place when the love mojo transforms either-or battles into relational marriages, enabling both ends to have interconnection along the course of one's journey.

Don't fight your enemy; love your enemy. Toma liked this idea, but added something else, "Love the ropes, for they pull your enemy into love."

> **"The ropes must be made stronger so that we are good to one another. We dance, laugh, and share in order to make our ropes stronger."**

This is Kalahari wisdom. The Bushmen know that it is about the felt ropes of relationship, not the linguistic scissors of discrimination, that bring our hearts together. Toma went on to say, "The ropes must be made stronger so that we are good to one another. We dance, laugh, and share in order to make our ropes stronger. If two people in the village are irritable with each other, we call for a dance and have them stand next to each other. This heals their ropes. Then they feel their relation-ship, and if they are husband and wife, they will now want to pull on each other's genitals all through the night, if you know what I mean!"

The men around Toma started laughing hard. |Kunta Boo answered, "That's right. Tell them that the secret to a good love life is to make your rope strong and hard, while insulting your wife so she'll get nice and soft." The women overheard this, and Ti!'ae shouted back, "Tell that to your stick because we're going to use it for firewood tonight. But, then it's probably too wet and won't burn. It's worthless as usual."

Everyone keeled over laughing as they insulted each other's meat. We knew it would be a good dance that night because the more absurd they can be with one another, the more likely the gods and ancestors will want to come out and play. Why? Because absurdity helps erase any and all differences, bringing everyone to the same ground level. Men and women, hard and soft, living creatures and ancestral beings are brought to the same playing ground.

And it is a good dance. Motaope and I are like two human pistons, pumping away side-by-side throughout the night. We are heart generators that bring light to the dark. Moving from power to love, we feel the vibrations of our voice reaching down to our heart. It is pulling our heart to rise even further. This ascension of the heart is made possible by the n|om rope that has a hold on us.

As our hearts rise, we become softer and softer. Whatever pains that our bodies may have brought before the dance have now disappeared. A Bushman who can barely walk to a dance will move without effort when full of n|om. It's as if the weight of the body and all its aches and pains are taken away. As the n|om brings on more light, you feel lighter. The strong tco-kxao are able to keep standing and pumping. Those less strong fall over and pass out.

Motaope and I are standing. We do not fall. As we get deeper into the n|om, our body becomes so light and pliable that we can feel ourselves stretching. We are now twenty to thirty feet tall, looking down over the dance. We can get even taller and see the village from the sky. We not only are able to stretch, expand, and reshape ourselves, we are able to shape-shift into other forms. If we look into the fire, we might see an animal that catches us. By this I mean that our heart catches a feeling for it. At that moment, the animal can jump out of the fire and dissolve right into us; or if it is a big animal like a lion, it can swallow us whole.

That's what happened to me when I became a lion. I saw the lion's head in the fire, which completely shocked me, but its beauty caught me. That lion jumped right out of the fire with its mouth open, and I went right down its hatch. I became a lion. My heart was the heart of a lion. A roar came out of my mouth, and my body stretched itself into the form that holds the movement and lines of that feline. Everyone felt and saw this new lion. A few screamed and ran away out of fear, while the others felt more n|om come into the dance as they clapped and sang with increased fervor.

Shape-shifting, called *thuru*, does happen, but it is another distraction, an exiting from the main highway. There is something to learn from being a lion or leopard, eagle, giraffe, eland, or any of the other creatures, but the main road will take you to other mysteries. If you find yourself desiring the power of the lion rather than the pulling of love, this can make your heart fall. Power bends the rope, and causes a sideways turn away from the straight and narrow road that goes to God's house.

**You cannot only bring back your ancestors,
but you can step inside their essence, their heart,
and feel them from the inside. In other words,
your heart can become one with them.**

Go past the animals you can become. See the ancestors. You might find your grandparents and other loved ones who have gone on. They might catch you when you least expect to see them. Yes, I was surprised to see my grandfather, and my heart was lassoed by my longing for him. I shape-shifted and became him. This is also a good teaching. You cannot only bring back your ancestors, but you can step inside their essence, their heart, and feel them from the inside. In other words, your heart can become one with them.

This is what the great longing of our heart desires. It is not only to feel the pulling to find our beloved but to become the ones we love. As we travel down the King's Highway, the road to God, we are constantly captured and absorbed by one teacher after another. These are the teachers who possess our heart. They will talk with us if we ask them a question. Don't forget to ask them whatever your heart desires; this is important. Sometimes they remain still unless we make a request. They may show you many things and bestow special gifts. If you want to learn everything they have to offer, you must allow them to catch your heart so you can step into them and become them. Then their heart is absorbed along with their wisdom and unique gifts.

"Stay on the rope," Motaope sends me a telegraph along the rope connecting my belly to his. "Don't fall off it."

He is reminding me to not take any exits. Go on by all the ancestors. They will help you, but don't be distracted by them. As I do so, an amazing transformation takes place. I feel all my materiality slipping away. I am no longer a living being with a body; I have turned into a cloud—a fog that pulses with vibrant electricity; I have become pure n|om. This is when a tco-kxao is fully awakened. Now I can see with my second eyes and all my other spiritual senses.

We have danced through the night, and the people have gathered to make coffee and breakfast. A few of us lie down on a blanket. I am still feeling like an electrical cloud. I know my body is there, but my consciousness is not defined by its typical way of being present. I get up and sit down on a camp chair. As everyone is talking, I hear something in the bush and turn to look. I see twelve women elders, all dressed in green robes, with eyes of pure light. They are not smiling or laughing. They are all staring at me, sending waves of n|om into me. It feels like they are directing me and testing me at the same time. I do not choose fear nor do I pass out from the intensity of their locked-on gaze. I receive them, all of them, these twelve queens of the Kalahari. They are touching me, rewiring me, preparing me, and teaching me right in front of the whole village.

"Yes, the ancestors have come to see who you are," Motaope, the old blind man, explains. "They have heard about you. Word has spread along the ropes. You have passed their test, and it is a strong test. It would have killed some people. Now you can expect them to show up all the time. They are going to visit you for the rest of your life. They will live inside of you. They will bring you n|om and love. A few may decide to make love with you—not on you, with you. You are now becoming a village, a place where the old African ancestors will come to dance and sing with you. Someday soon, I, too, will visit you in this way. Now eat some breakfast. The ancestors are hungry."

The Classrooms of My Learning

Several months after my experience with Motaope and the ancestors, I left the Kalahari and visited the island of St. Vincent. There, I went to

183

the spiritual classrooms under the pointing direction of Archbishop Pompey. The community ceremonially prepared me, bound my eyes with colored bands, and laid me to the ground in a fasting room. There, they left me for nearly a week. I was prayed over and sung over at every sunrise and sundown. In the Caribbean, I found another crossroads that enabled entry to the spirit worlds. Let me take you along for one particular multilayered vision that I experienced:

I face a long building. The middle part is a high structure, and the sides are lower wings. It is an airline terminal. As I enter, I see a gentleman wearing a white suit. He is standing on a podium and is clearly the director of this operation. What astounds me are all the lines that shoot out around him. They are like laser beams. Some are straight, while others are curved. They are everywhere, and they are made of many different colors. I walk toward him. He points to one of the lines. The second he does this, I look and—*swoosh!*—I am immediately picked up and shot along its pathway. I land at a new destination.

This is how you get to a spiritual classroom. Someone points to a line, path, track, or road, and you take one step toward it. The rest happens in a flash; you are sent there immediately. Sometimes you simply see a line and jump on it. The exact form of the pointer or the line may vary from case to case, but rest assured that there will be a line for traveling.

All who have entered fully embodied spiritual lives know about the lines. All Bushman n|om-kxaosi have used them, and all cultures that keep original spirituality intact have had access to them. Without these tracks, there is no way to get to a classroom. Without spiritual teaching of the direct kind, you are left with a guessing game. That's when trickster has you for dinner. Without direct infusions of spirit, you are easy prey for trickster's talk. Know that you must be filled with enough n|om to find your way to the classrooms.

The destination at which I arrive is the base of an enormous mountain. To my delight, my wife and son are by my side; we are there as a family. This makes me very happy because it shows my ropes with my family are strong enough that I can bring them with me. Bushmen also enjoy traveling together. A strong dance usually has several n|om-kxaosi going up the ropes side by side. There is a rock art image from South Africa that shows a group of Bushmen climbing a rope together. They are going up to the sky village, one of the great classrooms.

We look at the mountain and notice there is a lot of activity. A multitude of businessmen wearing black suits are walking down its slopes. Then, without notice, a gigantic gift box appears on the top of the mountain. It is larger than a building. It is a white gift box wrapped with a red ribbon. People start pointing at it and running, for they fear it may tumble down the mountain and crush them. The box begins to rock. It is teetering, and soon it starts to come down. It is sliding, as if skiing, down the mountain. As it gathers speed, the people cannot possibly escape its arrival. Thousands of people are slain by the moving box. I watch at the base, holding hands with my wife and son. I hear a voice say, "You are given the gift of n|om, what your grandfather called the Holy Ghost power. Use it to slay the people."

I recall how old country preachers talk about being slain in the spirit, and I am seeing it right in front of my eyes. My pointing father, Archbishop Pompey, is now by my side. I come back to myself, and he asks, "Did you see that?" I assume he was there too. "Yes, Father," I reply, because he is now my spiritual father. He is very serious about this incident and gives me further instruction, "Go back and ask why you are there. Find out your job."

Back I go, swept away to the mountain classroom. I ask out loud, "What is my mission? What spiritual job do you want me to do?" A rumbling can be heard in the sky. A voice fills the Earth so that every creature alive can hear it: "You are an ambassador of the Holy Ghost. You are to bring down the n|om, the life force, the Holy Ghost power. Open your gift."

The large gift box comes to a rest at the base of the mountain, and the lid slowly floats off. Out of the box, a silver shield is revealed. The voice speaks again, "This is your shield. It will protect you. There is nothing for you to fear. March on and do your job. I say these things in the name of the holiness that brought these things forth. Go among the people and share this gift. Never forget that these things come from a mighty mountain, the place some know as Zion. It is where the Last Supper was served. It is now serving the bread of life, the spirit that feeds the soul. In the name of all that is holy, we ask you to step into your mission and never look back. Take one step at a time. We will pull you through."

**Fill your heart with the songs of praise.
Dance along the way. This is how you stay on track.**

I come back to myself again and my spiritual father is patiently waiting. "Yes, my son, this is how it is in the classrooms. You have been admitted to school, and there will be no end to your education. Make sure your heart is pure when you go to school because the road to the schoolhouse is very narrow. Many people lose their way or take a wrong turn. Don't walk there quietly. Fill your heart with the songs of praise, and dance along the way; this is how you stay on track. Now get some rest, for there are other lessons tomorrow."

I am driving along the narrow bumpy roads on the island. I do not yet realize that I am heading toward another spiritual classroom. The road leads straight into the ocean. I keep going until I am underwater. There, a teacher welcomes me: "Go deeper and deeper into the spiritual sea. We gift you with this vest of weights that will help you go farther down. Do not be afraid even when it is dark, as it will be as you go deeper and deeper into the ocean." I remember my shield, and I hold on to it, allowing myself to sink, going all the way to the ocean floor.

I find a room, a holy place. It is another classroom for learning. "Look below," the voice announces. I see a bulge on the sandy floor. "Pick it up." I dig around and find that a musical instrument has been hidden underneath the sand. In this way, more music is delivered. A song, one of my grandmother's favorite hymns, begins playing: "Pass Me Not, Oh Gentle Savior," I hear the oceanly choir continue to sing, "Hear my humble cry; while on others Thou art calling, do not pass me by."

I can hear my grandmother singing it with them. She was such a gentle soul that, when I was a child, I named her Doe because she reminded me of a deer. She was a dear person for all the ninety-three years she lived. Now, in this classroom, she continues to sing what I always heard her sing and play on the piano, "Pass Me Not, Oh Gentle Savior."

This song was composed by Fanny J. Crosby, a devout woman who was blind since birth. As an adult, she dreamed that God walked among the people in her church and touched everyone who would go to heaven. As God got closer to her, she started to pray that He wouldn't pass her by. She woke up hearing this song. She also was able to describe in great detail all the people in her church, even though she had never seen them.

At the bottom of the ocean, where darkness and depth coexist, I am taught to see with spiritual eyes. My grandmother's love is a rope to a song that opens new eyes for my spirit. When I come back to myself, I am singing the song and weeping.

You never know when you will be taken to the classrooms, but you know you are ready for school whenever you get filled with n|om. The Bushmen cook their n|om in a dance, hoping that a rope will pull them into a classroom. It can happen in the dance or after the dance. Even days after the dance, you can lie down and go straight into an unexpected class.

I was once awakened in the middle of the night and got up from bed because the back door was open. Before closing the door, I noticed that a mountain was in my backyard. "That's strange," I thought to myself. "I've never seen a mountain in my yard." There was a dirt trail that led up the mountain, and I followed it. After a steep climb, I came to a little outcropping with a Japanese elder sitting on the ground. It was Professor Kato, a dear friend of Ikuko Osumi.

Whenever I wake up to find my back door open, I climb up to visit him. He doesn't say a word. He simply places his hands on my head, and gives me seiki and n|om. I wake up vibrating as if plugged in to a thousand megavolts. I also feel that he has downloaded some know-how into me—a knowing that goes past what can be conveyed by words. Our rope, our connection, is made stronger. I weep over how much I long to see him again and for gratitude to have been able to make contact in this way.

My classrooms have many teachers, from my grandparents to many elders from diverse spiritual traditions around the world. Sometimes I am introduced to new teachers I haven't met before, but the link to them is almost always through someone I deeply love. The ropes that take you there are ropes of love—the relationships we have for one another. My love for my grandfather connects me to him, while his love for his grandfather enables me to travel farther along the rope that goes from generation to generation.

The Classroom of the Original Ancestors

The original ancestors, the g||auan≠'angsi, are also waiting to teach you. Once, I was asleep, though I thought I was awake. I turned my body, and to my surprise, I twisted my spiritual self right out. I was hovering above the bed, looking down at myself. A voice spoke, "Let me take you all the way." I held on to a deep trust and was immediately shot out of the roof of my house. For a moment, I was an astronaut riding a rocket launch into the sky. I observed the Earth below, and then, without warning, I was in outer space, still flying. The Earth became a small globe. The sun came closer, and I felt its heat and power. There was a slight temptation to move toward the sun, but I remembered that this station of a spiritual journey must be bypassed.

This was happening as if I was completely awake. Had I been picked up by an alien means of transportation, or had I become an unidentified flying object? It didn't matter because the flight was so exhilarating that it brought rapture and joy just to experience the whole universe of planets, comets, stars, and galaxies. I could hear a marvelous symphony everywhere in the innards of outer space. It was celestial and moving—the music that provided the fuel for this voyage into the universe. It gave birth to n|om and provided the rocket-like thrust of a breathtaking momentum. I had hooked up with the original source of spiritual pulling. Creation itself had grabbed hold of my soul and was sending me to its outer edge. There at the end, I found the beginning.

The beginning spiritual landscape is the Kalahari Desert, which has one tree, sometimes depicted as a camelthorn tree and at other times a baobab tree, like the one on the cover of the book. This tree has holy water inside its trunk. It is the original source of the n|om that gives life to the universe, including its creatures and all their specific creations. At this place, I landed with my feet on the ground and felt them start to move in the old way of dancing. The original ancestors were there, unseen but felt. They were singing and dancing, and I was there to receive n|om from them.

The strongest Bushmen tco-kxaosi have been to this classroom. It is the end of the rope, where all spiritual mysteries began. This track prepares you to get fully cooked.

At this place, like all holy places that flow with n|om, we do not say God's name. Rather than uttering !Xon!a'an, we say a respect name, G≠kao N!a'an. When the Sky God of infinite love showers a n|om rain upon us, we do not even speak at all. We are back in First Creation, and trickster hasn't yet been born until we start speaking. Then we are sent home to Second Creation all over again.

To get to the classroom of the original ancestors, we must go past the station where fire tempts us with power. This station, called *n!aroh-||xam*, is where you meet and deal with fear. You must neither surrender to fear nor pump yourself up to fight it. You must go past it.

A second station, the place of the heart, awaits you. This place is called *g!a'ama-n!ausi*. This is a high station—a high rise—for your soul where healing takes place. If you keep going on a nonstop express train, you may get to the third station, *thara n|om*. This is where you arrive when you are soft enough to receive an arrow of n|om.

You can keep on truckin' and arrive at Grand Central Station. There, you can catch a train, hop a plane, or find a road to a classroom. You might even be taken to the beginning, the end of the rope.

The Eighth Mystery

Hold my hand and let's go visit a classroom. Let a song come into your heart; it matters not what tune comes forth. Sing it in the way a child would sing in a reverie of delight. Let's sing together while holding hands. Feel the fire of the Kalahari dance send a spark into the sky. Catch a feeling for its streak of light. Somewhere, somehow, loved ones are reaching out for you. They want to lift you on board their ship, pulling you out of your stormy sea. Allow your imagination to invite this pulling. Have it pulse with the rhythm of the song that is moving your voice, calling all this forth, and know that I have already surrendered to the ropes of my ancestors.

Into the classroom we go. This time we have walked all the way into the sky, halfway up into a cloud. I'm sure I just saw an angel pass by. A harp just played, agreeing with me. This cloud is not dark but bright. It has a desk with a large book sitting on it. The book is open, and I see that you are already reading it. There are no words on its pages, only lines that shoot out into the cosmos. Each line is a different color. Some of the lines are thicker than the others. We both hear a voice speak to everyone in the cloud, "There is a line for you." It's your rope and your road. Move toward it. If you even think of moving toward it, it will grab hold of you and whisk you along its path.

This is the book that matters. Its lines are lines of feeling rather than lines of thought. It connects you so you know where to go. It connects you so you can hear what needs to be said. It connects you so you can get the electricity to charge your journey. Feel the connection, follow the pathways, and receive the wisdom that presents itself to you, in whatever form. When you are ready, you'll return to yourself.

The spiritual classrooms are sweet just like the sweet love that comes from truly grand grandparents. Even when you are startled or lost in a teaching, ask for a helping hand, and it will come in the form of what you trust and love most. The setting will make you feel at home once you hold on to the hand that provides a secure hold. Put your hand in that hand. This is how you hand over your limitations and find yourself a link in a greater chain of being.

You can ask God to take you to a spiritual classroom anytime you want. Prepare yourself for the trip by singing sacred songs that touch your heart. Sing the songs that were sacred to your ancestors. Did your grandmother or aunt have a song that was important to her? What song do you think would open her heart? When you sing it with all your heart, she can catch you. You can then get a hold of her rope, and it can start pulling.

Do this before you go to bed. Sing in order to catch a rope that brings you closer to someone you love. Go to sleep with this n|om rope stirring and pulling inside you. Gently and sweetly ask to be taken to a classroom. Ask as if you were an innocent child, which you are, in spite of all trickster's efforts to convince you that you have already grown up and graduated. You have only just begun.

The teachers are waiting in their rooms. They are in the air; under the water; inside mountains; amidst the swamps, deserts, nightclubs, cathedrals, fire circles, baptism pools, ski slopes, and galactic orchestral halls.

Create a seat belt for yourself out of a beautiful piece of silk. Think carefully about what color it should be. Maybe a spiritual classroom teacher will tell you what color to wear. Wrap this seat belt around you before you go to sleep, and don't wake up until your school is out. Stay in your seat unless you are called to dance. Then wave your seat belt as you dance.

After you spiritually travel somewhere, hang the silk cloth from your bedroom ceiling. It is no longer a seat belt but a spiritual flag. It reminds you of where you have gone, what rope and track you have traveled on. Fill your room with silk spiritual flags. Consider these your spiritual diplomas. You only need one, but you might get lucky and find yourself with more. The Silk Road to China can also deliver you to Africa, the Caribbean, East Greenland, Egypt, the Australian Outback, Indonesia, Japan, Siberia, Jerusalem, Persia, Greece, and all stops in between, including New

Orleans. Start traveling the old routes. Only they can bring something new.

Welcome to the spiritual classrooms. I can only point you toward them. The rest is up to your finding a song and going to a n|om gas station. Fill 'er up and get on your way. If you stop for a station break, remember that more of the journey lies ahead. This is your pilgrimage to the holy city, the city of crystal. Along the way you might see the sea of glass, the enchanted forest, and the mermaids of Atlantis, but only if one of your loved ones—a relative or an acquaintance—already had a longing for such a place.

Maybe you'll find a new friend, a helper, a guardian angel, and even a private tutor; the spiritual classrooms have no end. You need to end your stationary ways and start traveling first class. There's a horse, a train, a ship, a plane, and even a rocket ship headed for fantastic glories. Hop on board the Love Boat, the Mystery Ship, the Starship Enterprise, as they are humming their engines, tuning their instruments, and preparing some dinner, all for your trip of a lifetime to Oz to meet the wizards of n|om.

Now I come back to myself.

9

HAVE A DRINK ALONG THE WAY

The Ninth Original Mystery

What makes the desert beautiful is that somewhere it hides a well.

ANTOINE DE SAINT-EXUPÉRY

The golden elixir is one of the names for the mystical liquid that flows from the fountain of eternal life. It can be ingested as you would drink a glass of water. The difference is that it doesn't travel down to your stomach; it travels through every part of your body. As it smoothly courses through your insides, it brings warmth and vibratory energy. This tasty treat is a n|om-shake. Believe me, there is nothing like being served this dessert at a Kalahari roadside diner. It is the most refreshing and inspiring shake on the planet. Once you've had a taste, you'll never reach for anything else to get high.

The first time I drank from the holy cup was in a visionary experience. Jesus came to me and held a glass filled with white luminous light. It looked like glowing milk. As I drank it, the life force permeated every cell of my body. It was an intense dose of the Holy Spirit. Without any doubt, this is an extraordinary experience beyond description; it goes past fantasy and science fiction. It is drinking the purest truth from the deepest well.

But the drink is not confined to the realm of visionary experiences; it is as real as n|om and just as potent. The Bushmen know this drink, and it sometimes comes to them in an exceptionally strong dance. |Xoan, |Chu|kun's grandmother, was a powerful n|om-kxao. She carried a special turtle shell by her side. When the n|om boiled during a healing dance, she would walk to the center of the dance space and hold the shell as high as she possibly could, lifting it toward the night sky. God would fill her Kalahari cup with a holy water—pure n|om— that she would serve to the other n|om-kxaosi.

|Xoan is a close friend to all my n|om wives. She and I have exchanged many nails and arrows of n|om. She grew up with Toma and |Kunta Boo, who remember drinking from her grandmother's cup. |Xoan also drank it on several occasions. All of them would get a super-boost of n|om that surpassed anything else experienced in the dance. It was such a strong beverage that they couldn't walk a straight line for the rest of the night.

This drink is handed to you by an |ae-N≠unhn, an ancestor who sends down a n|om soft drink from God. The Bushmen suggest that the drink is God's urine, though it looks like water. The Sky God's medicine water has a name: !Xo g!u. If you could bottle it, the billion-dollar pharmacology corporations would go out of business. The same would be true for the world's institutionalized religions and liquor businesses.

When that Coke bottle fell down from a comedy sky, maybe it was a subliminal cultural request. We are desperately thirsty for a drink from God. The Bushmen know where the soda fountain is, and our empty bottles are dying to get filled with some Coca-God-ola. Or maybe you prefer Seven-Heavens-Up or Dr. Pepper's Not-So-Lonely Hearts Club Band. These holy drinks come with a taste of heaven accompanied by some heart-and-soul dance music.

I have tasted the Kalahari cocktail served by the gods. In fact, I have tasted it several times throughout the world, and I took in every drop from the glass or turtle shell, no matter where I was feasting on the spirit. My oh my, what can I possibly say! Once you've had a taste of this juice, you can never be tempted by any con artist's snake oil. It's the real spiritual deal, not the mai tai of Trickster Trader. It is the holy white lightning of God's water. Tilt your head back right now and ask God to tinkle a few drops in your mouth. If you are sincere, an ancestor might take you seriously and send you down a kundalini smoothie. You'll be sorry that you didn't ask earlier.

The Hearts of the Spears

God is unpredictable and can decide without notice to serve a drink to anyone from Mozart to Moses, Annie Oakley, Mother Teresa, or Babe Ruth. There are no restrictions on who gets served. Nevertheless, the folks who get the most access to the sacred libation are the strongest n|om-kxaosi. We have talked about the beginners, healers, and transmitters. There is a final category that refers to a n|om-kxao who has been fully cooked. God takes this person out of the pot and throws the well-done meat into the world to spiritually feed others. These are the n|om beings.

The name for a fully cooked n|om-kxao is *g≠aqba-n!a'an*, which means "heart of the spears." These people have healed hundreds if not thousands of people, and have delivered as many arrows and nails. They frequently visit the spiritual classrooms and are constantly filled with sacred song. They shake at a second's notice. The greatest mysteries are all familiar territory to them, and this includes drinking God's water.

Most hearts of the spears have received the gift of God's ostrich egg called *!Xo dso'o-n!o*. As I explained in the introduction, the first time the egg came to me in a vision, I was nineteen years old. It was a large luminous egg, and I received a direct, multisensory spiritual transmission from it. More than a decade later, the egg came back. Again, I was in a visionary state, though fully conscious. What took place was very simple, but it was n|om shattering. This time, a large ostrich egg floated in front of my face. I stared at it, and the egg cracked open. One half had two colored lines circling it, one red and the other green. The other half had a pure white line around its circumference. Then I woke up shaking and quaking, filled with n|om and song.

The Kalahari elders were thrilled when I told them about these experiences. "You've received God's ostrich egg!" they shouted. "Let's dance tonight, for now you have all the ropes." The Bushmen believe that this visionary egg cracks open as a means of giving you all the nails, arrows, and ropes of the Sky God. It is a sign that you have been given everything. Furthermore, it enables you to communicate with other Bushman n|om-kxaosi through the ostrich egg telephone line. The Kalahari elders know when I am coming and what I am doing by their special dreams of an ostrich egg with me inside the shell. The Kalahari Television Network is broadcast on a big eggshell screen. It enables the n|om-kxaosi to keep in touch by a face in the egg rather than egg on the face!

Very few hearts of the spears are alive today. There are a couple of men and a handful of women, and I am regarded as one of them. This is why they pull on my chain so much, asking me to teach their young, make their doctors stronger, and tell the rest of the world about their endangered original way of being with n|om. It's not the n|om that faces extinction; it's the way people need to be softened and cooked in order to receive n|om and the ropes to the spiritual classrooms.

When I say I am a heart of the spears, I am not boasting. Yes, I am very happy with my chosen role, but to be a heart of the spears requires knowing that you are an idiot and always susceptible to trickster's pranks. We are all human, and we are all animals. We are also dumb as a weed. What a person skilled with n|om knows is how to soften hearts and insult the meat, followed by the production of a thunder and lightning show. We are troubadours of the traveling Life Force Theatre, the oldest guild on the planet.

Walking the line and following the track to God cannot be achieved by willpower. You can't get there by trying hard; if you're trying, it won't work. This is effortless work.

The ropes have nothing to do with rigid rules for how to behave. They are the highest expression of ethics in which good action and deed are pulled forth effortlessly and naturally. These are Tao ropes pulled by the Way. Don't ask me what that means because, if you have to ask, I'll have to pull your cord. It will probably be a dissonant chord to help you see that it is the cacophony, the crack between the major expectations, where the light of n|om jazz shines its ray. A heart of the spears is a n|om instrument ready to be blown by the breath of the ancestors and gods—a *wui-wei* wind. Sometimes you are blown as a reed instrument, and other times you have to sound the brass or hit the drum. It's all about n|om jazz.

Walking the line and following the track to God cannot be achieved by willpower. You can't get there by trying hard; if you're trying, it won't work. This is effortless work. The purpose, if there is any to be said, is to make yourself a sail to be moved by God's holy breath. A sail and a nail help God's mail get delivered.

The way of n|om is the way of natural goodness, effortless kindness, and wise love.

This way of the wild voyager is not irresponsible. It doesn't indulge in the pursuit of mirages and appearances that have no spiritual reality. The way of n|om is the way of natural goodness, effortless kindness, and wise love. Its ropes are strengthened by commitment and loyalty, while nicely seasoned with the appropriate spices. Similarly, master therapist Dr. Carl Whitaker used to say that a healthy relationship, especially marriage, needs vulgarity. He is saying that you need to get some dirty rice as the spice for kicking your relationship up a notch. In the same way, you need to get dirty for the Lord. There simply isn't enough spice and life in a sterilized piece of leather binding, whether we are talking about the meat in our significant relationships or the words in our holy books.

A heart of the spears teaches us to never judge another person. What anyone has done, we too are capable of being tricked into doing. The compassion we offer is not one that sits still. It invites the fallen to come to a dance where they can be shaken up all over again. Here, everyone is given a fresh new face like the screen of an Etch A Sketch when it is shaken to clear the previous efforts at making and following lines.

**Never judge another person. What anyone has done,
we too are capable of being tricked into doing.**

Love your neighbors by helping them make their ropes stronger. This means the relationships in their lives. Help them find a way to love their mommies, daddies, children, grandchildren, brothers, sisters, aunts, uncles, cousins, partners, and neighbors, no matter how young or old any of them are. If you don't feel the longing for a loved one, then there will be no ropes. You have to sing in a way that pleases your ancestors rather than impresses your uppity trickster-self. You have to make an odyssey to get down to your hometown in order to find your ropes. The beginning is what is needed to help you find the end.

At the same time, we are all one colossal family. Every culture is filled with many brothers and sisters waiting to hold hands and make our ropes stronger. My songs come from many traditions. My heart connects with my family of origin when the old gospel songs are sung. Those are my strongest ropes and lines to them. The Bushman n|om songs connect me to my Kalahari family, while the sacred songs of Bali, Native America, Japan, Mexico, Brazil, St. Vincent, and many other places in the world sing through me when inspired by all those relations.

I was named He Who Catches the Songs by the Guarani shamans. I like that name. It makes me feel closer—like I have a stronger rope— to my earliest heroes, the great American songwriters like George Gershwin and Jerome Kern, among others. They knew how love, song, and pulling were all tied together.

**A heart of the spears never gets off the ropes.
You live in a constant immersion in n|om.**

When I was a young boy, I wanted to be George Gershwin. It should be no surprise that his songs are among the strongest ropes in my life. "Our Love Is Here to Stay" and "Someone to Watch Over Me" are two of my favorite ropes. I had the opportunity to get to know George Gershwin's niece. Her mother was George's sister, a Broadway singer for whom George often premiered his latest composition. I took George's niece to meet the Bushman n|om-kxaosi, and she gave me the gift of a story about her uncle. What she told me suggested that George had a love for the African way of expressing life through movement, and he surely felt what the n|om-kxaosi experience in catching a song.

A heart of the spears never gets off the ropes. You live in a constant immersion in n|om. Most of the elders I have been led to were these hearts, even in parts of the world where they did not know that term. They had gone to the spiritual classrooms and knew about drinking the holy n|om water. I also met many spiritual teachers who did not know about these mysteries. It helped me understand how some cultures have lost or disconnected their hookup with the divine. It can happen to any culture, especially if it gets too wordy and top-heavy.

A n≠u'uhan is someone who pretends to be a n|om-kxao, and there are many great pretenders in the spiritual marketplace. If you want to check their authenticity, turn on some music or, better yet, ask them for some music. If they are connected to God, they will jump at an opportunity to be a DJ for n|om. Then watch what happens when the music is played. Does n|om grab them and pull them all over the place? Do they allow themselves to be ecstatically shaken like a fool hanging out at God's highest bar? Do they love n|om, and do they enjoy sharing it? That's all you need to notice. Everything else said about their expertise is just that: words. Look for n|om that rocks them and for n|om that energizes their words, tuning them in to language that softens hearts and minds. You want the soft, insulting teachers who can cook your meat.

Strong ropes connect you with everything in the universe, and when it is important to know about the other end of a rope, it will tap or pull you.

A Little Taste of God on Tap

All Bushmen know about the tapping that touches their body. When it is time to hunt, a hunter feels a tapping called a *kxaetci!hun*. It tells him it is time for hunting. It is the ancestors or God that tap and pull the ropes on his body. In general, their tapping is called ≠a'am|'an. It can be a shock on the fingertips that says that a lion is near. Or the palm of your hand can tingle because you feel someone is coming with a gift for you. Even the place between your legs can get stirred when your loved one is a day away from returning to your home bed. Strong ropes connect you with everything in the universe, and when it is important to know about the other end of a rope, it will tap or pull you.

When you are fully cooked, you receive a rope to the water fountain in the heavens. When you need renewal, this rope becomes a pipeline for the n|om water to pour into you. Bushman spirituality is all about the ropes and the n|om that makes everything flow, from love to a sacred drink.

"There's nothing like a drink of God's water," Toma exclaims. "It is the best! It makes you feel reborn. I love that drink. I hope to get another one soon. Do you have a cup on you? If so, let's fill ourselves up."

"Yes, Toma, I have a sip for you, but don't spill it. If it drops on the ground, the Earth will think it's from you. Then you might find a tree root coming after you, so be careful. Are you sure you won't spill it?" I tease him, acting like I am wobbling with the cup, ready to spill it near his feet.

"I think you have had too much to drink," Toma answers back. "You got so excited thinking about it that you wet your pants."

We both start laughing even though we could jump and scream in delight simply thinking of how good God's water is to drink. It isn't the taste that exhilarates; it is the feeling that pours through you. When it flows down your throat, it makes you want to leap into the air and scream, "Hallelujah!"

"I wonder what your friends will think when they hear that you have developed a liking for holy pee," Toma pretends to be concerned. "Will you tell them that God has some drops that are tasty, or will you say that God makes a good stream?"

I never imagined that anyone would think that the golden elixir is urine. I had drunk it before I knew the Bushmen's explanation and name, but today I don't care what anyone thinks it is. All I can say is that it rocks your soul and knocks your socks off, for it distills the whole essence of life's satisfaction into one sanctified sip. If its transformative effects were known to the world, people would pay a fortune for it. But it's not for sale. It is free for those who allow their whole being to be insulted and softened, made ready for the mysteries of n|om.

There is a classroom that is a water hole; it is called *!'han-n!ang*. Our friend |Kunta Boo has been there. When he received his first big arrow of n|om, he was sent to this place and found that going underneath the water can take you to the same classroom that is in the sky. It's just a different way of getting there. Here, everything is a circle, so you can go down to get up. Similarly, you have to ridicule your everyday habits and make them unimportant in order to be filled with the largest and most important gifts of n|om.

"Belly up to the bar, mates. God is serving some grog; don't ask what it is. Just drink up and get yourself loaded to the gunwales. This is better than grub. It will give you sea legs you'll never forget. Step right up. God's got some grog for you!"

What more can I say about a life lived on the high seas of n|om? You'll walk away from the constraints, but not the love, of every major and minor religion. Newfangled spirituality will become a bore. You'll head for the sea where the deepest water exists. There, you'll feel closer to God and, with a good compass and a bit of luck, you might get a little taste of God on tap. That will make you tap dance on any dangerous water. Pause and imagine a bar on Bourbon Street that sells God's water. The line of people waiting to get a sip would cross the country from every direction. Everyone would see where the crossroads are pointing and head to New Orleans.

In fact, there are some poor country churches out in the Louisiana swamplands that can hook you up to this brew. This is God's hurricane, a spirit julep, Pimm's holy cup, a soul-zerac, brandy milk n|om punch, absinthe lightning, and a Creole bloody Virgin Mary. If you thought I was telling even a tiny particle of the truth, you'd pack your bags tonight and head down here. But I *am* telling the truth, so grab your cup, close your eyes, and wait for the rope that will carry you to the highest bartender who waits with the healing salve for tender souls and thirsty spirits.

> **Once you get a taste for God, everything else**
> **is mere tap water. If the world knew that this is the**
> **drink that can quench our deepest thirst,**
> **we'd have a different way of relating**
> **with one another.**

I have had the pleasure of serving this drink to addicts and drug abusers. Those who opened their hatch so the medicine could go down found the best ecstatic mix of their dreams. They immediately became bored with the stuff sold on the street. Once you get a taste for God, everything else is mere tap water. If the world knew that this is the drink that can quench our deepest thirst, we'd have a different way of relating with one another. We'd be doing everything to hunt and share n|om.

When the N | om Gets Flowing

N|om not only gets into the water, it gets into every aspect of your life. When you catch the feeling for God's love, it gets pumped and mainlined into your innards. The n|om flows whenever it is needed. As you become more intimate with n|om, it goes to work with you and even sleeps with you.

Yes, there is n|om sex. It is what tantric practitioners can only fantasize about, but it is not pornographic. The latter is problematic because it is graphic. As any good marriage and family therapist will tell you, sex is about feeling, not seeing. Furthermore, sex is most alive when it has a rope to pull, and you don't get a rope unless you love the other. Sex with the love of your life knocks your room lights out and turns on God's spiritual light show.

Porno has to do with watching a recording of the action of sexual intimacy, observing it from the sideline rather than being inside the mainline. It is a rerun, a pretend encounter. There is no rope and no relationship. It is pushy with little pull. Porno is an imitation, a false reproduction of a creative act.

In the broadest sense, reproduced imitations of sex are not the only things that can be pornographic. Observing a fake copy of sacred love might also apply to how we express love for God. If it isn't real but only feigned talk, then it's porno-religion. Shamanism without real love is a porno-sham(anism). Love without a strong rope moves toward porno-love. A God without infinite love and forgiveness is a porno-god. Perhaps most of the super-successful mega-churches are profiting from the sales of porno-Christianity. To avoid the trap of porno, we must make our ropes stronger, and this can only be done by devotion to our beloved and a commitment to pulling one another through both the best and worst of times.

"I love that n|om sex," Toma says while talking privately with me. "Women always want to marry a strong n|om-kxao because his ropes are the strongest. Men also want to spend their lives with a woman who is in the medicine way. Her ropes can pull him into another world. When both a man and a woman's n|om is hot, look out. They can love themselves right into First Creation. They have to be careful when they are fooling around because in First Creation they can change at any moment. They might look down and see that there is a giraffe inside of them. That could get dangerous."

N|om yanks the rope of two people who have a true heart-to-heart commitment in their relationship. It can transform their intimacy.

Toma is not teasing this time. N|om sex is what he says it is, and there is no other way to describe it. Let me say that differently: He is teasing, but there is a truth in his play. N|om yanks the rope of two people who have a true heart-to-heart commitment in their relationship. It can transform their intimacy. It utilizes both their similarities and their differences. It is the pulling found inside a complex relationship, one filled with many contradictions and paradoxes.

It is not the simple, sugarcoated filmed rerun of a graphic, romanticized scene. There, you are play-acting. In n|om love, a rope pulls your relationship into the depths of an infinite complexity of interaction. It dances you with someone alive and unpredictable—a complex, multileveled whole ecology of beauty, not a flat and postcard-like simpleton. A complex and rich lover is capable of both caressing your face and ripping off your head. Complex love is a crossroads, impassioned by the tensions between life and death. Toma is correct. First Creation sex is for wild animals. It plays at the borderlines of danger and safety, an intercourse that holds all the contrasts that pulse and throb a ride on n|om.

N|om not only pumps up your sex life, it infuses itself into all daily activities.

All aboard! There is a n|om brothel waiting for all holy marriages. Come on in and find your pump. It's hot. Take off your self-esteem and feel the sweat of the nighttime steam. Experience God's way of making your ropes stronger than steel.

N|om not only pumps up your sex life, it infuses itself into all daily activities. The great Bushman hunters may appear to be hunting an animal for dinner, but underneath the surface, they are hunting n|om. They are pulling the strings of the bow to make a connection with another arrow of n|om.

Cwi, one of the last old-way Kalahari hunters, talked to me about what it is like to be a n|om hunter:

When there is an animal in the bush, I feel a tapping on my arm. My heart also starts pounding, and I say to myself, "Am I going to hunt?" My grandfather took me into the bush when I was very young. That's when I learned to hunt and feel the tapping. My grandfather would ask me, "Do you feel that?" That's how I learned to feel the rope pulling me.

The tapping can also be along the chest or on the wrist. If the animal is a female, the tapping will be on the right arm, whereas the left arm will signal that it is a male animal. The tapping will tell you whether it is a young or old animal. It also tells you if the animal is small or large. The tapping is stronger when it is a big animal.

If God gives you an animal, that animal will speak to your heart. Your heart will be happy—will quiver and vibrate—when the animal is nearby. God brings the animals to us; it is God who makes these things happen. God makes the animal come near us and cause our heart to vibrate.

It feels like God pulls me toward the animal and pulls the animal toward me. It is a pulling in both directions. The n|om-kxaosi say that God has a rope attached between the animal and me. That is what God pulls. I feel those ropes pulling me, but only the n|om-kxaosi see the ropes.

Sometimes I have a kabi where the ancestors show me an animal, and when I wake up, I know it is time to hunt. The ancestors say, "In the morning when you wake up, you must get up and kill this animal. But don't tell anyone. Otherwise the animal will go away." When the animal is shown to you in a kabi, you must go and hunt alone. Otherwise the animal will not be there.

God or the ancestors can also tell you where the poison is—where the trees may be found with the larvae that we use on our arrows. God can choose a person to be a hunter of a particular animal; God gave me the kudu. That is the animal I am connected to, and I am pulled toward it. God made me a kudu hunter. God gave me the kudu so I can hunt it. The kudu and I walk side by side. It's like God made a special connection between the kudu and me.

The kudu gave me a song. When I feel a pulling toward a kudu, I sing that song. I keep singing it in my heart as I am pulled toward the kudu in the hunt. I sing it during the whole hunt. Sometimes in a kabi, I will look into the eyes of a kudu; it makes me shake and feel n|om. I sometimes see my own eyes reflected in the kudu's eyes. That makes me jump and feel hot. There are times when I touch the kudu.

When I pull back the string of my bow and move it up and down, I am trying to find where the pull is strongest. I could close my eyes and still shoot the animal because it is the pulling that aims the arrow. Shooting is more feeling the pull than aiming with your eyes. God makes all of this happen. I know God is present when I feel the pulling. This means that God has brought the animal to me.

God is the hunter, and I am God's bow and arrow. I feel closest to God when I feel him shooting me. When this happens, I know the animal will die and provide meat. This makes me very happy, and it makes God very happy. This is God's work.

A hunter is a special kind of n|om-kxao doing work for God. I am now old and my eyes are getting bad. There are only two great hunters left—my son and me. All the other great hunters have died. I still make my arrows out of bone. I like talking about these things. It makes me happy.

Tracking God is the hunt for an extraordinary ecstatic peak of affection in ordinary everyday life.

All of life is a hunt for the Bushmen, and what they hunt most is n|om. Hunting an animal is not only hunting meat to eat, but it is hunting the heartfelt and inspired spiritual food of the universal life force. The tracks to God are everywhere an awakened heart leaves its markings of love. They lead to extreme love with its highly charged n|om. Tracking God is the hunt for an extraordinary ecstatic peak of affection in ordinary everyday life.

On the Rope to God, Stay Focused but Never Isolated

A heart of the spears lives to be pulled. It is pure Taoism with all the strings attached. You wait for something to get a hold on you, and then you get out of the way and let the current move things along. Wisdom is spontaneously pulled out of your being. There is no judgment of others because a splinter in the eye is not as important as the rope between your bellies. When you have a strong rope, you may ask the rope to find the truth you seek. When you ask for something important and send the request through the rope-vine, it will be received. When you tap and feel the knocking, the doors will open.

If someone asks you for meat, don't reply with empty abstractions. Feed others with n|om. Give them spiritual food rather than stoned explanations. Do not fully open your heart to someone with whom you do not have a strong rope. That is like offering pearls to swine. Pigs don't appreciate jewelry. If it can't be eaten, they'll trample it—and you along with it. First make a rope, an authentic relationship, with another person, and then deliver the truest gifts and offerings. Share what you want them to share with you, but know that a rope of relationship is required as the bridge of transport.

The track to God is narrow, and few stay on course. The wide roads get fatter and wider until no road at all can be discerned. They take you down the side ways that distract. Don't stop for sightseeing or window-shopping; keep on trucking down the main road. Trickster has many roadside signs promising all kinds of delights. But it is all false advertising. Trickster is a skin-walker dressed like a sheep, but underneath is a rabid wolf. Be careful not to be hypnotized by trickster's sleight of hand; his hand picks inedible fruit. Though it may appear one way, it is the opposite. Trickster's world is the world of opposites: Here, trickster is God and good fruit is evil, and a good tree is corrupt. Trickster offers the grapes of thorns and the figs of thistles. They are dirty thorns, not the clean arrows of holy n|om.

Not everyone will stay on the straight and narrow track; they will follow that which distracts. Hold on to the ropes. Rather than judge a preference for any side, strengthen both sides of a rope. The ropes of God will pull you up the high road. Strong ropes become as strong as a rock. They will not break even when there are high winds and floods. With these ropes, you are able to go all the way.

"Grandson, everyone has a calling. Make sure that you follow God's calling for you. Only it can bring you the treasures of spirit." My grandfather, the Reverend W. L. Keeney, was talking about the Kalahari pulling of the ropes. As the Bushmen say, God has made a rope for each of us; it dangles over our head. We simply have to reach and grab hold of it.

It's not faith that we need, it's n|om. Faith is contrived in the mind; N|om flows through the heart. With n|om, you feel the pulling of God's rope, but be careful, for there are other ropes that can get hold of you as well. Trickster has his ropes, and they are trying to catch you whenever you look off course. Keep your eyes looking straight ahead. You can walk on water if you are not distracted.

We need to help each other stay on that highway; together we can make it. On our own, without relationship, we can only get lost.

When a heart of the spears receives God's ostrich egg, the left side of the egg has a red line and green line on it. The red line is trickster's; be careful about it. The n|om-kxaosi are always looking out for one another. When they see someone get on a red line, they send out a rescue team. They throw out a lifeline and reel the lost soul back in. The green line sustains life. Our healthy relationships with one another are green lines. The white line—found on the right side of God's ostrich egg—goes straight to the sky. It is the track to God. We need to help each other stay on that highway; together we can make it. On our own, without relationship, we can only get lost.

There are no lawsuits in the Kalahari. Bushmen hire neither assassins, soldiers, nor lawyers to get even with someone who has wronged them. They pick each other up when someone stumbles; this is compassion in action. All misdeeds are seen as rope problems. The Bushmen help each other get back on the right track, and then they make the ropes stronger through the ways they ecstatically awaken the feelings that build relationship.

The idea of community healing also takes place among the Diné culture, the residents of Navajo land. Navajo healing resides in the whole community. When someone gets sick or acts badly, it is taken as a sign that the relations holding the community have been disturbed. The sung ceremonials aim to bring the whole community, not an isolated individual, back to health.

What is healed? It is always the lines of relationship, the ropes that weave a unique web of experience. These lines are repaired by the way we feel and emote. To be in a relationship with another means to be inside enlivened feelings with one another. Love is the only medicine. All other names for a remedy come from trickster talk.

Drinking God's Water Is Drinking Love

My grandfather often said, "God is love," and he was right. God is the source of life and healing, and love is its rope. The feeling for God is the pulling of a rope for infinite love. When we get disconnected from this pipeline that goes to the well of well-being, we get sick, disoriented, and stressed out. The holiest water is blessed by love. The prayers offered by a healer are simply requests for God's holy water. Whether or not you receive the golden elixir in visionary or spiritual experiences, you can start serving it to yourself.

Hold a glass of water in your hand and project your prayer into this body of water. Say a prayer as an expression of love for God. Make your prayers the conduits that enable God's love to course through you. Pour that love into the water. When you finish the prayer, have a glass of water. Drink your blessing, and make it a part of you. This is how you start movement toward God's fountain of life.

Throw away your vitamins and start drinking a single glass of holy water every day for the rest of your life. This will make your ropes stronger, and your link to God will be more able to receive a shower of blessings. It will also help you to wake up your good feelings. See your praying as a feeling workout. This is the time for you to throw some n|om heart and soul into your prayer life. Sing your prayer, rock and sway as you give voice to praise, and allow yourself to get closer to the n|om drinking fountain.

The recipe for the golden elixir is this simple. Pour a glass of water, and then add your most loving thoughts and feelings to it. Lift the glass up into the air, as if offering a toast to all the ropes hanging from the sky, and have yourself a sip. Don't believe me? Your belief doesn't matter. I am not asking you to believe. I am asking you to feel it.

Drinking God's water is drinking your feeling for God; it is drinking love. We are created from the wine of love. Grow these grapes, turn them into wine, drink it, and share it so that the world becomes your beloved.

God's tree holds the medicine water—the love that becomes a wine when our hearts drink it. It is the infinite ocean, the source from which life arose and to which it will return. The tree of life found in the first Kalahari is a tree with thorns—thorns that turn into beautiful flowers because the water of love makes it so.

How fitting that the oldest Bushmen spoke of the thorns of n|om. The tree of life holds these thorns, and as painful as a thorn can be, it is the very thing that delivers the greatest love and ecstatic joy. Perhaps this is the greatest wisdom of all: To change a thorn into a flower is the first and final teaching. All that comes to you with the promise of a sting and pain is that which you should welcome and offer thanksgiving. It is there for you to love. Tears may fall, but if they come from the heart, a transformation will commence. Turning painful thorns into Cupid's arrows of love is the Bushman calling. It is what God originally asked us to follow.

We are meant to shoot one another. We shoot all kinds of arrows because we are human. Some of them are dirty due to our selfishness, jealousy, frustration, and anger. If we learn to doctor those arrows with holy water rather than destroy them, we can change sickness into health, ugliness into beauty, and death into life. Doing so makes the arrows shiny clean. As the arrows of love start to pour from us, we notice a steady stream of arrows. There are so many arrows that they look like a column, a bundle, even a rope. This is how we bring relational life into the world: through love, and the embrace and healing of everything that is shot at us. Love your enemy's dirty arrows. If you clean them, love will follow.

Sin is not the problem. What bogs us down is worry. Trickster stops the flow and puts out the fire of love by tricking us to worry.

Sin is not the problem. What bogs us down is worry. Trickster stops the flow and puts out the fire of love by tricking us to worry. When we worry, our mind immobilizes the whole of us. Our heart is paralyzed and afraid to come out and play. We are frightened that something is wrong, either in ourselves or somewhere outside. We desire protection. We mobilize anger. That's when *ju!kag!ua*, a liquid that surrounds the heart, starts to form. Anger creates this toxic fluid, causing a shutdown of our spiritual heartbeat. Worry leads to anger, and then the heart starts to drown in a toxic cesspool.

We cannot talk ourselves out of worrying; we can only sing and dance ourselves out of it. No one escapes being tricked into worrying because trickster knows what buttons to push. The same is true for all the other emotions that weaken our hope and destroy our joy: it will happen to you again and again. There is nothing you can do to stop being tricked. However, there is something you can do about it. Rather than giving in to paralysis, lift yourself up to your inner stage, the Kalahari dance ground, a sanctified church, or Preservation Hall and let some music roll. Music that has soul, your most sacred songs, is the medicine that frees you from trickster's imprisonment by washing away worry and the emotional sludge that comes along with it.

The song is the channel that brings down the holy water. Next time you find yourself worrying too much, even if it is in the middle of the night, get yourself another glass of water. As before, hold the glass and serenade it with a holy song. You can sing it inside your mind and the glass can be invisible as well. After singing your song, drink the water. It is now holy, for it has been infused with soul and love.

Sometimes trickster will help you, but never trust it or challenge it, for trickster can easily find a way to get you stuck in the quicksand

211

of worries, the forest fire of anger, and the ice storm of jealousy. Welcome trickster, but be smart as a fox. Serve it a drink of holy water, for even trickster is thirsty and part of God's plan. Dance with trickster, but don't spend the night with it. If you wake up with worries, know that trickster snuck into your bedroom. Don't ask it to leave. Offer it a song and a glass of water. Trickster, my friend, is you.

Saying these words sometimes trips me and takes me to the crossroads of love and absurdity, where I fall into the crack. There, I hear the whispering of the old ones as they teach their lesson about mystery.

The Ninth Mystery

You, trickster, have been tricking yourself out of having the best gig ever invented. You were born to love, and love was born to create you. You knew this in First Creation, but the naming changed all that. With words, you talk yourself out of life. You talk a worrisome line when there is nothing to worry about. Everything, from life to death, wants your love. You cannot discriminate because love does not discriminate. Yes, you can be wise and know that there must be a rope before you can climb anywhere. Otherwise, you will fall and get trampled by other folks who have fallen because they forgot to hold on to their rope.

Make a bumper sticker for your bed that says, "Born to Love." It doesn't matter how you make it or how you attach it to your bed. It doesn't matter where you place it. Simply do it or risk being lost for the rest of your life. You, like everyone else, need a love life; it's being offered to you. Choose it. Do not reach for it with your mind, for your thoughts will shred it apart. Open the door of your heart and invite this love quest in.

The holy pilgrimage is a trip to the wine country, and we are talking about God's wine. Whether called holy water or Kalahari pee-pee, it is the

finely distilled wine of eternal love. In these vineyards, the thorns are insepa-rable from the grapes. With this wine, a thorn in the flesh awakens a heart that loves God.

Take the first step—the step of a n!aroh-ma, a beginning learner of n|om. The next step takes you farther into the wine, the love that will anesthetize the influence of trickster mind. God's tree lives in the bush; the Bushmen call it !ku. Its water is the wine of love. Travel all the way to this vine and find that it, too, is a rope. The world is a vineyard that makes God's wine. Fill your heart with its sacrament and feel the vines, the veins of love.

Here, you will find your beloved. Embrace the vine and drink the wine, for love has found you. But it never lost you. You tricked yourself into believing that you were not on track but lost in the woods, parched in the desert, and starved for a serving of a good old-fashioned home-cooked meal. God wants to serve you. Come break some bread with the ancestors and have a cup of tea.

Somewhere in a tepee in the wilderness of Canada, a friend of mine starts to feel something shake. The tent is wildly moving back and forth. The spirits have arrived, speaking to him as he shakes his rattle. They are saying, "We are thirsty for your thirst. We want you to want us. This is how love seeks love. This is how God brings us a drink."

Come close to this tepee. Open your hand and make a cup. It is raining; catch a drop or two. All you need is a single drop, a single molecule to get clean and be reborn again. This old-time baptismal pool wants you to wade in the water. Come on in, whether the inside is a shaking tepee or the River Jordan. The current is everywhere. You have to take off those trickster glasses that block the light. See the world for the first time by immediately seeing all the cups. The cups are everywhere, waiting for the holy drops. Every single living creature is a cup waiting to be filled. Just like you.

Open your hands again, palms together, forming a cup. It's always raining God's water, so go ahead. Nothing can stop you from taking a drink. The desire and longing of your heart is stronger than the knee-jerk chitchat of trickster's small talk. Feel the water calling you. Feel it coming. It is God's gift, the love that overflows.

Now I come back to myself.

10

GOD WANTS YOU TO HUG

The Tenth Original Mystery

You can't give a hug without getting a hug.

ANONYMOUS

Celibacy makes no sense to a Bushman. "You've got to be kidding!" Toma shouts. "Are there really people who think that not having sex makes them closer to the gods? What god would want to hang around them? Maybe it's better if you don't go home. Your trickster gods sound boring because they don't know how to have a good time. Hang out with us and you'll learn that God loves sex!"

Love transforms and anger attracts. What you angrily protest, you become. That is the Kalahari law of attraction.

The beginning cultures never had a sexual hang-up, and there certainly was never a phobia about touch. That's a new development in the human scheme of things, and it seems to have started as a word game. Mind got separated from body. Good was separated from evil. Mind married good, while body married evil. Thereafter, whenever mind experiences itself as inseparable from body, a sin of inappropriate union is declared. Being touched by God shifted to being heard by God. But God isn't listening to your words; God wants to be touched. The same is true for you, so go find someone to hug.

In the Kalahari, touch is the primary instrument of sharing n|om. In samurai Japan, touch is the beginning of healing. When your body is shaking, a vibration can be transmitted. When it is connected to a voice and torso that pumps, your hand can pull out sickness. When you touch people with n|om, they can ecstatically awaken. Without touch, a healer is rendered impotent in the Kalahari–Mount Fuji circle. Outside the ancient ancestral home grounds, touch is feared, and that too often is inclusive of all encounters of the tactile kind.

Turn on your television and watch a random sampling of the well-suited evangelists. They usually sound angry and upset, don't they? Do they embrace anyone with loving touch? I can assure you that they are not attracting the Kalahari gods. In fact, more than a few trickster forms, maybe those with horns and tails, are most likely egging them on. Their pitch isn't inspired by love. It is spoken with a forked tongue, and it makes them as cross as a rhino whose horn has been broken. They are not bringing anyone nearer to the crossroads.

Love transforms and anger attracts. What you angrily protest, you become. That is the Kalahari law of attraction. What you love, you transform into being more loving. Call this the Kalahari law of transformation. Teasing is the way to soften rigid dualities not war. What in God's name has happened to people that empowers them to call upon God, the infinite source of loving wisdom, to justify greed, hatred, and war?

We exist to radically help one another, hold each other up, forgive, heal, share, inspire, and love.

Recall what was asked of Jesus: "Teacher, which is the greatest commandment in the Law?" He replied, "'Love the Lord your God with all your heart and with all your soul and with all your mind.' This is the first and greatest commandment. And the second is like it: 'Love your neighbor as yourself.' All the Law and the Prophets hang on these two commandments." The same may be said about the core wisdom of all religions founded upon the love of God.

We exist to radically help one another, hold each other up, forgive, heal, share, inspire, and love. There is no spiritual justification for invading a country with weapons, or launching a pious attack that spreads fear and motivates the diminishment of creative expression. The Bushmen don't even need the commandments to get this wisdom. They live it because it is the natural pulling of God's love to be this way. When they have conflict, they shake the n|om free so that love flows again and rules supreme.

A Kalahari patriot is a solder marching for love with n|om arrows packed on his back. A Kalahari lawyer mediates with love inspirations, not legal dispositions. A Kalahari priest embodies and advocates the stewardship of love in all the relationships that constitute social living. In the Kalahari, people have chosen love over law, forgiveness over swords, humility over hierarchy, and humor over hell. It has worked for over sixty thousand years. What can we say about the spiritual state of the dissociated and disunited mind of other cultures?

A heart of the spears knows that the most important teaching does not come from the lectures of a learned scholar but from interactions created through mutual loving.

A heart of the spears knows that the most important teaching does not come from the lectures of a learned scholar but from interactions created through mutual loving. This reaches a new height when two hearts of the spears give n|om to one another. In this circular sharing, they create a bigger heart greater than either person's alone. In a vibrant embrace, two hearts sing and enter into a mutually conceived high-frequency vibration. This is a vibrant connection, a harmony of spheres that requires surrender and trust by each person. It is a spiritual union of two fine-tuned hearts whose lives are devoted to healing and transformation. This co-resonance does not involve any hanky-panky. It is a holy joint prayer.

Love and Caring the Whole World Over

Can you imagine if the entire world pledged itself to absolute obedience to love and laughter? Forget the treaties that try to slow down the arms race. Let's escalate the arms that embrace. Bring all deal making back to a handshake and a hug. Why would that be less effective than the stacks of treaties and contracts that few read and few rarely follow anyway? A handshake and a community shake gets to the heart of the situation. If hearts don't agree, trickster will have a field day with mind-made agreements.

Let's have a love embassy in every city. It doesn't even need a building; a few trees in the corner of a public park will do just fine. That's where people could come for a n|om hug and ask God to make their hearts one. Why not? Whatever reason you come up with to negate this proposal is simply a reason, and it doesn't have anything to do with the season of the hearts. The hearts want their time and place. They need to be felt. This is how medicine can be brought to the problems and challenges our minds have produced.

I want the world to fall in love. Let's have countries court one another. How about serenading France? Send a box of chocolates to Uganda? A simple telegram to Argentina that says, "We love you." Make the news by making this kind of international love that has no boundaries or borders. Send a love boat to the Navy. Declare that the love-ins have returned. Let the sixties pick up where they left off: make more love and stop all war. What the world needs now is pure honey love, not artificially sweetened love. "Bee for love." Smell the sweet madness of transformative love. Love a thorn into being a rose of many names.

Call for the creation of another branch of the military that is called the Love Force. Make sure it is sufficiently armed to beat the agape out of the Delta Force. Insult anyone who doesn't get it, but do so in an absurd, loving way, making it impossible to rationally arouse anger. Awaken confusion that makes us fall, for in the falling, we may fall in love.

There is a mountain that wants you on its side. It wants you to see the other side, the land of milk and honey. All the parts of you are waiting to be taken to the other side of the rainbow. You need a leader to carry the whole of you over. I'm going to suggest something completely ridiculous, and that's why it might work. If it makes sense, you aren't going to budge. But if it is not expected, then it has something in common with you. You are not expected to move to paradise, are you? So meet your relative, and see whether the two of you can join forces to tinker with your familiarity of that which is unexpected.

Here's the deal: if anyone in the history of the world could take you to the fantasized Promised Land, however you define that place, who would it be? Would it be your grandmother, Moses, Mr. T, James Bond, the Virgin Mary, or the Blues Brothers? Who pops into your mind? Choose anyone. (It's good if it is someone inspirational, and it's as good if your choice makes no sense.) Now find a photo or drawing of this person, and copy it or cut it out. Tape this image to your suitcase, and pack a single change of clothes.

Expect the world to change in some way. The moment you think you notice a change, promise to wear whatever you packed in the suitcase as soon as you arrive home. Try this several times. Enlist a colleague to join you. See whether you can find creative variations of being led by absurdity to find other sides to your everyday reality that you have never brought forth before.

This is a way of embracing love, and it is potentially as transformative as two hearts of the spears getting it on in the Kalahari. It doesn't matter whether you embrace your habits, thoughts, pet, or loved one, simply embrace whatever comes to you. Stop asking what is wrong with your life. Start asking what is interesting about it. Then explore it further. Tinker with it, toss it about, and utilize it to do something you have never considered doing.

Embrace all the light, both what is luminous and what is lighthearted. Do this with all the creative energy you can muster. Why was the kingdom of heaven compared to a mustard seed? A small seed can represent a new beginning in your life, one step closer to your appointment with God. Have the faith of a mustard seed. Though it is one of the smallest seeds, the mustard plant grows to an extremely large size. Its growth is powerful enough to crack cement, and it can open the cracks that bring you to the crossroads.

Are you aware that the aristocrat Nikolaus Ludwig von Zinzendorf founded the Order of the Mustard Seed in Germany in 1715? It sought to be kind to all people as a means of spreading the gospel of love.

Carry mustard seeds in your pocket or purse. When you feel that someone needs a boost of faith to help stimulate some growth, hand over a seed. Tell them that you are following in the footsteps of Nikolaus Ludwig von Zinzendorf by spreading the seeds of kindness. See what kind of conversations this brings into your life. See this as embracing another person with n|om. Allow the uncertainty of what might happen to loosen the grip of your rational, overcontrolling mind. Believe in the strength of your mustard seeds. See how they help you cross the relational divide that keeps you separated from caring more deeply about others.

Play Is Flirtation with God

N!yae and I have been embracing the n|om for the entire afternoon. We are drunk, unable to walk. We are dizzy from n|om, what the Bushmen call *kaakare*. She looks drunk as a skunk, and I don't look any better.

"So this is what you do for God?" Ti!'ae teases. She looks drunk too but continues with another barb. "You two should be locked up; it's not safe for you to walk home. You might crash into another pedestrian." She has heard about our law that does not allow for one to drink and drive. She is using it to tickle us. I wait to respond, for I know this is just the beginning.

"You two should be ashamed. That's too much n|om for anyone to drink. You should have shared some of that with me."

N!yae is ready for her, "What are you talking about? Look at you. There was barely anything left for us after you had your drink. We're going to call the police. You should be locked up for good."

I join in, "You two girls can't hold your n|om. Next time I'm going to have to drink with the boys."

"The boys can't even stand up after one drink. You know they can't handle their n|om. It takes a big little woman to handle this stuff." This goes on, moving us to return to the village. There, we come back to ourselves.

Play is flirtation with God. God wants you to be tickled by the heavenly powers. Get slain, laid, and knocked up by the jokes hurled by God's stand-up comedy. Did I really say that? You bet I did. God wants there to be more creation in Creation. Otherwise the n|om can't circulate in and out of every pore of your leaky boat. Go for the whole-bodied stimulation of holy ascension. Holy cow! Holy cat whiskers! Did you read that? Never mind, maybe it's not your subject matter. But did you know that God is sexy? Why not? Where do you think all that beauty and life came from? God is hot! Get burned by celestial love. The gods need their meat insulted as well. If you can't soften your relationship with them, you aren't going to get a booking to any inn in heaven.

Any true lover is teased because that is part of love. Tease God. Do not fear God.

I can tease God because what I say is a way of freeing myself from all things said. I don't want to be attached to any words; I only want to own the feeling of love for God. The words for God are for the trickster side of God, one side of the whole God. My ideas about God need to be shaken up and liberated so there is room for God's light and love to enter my heart. When I believe that God is real because of the love felt for the divine, I can say that I have ≠um !xo kokxui: love is what is real, not the words.

A heart of the spears is free to exercise the right to speak freely because the voice of n|om lives in a spiritual democracy. It needs no bill of rights because it has the right bill—a theater bill—that announces each and every spectacular performance of God's Big Top. This circus shakes and loosens our stillness, inviting us to move more freely toward an ecstatic union with the love of all loves.

Any true lover is teased because that is part of love. Tease God. Do not fear God. The latter is the Old Testament huffing and puffing, threatening to blow your house down. Jesus came to kick the ass of that wolf's cry. Stop and think about this: why would you love a God that induces fear? It makes no sense. Don't even fear fear; make a pass at it. "Come on, fear. Why don't you come up and see me sometime?" Insult your fear. Tell it something that will shock its socks off. "Fear, you're sexy too." That will take the wind out of fear's sails. Send some flowers to your fear; a dandelion will do. Imagine how fear will run away when it hears the laughing roar of that lion. Then blow the lion's mane and watch fear scatter in all directions.

Life's heart is sweet. It wants to have fun with your whole family. Can you all come out and play? Teasing is awesome, and it must be done in the name of liberating all hearts to feel the less trivial, more outrageous love. As promised, this is a pirate's journey. Expect a mutiny at any time.

"Those mutineers need to get the flag o' nine tails! By the powers of Long John Silver, I say tie the scurvy dogs to a rope. Any son of a biscuit eater deserves to dance with Jack Ketch."

Mutiny in the name of love! Mutiny for the sake of doing everything that must be done to release your heart so it can soar with the wind and land in the hands of God's embrace. Life is like a box of feathers. Let them fly and sail away. "Walk away, landlubber, and dream of being a sea dog."

I'm reminded of the popular song "My Foolish Heart." It pulls my ropes. "The night is like a lovely tune. Beware, my foolish heart!" Beware, a foolish heart is always ready for mutiny, overthrowing everything in order to place God's love in command.

When a fool is in love, all words make sense, even what is absurd. A fool's love is what God loves best. It represents the ready and available heart of a child at play. Unless you become like a child, forget it. The gate won't open. Now think twice about holding back. "Mutiny for the sake of kicking open the hatch!"

**When a fool is in love, all words make sense,
even what is absurd. A fool's love is what God loves best.
It represents the ready and available heart
of a child at play.**

"Matey, you want us to make you shark bait?"

"Aye, aye, Brethren of the Coast. Cap'n send me to the locker. That's where the treasure is. You can't see it from the crow's nest, but it's down there. Use your deadlights. Only an old sea salt knows that you have to go below to find the swag."

"Shiver me timbers!" The Jolly Roger is hoisted again. "This time we're ready to sail for the spiritual lands."

Your heart can't move anywhere unless you are willing to risk everything, including any seriousness that paralyzes your creative interactions with the beloved. Insult the meat, all of it. There is no other way to bring you into the deeper, vibrant currents that promise to get you closer to feeling God's love.

**When several gather to love fully,
they become a vibration for God's love.**

The formula for getting your ship moving on the holiest sea is paradoxical: the farther you want to travel, the more you have to insult all the meat. Want to meet God? You'll have to insult the divine with a heart that breaks the grip of all remaining reason—that which takes up too much room in your cup. Your cup must be empty in order for it to get completely full. Go ahead and tease the gods; they are more than ready for a good joke. Their laughter will shake the universe.

Plugging into God's Love with a N | om Hug

N!yae and Ti!ae are holding on to me; the three of us are a pulsing amoeba. Our conscious mind is diminished in favor of the deeper expression of that which is unconscious. We feel like we have merged our hearts into the heart of God; this is the truest composition of church. When several gather to love fully, they become a vibration for God's love. We are making the wild sounds of n|om, with improvised songs interspersed. The shaking has a cycle. It intensifies at an accelerated rate and then hits a climax where a sound of release is voiced. Then it starts all over again. This may go on for five minutes or for hours.

"The strongest n|om-kxaosi always did this in the past," Twa once told me. "You have to be very brave to be with each other in this way. It is very good. It makes God happy."

The old timers talk about the early days when they were hunting and gathering all their food. At that time, it was not uncommon to see the strongest healers shaking throughout the day and night. They were so plugged into the source that they shook each other into the heavens.

N!yae and Ti!ae have made the same hookup that their ancestors once did, and we are pulsing ourselves into the bliss zone. What is going on here? What is behind this holding each other and shaking in harmony? Call it a n|om hug; it is a way of plugging in to God's love. But it's easier said than done. Your vibrations must be at the same frequency and perfectly in tune with each other for it to work. There can be no presence of ego-self or willpower in this encounter. No purpose, no goal of excitation, no solely below-the-belt stimulation, and no intention for a specified outcome can be present. Only the hearts of the spears whose vibrations are the purest can join together and spontaneously cocreate a mutual heart of vibration.

Rumi points a finger at our motion and says, "A secret turning in us makes the universe turn." The Bushmen, Sufis of the Kalahari sand, experience this turning. The pulse of vibration, the heartbeat of n|om, is the secret behind the turning. The circles of life turn within other circles of life. All are interconnected cogs and gears inside the timeless flow of n|om's heart-ticking clock. There is only changing, pulling, and turning felt as a beat that inspires the motion. I circle around myself. I move around the hundreds of me. We circle together around one another, and that includes the hundreds of us.

In the circle of held arms, we embrace the turning, the shaking that moves us into the mysteries of divine love. Here, we find the dance that opens, tears, fights, bleeds, and frees. Here, the longing moves through the emptiness so that it may move around the fullness. This is the dance circle held by gathered hearts of the spears as they feel the love for all their relatives and family.

Ti!ae, now tired, sits on the ground. She is pulsing and spiritually traveling as she sings her song. N!yae and I deepen our hold on one another. We are holding each other up, allowing the n|om to overtake us without it overtaking our firm stance upon the ground. We are paradoxically both grounded and without any earthly anchor. The revolving doors keep opening to deeper openings with each turn, and we are becoming empty shells available for the gods. We are holding and moving the space of emptiness. This vibrating interaction sweeps away trickster-mind, the inner observer and commentator, and all that remains is the spinning and the concentrated gathering of substance-less, circulating n|om. We belong to the whirling.

Now the mystery of vibrational union is ready to begin. This mystery can't be articulated with words or it will not be understood. It must shake and quake, causing a crack in our norm for ordering things. Only n|om can pull out the words that point us toward it.

The Tenth Mystery

The two make themselves available for the sacred matrimonial dance of the gods. Each has become empty of flesh and earthly desire. The sacrifice has been made. The gods, waiting with hope and anticipation, are ready to come down. They shall enter the bodies, the hearts of the spears who hold on to this moment for divine visitation. These bodies are ready to be used by the gods to bring forth the circle of changes, the first departures and final arrivals of First Creation. In the shaking is an emptying and then a filling. In the crossing of the line between gods and flesh, the world is re-created. Back to the first world and then on to the second.

It is a fulfillment of the secret of turning that is enacted. The Mother God steps into the woman, and the Father God steps into the male. Now the gods dance themselves across the line, through the line, around the line. The crossing goes both ways: spirit to human and human to spirit. The flesh and n|om go back and forth. The hearts of the spears are hearts because they are used in turning the wheel of life. This turning is the return of the eternal present made still by the turning, but only in the universal moment. This is the whirling; it belongs to you. And you belong to the whirling.

N!yae knows what is happening, and I do also. Our meeting is no accident, for we were born to help the turning. She turns with Rumi and howls with his dogs. I am both of these things as she is everything and every creature with me. We are nothing because we can be anything, but only for a split second—the effervescent moments of eternity.

Every surrendering to this holy embrace deepens our heart and sharpens our spears. The hearts of the spears know that their hearts must rise more, or as they say, !ka tsau |'an. Here, there is a time for all things, as it was sung from the Book of Ecclesiastes:

To every thing there is a season, and a time to every purpose under the heaven:

A time to be born, and a time to die; a time to plant, and a time to pluck up that which is planted; a time to kill, and a time to heal; a time to break down, and a time to build up;

A time to weep, and a time to laugh; a time to mourn, and a time to dance; a time to cast away stones, and a time to gather stones together; a time to embrace, and a time to refrain from embracing; a time to get, and a time to lose; a time to keep, and a time to cast away; a time to rend, and a time to sew; a time to keep silence, and a time to speak; a time to love, and a time to hate; a time of war, and a time of peace.

226

Everything, both left and right sides, is included as part of the vibrational embrace. I am not holding N!yae; I am holding my wife. I am holding the same whole of holies that was held by my mother and father, my grandparents, and all my ancestors. We are holding the sacred holding. This is the love that includes rather than excludes. This love is complete with all forms of incompleteness included.

To everything there is a season, a context, a frame of meaning that makes sense and confirms reality to whatever is happening. There is also a time for every purpose under the heavens. Somewhere there's a place for us and everything else. The challenge is not in whether to do it, but when and where to bring it forth. The ropes bring forth the season and the time. All ecstatic shakers know, even when they don't know, that all things—from thoughts, meanings, and even existence—have a time to live and a time to die. All the opposites, whether up and down, killing and healing, weeping and laughter, mourning and dancing, getting and losing, silence and speech, love and hate, war and peace, are movements in the interactive whole.

When two people shake together, we call it djxani-!uhsi. It allows the gods to make spiritual love, not the intimacy that hurts anyone. It is the love that honors all love. It is a testimony given at the front of a Kalahari church, an honoring of the transformative power of God's love in all its forms. Praise the name of this love. It is n|om, but as I feel it so strongly now, I cannot even say its name. It might overpower me. I must say tco, the respect name for n|om.

All n|om-kxaosi feel gua, the beginning of !aia, when our feelings start to wake up. As we step into our second eyes, we can see what we feel. We see the feelings. This is called kxae≠xaisi. After further cooking, we enter First Creation. When we first see it, the world appears to be whirling. We call this moment !kabi. It is the crossroads between First and Second Creation. We cross over, back and forth, in a movement that shakes the two worlds. All of this is participation in the turning. Second Creation sometimes is referred to as manisi n!a'an-n!a'an, meaning "the great turning around." It is not the end of First Creation; it is simply part of the never-ending turning. If we try to stop the turning, we get sick or we die. We must keep turning and crossing over the lines. Like a whirling dervish, we spin to experience the perfection of love.

If you have a loved one, honor your relationship even when it seems difficult. The love you desire cannot be received or given unless there is a bridge for it to cross. You must build this bridge and make it strong. The other person does not want love that can be deposited into a heart account; this is not a counting matter. The love that makes the world go round needs to be able to cross over the divide between you and the other. Build your bridge and the love will flow. It will be wrapped with n|om, and it will come with a song and perhaps a giggle, a flirtatious tickling of the absurdity that underlies how two people can pull one another into the mystical realm of love.

It is time that you obtained some mojo to plant the seeds for vibrant union. Go shopping for a string, thread, cable, or rope. It can be yarn, ribbon, copper wire, or it can be a pencil or a tree branch. What road do you want for carrying the delivery of your love? Whatever you select, consider it your love highway. Place it on your wall and put a sign underneath it that says, "Highway L." Explain this to no one except your lover. If you don't have a relationship of the intimate kind, then place it there as bait. It might help you catch some love.

Stare at this highway at least once a day. It is better if you do it at both morning and night. As you look at your love highway, believe that this is what you desire. It is not about the object of love but the highway for love. When you have a love highway, the love can move and cross over. It is a two-lane highway, so the love flows both ways. Change how you think of love. No longer think that you are looking for love. Believe that you have found the highway and that your love is on the move. See your love as an arrow with wheels. It's zooming down the road on its way to an ecstatic destiny. Get those love arrows on the move. Hit the road, Jack!

Love is a many-splendored thing. It is never lost, though it may seem out of reach. It is always at hand, ready to get on board any means of transport. When a road is in sight, the love can move, and when it's on the road, it feels good. L is for the lane you're driving in, O is for the odometer that tells you how many miles you have driven, V is for the velocity that promises a safe delivery, and E is where you want to end. After all, all's well that ends well.

You know the love that binds and transforms when you hold your child in your arms. You know it when you feel a magical connection with the rise of dawn. Movement is love. Anything that flutters its wings and carries a beat sounds the beginning of love. Love is stronger than death. It goes past any purpose of life. It is a mighty wind that blows all the dead words away, making us freer to speak freshly arisen words that touch the hearts of others. Love delivers the word souls—the liberating ropes that pull us to newborn freedom.

Be a love beam that shines on the darkness of unlit souls. God is waiting to hold you and be your beloved. In this embrace, feel the vibration stir an awakening within. Participate more fully in the creation of life. Whatever you come across, breathe life into it. Sign up to be a sunbeam for the Lord.

The love of God is a miracle. Our God is a joy to behold and celebrate. Every day should be a party that rejoices in the grace that rains upon us. We are not lost; we are confused. The way out of the quagmire requires no calculation or reason. It needs a feeling—a wave of joy—that celebrates that it doesn't matter whether we are lost. Only our mind is lost. Forget your mind, and celebrate the wisdom fact that your uncertainty is a confirmation that life is a mystery. The more mystery you encounter, the closer to God you become. Don't despair. Party like it's a homecoming. You are coming home to God's ecstatic embrace. This extreme love will set you on fire.

Now I come back to myself.

11

THE LIBRARY OF MYSTERY

The Eleventh Original Mystery

Some books are to be tasted, others to be swallowed,
and some few to be chewed and digested.

Sir Francis Bacon

After the classrooms, there are no teachers. What remains is the library of mystery, where all wisdom is held. It is eternal wisdom, which means that while its holdings are changing all the time, its infinite reach never alters or falters. This library holds all the ropes, and they are cross-referenced at every intersection. In this archive, there are no volumes of words, but feelings ready to be amplified and heard with great volume. Many have tried to make their way to this palatial space, but few have entered its doors. One must be cooked many times until nothing is left but a vapor of steam that can pass through the keyhole.

In the Kalahari, there is no public library built by the Bushmen. Until recent interactions with outsiders, they had never seen books. There also has never been an oral custodian, someone who memorizes all the previous knowledge base. Instead, the Bushman n|om-kxaosi keep the n|om fire burning, knowing it will deliver whatever teaching is needed. The Bushmen have learned that when n|om cooks you, you are taken to the spiritual classrooms. Those who graduate don't get a paper diploma. They receive an invisible library card that permits admittance to the library of mystery.

What is required to get your library card? All the classrooms essentially teach you the art of handling vibrant love. Your final examination is an invitation to love with all your heart. This (and it can be nothing less) gets you inside the building. This expression of love includes the n|om hugs that are a heart-to-heart transmission, a ≠ara-khoe. The hearts of the spears learn that the wisdom fruit harvested from shaking themselves into God's love is an open door to the extraordinary library of n|om's ancient eternal mysteries. Once you enter, you are able to return for the rest of your life.

When you fall into the ecstatic grip of a n|om hug, the amplified co-vibration can get into your spine. When you are released from its physical embrace, the vibration does not drop away. It continues on both the outside and the inside. It's the deep, internal spinal tapping that announces admission to the library. When you feel it inside you, it's an amazing plug-in to God. You lie down at night knowing that tonight might be that special night, a time to go to the mystical library. When it happens, you feel your spiritual self slip right off your skin. It's like a thin, luminous covering that gently slides into another dimension.

As strange as this sounds, it does not feel weird. It is natural and effortless. When the outline of your body, the spiritual cover, slides off, all the weight of your life is let go. There is no gravity to hold you down. Neither excessive worries nor desires are a burden. You are free and unattached to trickster's ropes. Without the friction of any mental debate over fact versus fiction, you smoothly glide into the library door. Though you get there by flight, you firmly land on the substrate of mythopoetic ground.

You know you are in the library because there is no classroom. There is direct contact with an essence that will dissolve into your being. Here, you become an original ancestor and experience the world of First Creation as they have always experienced it. Maybe it's less a library and more a theater where you behold the productions of the original world.

Into the Heart of the Bee,
One of the Kalahari Library's Rarest Holdings

It's been a long day and night of shaking in the Kalahari. As I prepare to get into my sleeping bag, I feel the deep vibrations inside of me. They are pulsing in my spine at a high frequency, and I know I am being tuned in to some kind of guidance system that will pull me to the other side. Even before falling asleep, I feel my form leaving. Without effort or resistance, it slides out of the top of my head, and gently and smoothly goes right through the tent wall. On the other side, the library door is open. My heart enters.

There is a single golden flower directly in front of me. Its petals comprise a beautiful universe of perfection that is completely whole. The background of this scene is black space, whereas the flower is radiant and vibrantly alive. It absorbs all my attention. Then the bees come, one after another. They fly and dance around the flower.

The music begins; it is an old n|om song. I can tell it is old by the way it is sung, though I have never heard it before. The bees are changing into the ancestors. Back and forth they shift, with a blur at the crossing between ancestor and bee. I am singing with them, changing with them, and feeling the nectar of a splendid n|om. My heart is being pollinated with a dance. It moves me to tears, and the stream takes my heart with it. I come back to myself.

I continue singing the n|om song, and it wakes up the village. They gather around my tent and sing with me. Toma is weeping. It will be awhile until he can gather the words to speak.

"I know that song; my grandfather used to sing it. You received the 'Bee Song.'"

"Yes, Toma, that is true," I say with tears of delight, feeling the rope that is pulling through me. I am connected to his grandfather through his longing for him. Our relationship as n|om brothers connects me to his other ancestors; this is how the ropes work. Twa once told me, "Our power comes from our tears, our longing for the ancestors who have crossed over. We miss them and want to be with them. That is where our ropes come from. That is the source."

Toma directs me, "Get up and show us how they danced." I start dancing, and the women clap in syncopated time with the song. Toma is nodding his head up and down in affirmation as he says, "Yes, this is how the old ones danced it."

We dance through the night and celebrate the fact that I brought home something from the library. It was loaned to me so it could be shared with the community. Since all who have gathered own the feeling for the song and dance, it belongs to all of us. This is how you check something out at the library of mystery.

Months later in a South African university, I am told a version of the creation story of the Kalahari Desert's people. A bee once tried to carry a mantis across a river. The river was very wide, and it tired the bee. It couldn't make it all the way across. Somewhere in the middle of the crossing, the bee left the mantis on a floating flower. Before departing, the bee planted a seed in the mantis's body. That seed grew to become the first human being.

The ancient Egyptians taught that bees were created when the tears of the sun god, Ra, landed on the desert sand. Yes, the ancestors also long and weep for us, and in our missing one another, we pull each other with the longing. The tears of the ancestors are filled with love, and the gifts of song and dance. Is it an accident that the Bushmen's Mother Goddess is a bee?

Over the centuries, each world religion has shape-shifted the original forms, while creating a different myth to hold the same ancient truths and mysteries of n|om. The Hindu goddess Kamadeva carries a bow, and it has a string made of honeybees. Of course it does. It is made to shoot n|om so that the sacred songs can spread throughout the world.

Listen to the voice from the wilderness as transcribed in Deuteronomy: "Thou makest him ride on the high places of the Earth, and he eats the produce of the fields. He maketh him suck honey out of the rock." God's timeless wisdom is sweet honey whose source provides us with a solid spiritual foundation. With n|om, "Pleasant words are a honeycomb, sweet to the soul and healing to the bones" (Proverbs 16:24). When a heart of the spears is charged and speaks, we say, "How sweet are your words to my taste, sweeter than honey to my mouth!" (Psalms 119:103).

In Greek mythology, the nymph who ate honey turned into a bee. She was the daughter of Melissius, the honey-man who became the daimon (spirit) of the bees. Here again, the Bushman n|om was carried from the Kalahari flower by the first bee goddess, Mother God / "Mother of Bees," named |Aqn-|aqnce. From one flower to another, the bees have carried original spirituality all over the world. The honey of God's love has flowed everywhere from the Middle East to Australia, Tibet, Peru, and the Arctic Circle.

In First Creation, we can own the feeling for the bee and receive its song, dance, and honey. In this way, we are pulled to step into the heart of the bee. We become its buzzing heart. When we come back to ourselves, we find that our rope with the bee has been made stronger. This is the work of the n|om-kxaosi—traveling on the ropes, the tracks made by God, so that all our relationships with life can be strengthened and given more life.

This is why you were born. You are here to find your ropes and to be pulled by them. You will be pulled to a bridge that is a crossing, an entry to the other side of a relationship. The crossing is the movement of love. It moves through the music that inspires a sacred dance. Unless you are hit by some holy music, your feet aren't going to dance down the aisles. That's how you get a solid relationship. It's also how you find your way to heaven. You get there by becoming a dancing bee.

**Rather than finding a book on a shelf,
you are brought directly to an experience that downloads
timeless n|om wisdom into your whole being.**

The Western philosopher Martin Heidegger would criticize our romanticizing the bee because, to him, human beings are more present in the world than bees, animals, and plants. Mahayana Buddhism tries not to separate human beings from other organisms, saying that all sentient beings have *bodhichitta*. A Bushman might define the latter as anything that can soften the hardest heart in order to awaken all that makes us light. The Bushmen find a familiar voice with Antoine de Saint Exupéry: "It is only with the heart that one can see rightly; what is essential is invisible to the eye." The n|om-kxaosi go further and add, "This seeing with the heart pulls the invisible so it can be felt."

This is what it is like to go inside the Kalahari mystical library. Rather than finding a book on a shelf, you are brought directly to an experience that downloads timeless n|om wisdom into your whole being. It fills your body, mind, heart, and soul. All of you reads this teaching. Here is the truest form of holistic education connecting us to the ropes of relationship that comprise the ecology of our living. All our relations are found in this body of knowing, from the honeybee to the Great Being of the cosmos. This is where the gods teach us the original mysteries.

The Ropes Are Made of N | om, Not Words

The library of mystery does not contain volumes of words. Words have great benefit when they are used to shake and waken ourselves, but they can also lead us off track. Trickster has convinced book writers and their readers that the more abstract they get at handling language and elaborating the proliferation of fine distinctions, the more they evolve their understanding of spirituality, passing from lower stages to higher stages. They believe that there is a progressive road trip that began in the Kalahari. There, the primitive mind practiced animistic shamanism. All of this evolved over the years to become the more sophisticated textual forms that the writers now exemplify in glorious fashion. For example, it's not enough for some highly educated folks to simply say that God is love. Instead, they believe that you get closer to the gods by pontificating highly abstract arguments that address hermeneutics, epistemology, ontology, eschatology, and so forth. With this presumption, only a philosopher or theologian would be able to enter the holy realms, but certainly not a child lacking sophisticated verbosity.

"Yes, that is how trickster would want you to see it," Toma responds as I try to explain this devoted attachment to words and elaborated explanations. He goes on, "The wordier you become, the closer trickster comes. The track to God doesn't move from station one to station two and then three and four in that way. Those are trickster's stops, and they make a person more stuck at each stopping point. The track to God goes the opposite way."

I think Toma is starting to understand the straight-line people, the name he sometimes uses to describe outsiders. Twa adds her voice, "We call them !huijuasi, the people who see everything moving forward in a line. I'm sure they try to hide their line by rolling it up or curling it, but it doesn't fool us. We'll throw it on the ground and stomp on it, revealing that it's just a plain old straight line, a line of lies."

Toma continues his talk, which is becoming a rare lecture from a n|om-kxao: "The track to God goes the opposite way. Whatever you think is the big truth must immediately be teased apart and shown as trickster absurdity. It is not in the saying. This is why the dreams and visions of wordy people are so complicated. They sound like one of those moving pictures. Did you know that they made a movie out here?"

Of course I know that. Toma and I have discussed it many times. I see that he is starting to get bored and that he'd rather laugh at how a film crew shoots a movie than talk bout how the line people aren't able to shoot n|om. However, I ask him to continue. He smiles and indulges me. He knows this is important.

"The wordy people string together one word after another, and the line gets longer and longer. Then they twist that line in all kinds of directions and end up with a bunch of broken sticks. Then they make other sticks until they have a stack of sticks. The only thing worth doing with this stack is burning it. It would make a nice fire for a dance."

I try to keep on track. "Toma, before we dance tonight, please tell us more about the track to God. Is it the same track as the one that goes to the library?"

"It can be, but sometimes it's not. It depends on who is walking on it. Seriously, when we graduate from the classrooms, our kabis and cunkuris get simpler. They move toward being pure feelings. They move toward the white light."

I am tempted to remark that the highway to God goes from the Kalahari to Tibet, not the other way around. I don't say this, because I already know what Toma would say: "It's the same no matter where you begin."

**Behind everything is the great force of change.
We call it *n!o'an-ka│'ae*, the original force that
changes everything. It is our most important word.
It is that which creates.**

The lines the Bushmen talk about and travel on are not geographic lines, and we keep forgetting this. There is no physical geography in the spiritual lands. It is heart geography. When my heart is on fire with love, I am with you, no matter where you are physically. When I feel an awakened love for the ancestors, they are with me, independent of time and space. Similarly, there are no words, theories, or theologies in the spiritual heartlands. All of that is trickster messing with you. In God's world, there are only songs, ropes, arrows, and love.

"I know what you are thinking," Toma responds. "This does not mean that we should be silent and stop using words. Words and trickster both help us. They help us change. They are the agents of change. Behind everything is the great force of change. We call it *n!o'an-ka│'ae*, the original force that changes everything. It is our most important word. It is that which creates.

"Trickster is half the side of God. It is God's changing side. The other side remains still. Whatever you say about God can only refer to the changing half. This is because all naming takes place in Second Creation. There, the gods and everything we say about them are changing. You can only talk about the God whose love remains constant when you are in First Creation. The trouble is that you can't talk in First Creation. There are no words there. That is God's village, and no one is going to be talking when they can be dancing and singing. That's the whole of it, but keep in mind that I have told you these things with words, and they may not have anything to do with God."

"But, Toma," I insert, "if what you say shakes me up, then might I feel First Creation inside the shaking?" I feel a bit dizzy even thinking about what this means.

"Yes, that is it! Your rope has been pulled into God's world as we speak. That dizziness is the first thing you feel when entering First Creation. It is !kabi, the constant whirling of God's world. We're in it

238

now. See how nice words can be? They can be used to shake us up and provide a crack here and there, momentary openings into the crossing."

"Toma, God's world still exists, doesn't it? We haven't evolved from First to Second, have we?" I can't imagine that First Creation is like a booster rocket that drops away as we are hurled farther into outer space.

"Yes, that's correct for the moment. But if you think about it too long or talk about it too much, it will be wrong." He finally gets me to laugh. This is as long a time that we have talked without laughter disrupting any serious line of conversation.

"Second Creation sits in First Creation, and trickster resides within the Sky God. We, the n|om-kxaosi, step out of Second Creation, one foot out and one foot in. That is what makes us shake. We stand at the same place that those people you told us about go to get their musical instrument doctored. We have one leg on each side of the crossroads."

If trickster is inside God, then so are we. When we forget this, we tie ourselves up with verbal strings and are unable to move anywhere. When the songs blow in from across the border, the words are unlocked and another rope drops into our hands. It is not made of words; it is a n|om rope. That's when we wake up. When the n|om starts to whirl, something starts moving, and it better include us or we'll miss the ride to the library.

In the name of the changing of the names, let us declare a newborn relationship with words. Let them shake us up, insult our meat, and inspire us to transpire toward first base. In this ball game, a single that gets us to first base is actually a home run.

Are you beginning to see that Lewis Carroll's Alice was a Bushman prophet? The way out is through the door or the window, and a rabbit hole will work just as well. Let's dive in.

The Eleventh Mystery

The library of mystery asks you to pay it a visit. There, you might find yourself staring at your grandparents' house while hearing a song that touches your heart. This pulls you to enter the vision more deeply. As you walk to the front door, you find a note has been attached to the doorknob. It reads, "The key is by the basement window." Sure enough, the front door key has been left for you, hidden in the ground next to the foundation of the house where the basement window is located. Go ahead and pick it up. Unlock the front door and enter.

The room is empty at first until the music starts again. Someone is sitting in a rocking chair. Who is that? Is it your grandmother, mother, uncle, child, best friend, or an old ancestor you have yet to meet? This person is rocking gently, back and forth. As the music plays, you feel something: the longing to feel the love of familial intimacy. Rock ever so gently and tenderly. Is someone softly singing an old song, slightly changed to give it more n|om? Let's listen: "Softly and tenderly someone is calling, calling for you and for me. See, on the porch, she's waiting and watching, watching for you and for me. Come home, come home, you who are weary, come home. Earnestly, tenderly, someone is calling, calling, oh children, come home!"

It's all right if you want to weep. Feel the pulling of those tears, the release, the beginning of a new stream. As Tennyson wrote, "Tears from the depth of some divine despair / Rise in the heart and gather in the eyes." This rising is the uprising revolution of your heart. Let those tears help it float all the way up, breaking new ground for your relationship with the missed ancestors. Their ropes are pulling as God is calling. Softly and tenderly, your heart is coming home. Then you come back to yourself.

Let's visit the library again. I see you are already there, or at least a part of you has arrived. I wonder whether that is your conscious or unconscious part. It doesn't matter whether you know because you are there in a way that is perfectly designed for the moment. Your life has arranged some more personalized nonbook learning. Whether you will remember being here is another thing altogether. But let's not worry about that.

I see you have found your pet dog, or is it a pet cat? I'm a little too far away to see clearly. Yes, that's right. Now I see. It is the pet you had as a child. Maybe it was your best friend. It has a song for you. It's a simple song, tender and sweet, perfect for a child. It sings about God loving all the children and all the pets of the world, red or yellow, fuzzy or not. The song says that God loves the little children and all their little pets wherever they may be on the playground.

Are those your playmates from elementary school? They also have their pets with them, and it seems they are quite moved by this song. Go ahead, you don't have to see anything or hear anything; just feel something. Whatever it takes to get you on that rope, experience it. Allow yourself to cross to the other side. The others have something to place inside your heart. Are they showing you something or telling you something? Maybe it's a good feeling you have forgotten. Maybe you left that good feeling in the locker room at school and forgot to take it home. Has it been missing? Pick it up and place it in your heart. It's nice to see it come home again. Now come on back to yourself.

The library of mystery is happy you have come for a visit. Its librarian has a rope on you. She wants to take you to another section where other subjects reside. Let us take a look at another one. What's that? Is your unconscious, the part of you that you seldom pay attention to, suggesting that we go upstairs? I wonder what we will find there.

Why is the sign to the upstairs pointing to the downstairs? Let's see where it leads. Very interesting, it is leading us to the rare collection of ancient treasure maps. The room feels like we are inside a pirate's ship. Do you see the parrot in that corner? It has a patch over its eye. I think we must be dreaming.

"Stop dreaming and wake up," the parrot shouts. "What do you think this is, a cartoon?" The parrot is irritated, and I don't know why she is talking to us like that. "Sit down and keep quiet," the pirate parrot chirps on. "My name is Pointed Beak, but you'd better not laugh at that, or else my point will fly over there and peck your noggin."

We sit in the hull of that basement and listen for hours to Pointed Beak. She tells us that all navigation in the highest seas requires moving in the opposite direction. To go up, you have to go down. As the bird says this, we hear an invisible choir sing a gospel song I've never heard before. "The farther you go down, the higher you will lift. Come on, children, get on down, let that gospel bring us all uptown."

Pointed Beak suddenly flies to the table and lifts a map, exposing an older map underneath it. She says, "This is what you came to see. It is a map of the track that takes you to God. See how it goes backward rather than forward. This is the secret that will lead you to the treasure. You'll have to figure out the rest of it on your own." Pointed Beak flaps her wings and disappears, going right through the hull. She is gone, but the map remains.

Look at it. Do you see what it shows? The map reveals that the end of the trail is the beginning. The map is simply a giant circle. There are these instructions printed on the corner: "Start anywhere to get everywhere. Keep on moving to find the end. That's where the treasure begins." And then we return to ourselves.

The most hidden of all secrets held by original spirituality has nothing to do with esoteric knowledge or bizarre rites of passage; it involves the profound way love pulls us to the gods. We have been taught to "get over" love whether it is associated with the grieving of a departed loved one or the sickness of romantic love. We should have been taught the opposite: hold on to the embrace of extreme love and never let go. Then and only then can the pullings of the heart be fully experienced. We are pulled by our longings, and what we long for most is to be pulled by the greatest love. When your heart finds its way to the ropes, you are taken to the library of hearty n|om wisdom.

I often ask elder women n|om-kxaosi what makes them so strong in matters of n|om. They always reply, "We are this way because of the tears we have wept for the ancestors who have passed on." The deepest longing human beings experience often comes from the loss of a loved one. Rather than trying to emotionally get over it, these Bushman elders keep the longing alive, feeding it until it breaks their hearts wide open in an awakened way, bringing them inside a more expansive and intimate relationship with their ancestors. In this connection, tears flow along a channel that keeps their relationships strong, and permits a never-ending expression of love and soulful guidance.

Another intense form of longing is familiar to all lovers who fall deeply in love. In this infinite ocean of Eros, we find there is more than simple love; there is loving love. When we become lovers of loving, the ropes are inseparable from us, carring our hearts into the highest realms. We become roped and swallowed alive by love in order to become living love.

Loving each other, we find ourselves in the space between what we are and what we are not. That difference inspires an infinite circle—a new course toward ecstatic love-burn and its longing for more longing. The motion sickness of recycled devotion pulls you, Kalahari way, into all reentrant forms. Bring forth the four-cornered wind and the weaving of love!

This is what it is to live with the n|om of love and the love of n|om. You feel the Kalahari ownership of a relational way of being: you vow to be moved, pulled, and organized by it. When you have this kind of heart ownership, the ropes of relationship become your teacher. The ropes are responsible for bringing us forth in the embodied expression of love. N|om love sets everyone on fire. We lose ourselves in the burning, and it alchemically transforms us from the power-pushing games of the belly to the love-pulled movements of the heart.

When our hearts are on fire, life takes place effortlessly and naturally. In the burning, we rise above the fixed categories. In the burning, we become one another. When we step into First Creation, we let go of any preconceived notion of identity. Here, everyone can change into any role: queen, king, giraffe, warrior, lover, lion, hummingbird, honeybee, or tree. This is the serious shape-shifting, context-shifting, identity-shifting, love-shifting play of awakened n|om. This is how we get cooked by the gods, and this is how we cook one another. This is the fire of n|om. N|om learning means finding your way to the roads leading to the mystical classrooms and library. In eternity, one is wed, conceived, born, slain, and reborn all at the same time. In the eternal library, it is the same.

The most important word for a Bushman love doctor is are. *It means "love."*

Do you remember why pirates are called pirates?

Because they ARRRRRRR.

Let us be love pirates sailing the endless seas, shaking rather than stealing the booty so that all may be set free to fly while howling at the moon. May every light ray trip you into being less than you knew possible. May your heart be stung by |Aqn-|aqnce, the Mother of Bees, so you may become her in flight, dance, and song. These things I dedicate myself to serving, a wild promise of the heart to swim in the depths of are.

The n|om-kxaosi say:

There are only ropes, lines, tracks, roads, threads, and highways.
They are made of God's heart.
When you are on one, you feel pulled,
You thirst,
You long,
You wonder which way to go,
You find obstacles along the way,
You must keep walking,
Until the sign says go,
For the green of life is the lifeline around God's ostrich egg.
It takes you to the library door.
Open it.
There, the light quenches everything.

Now I come back to myself.

12

BEING TOUCHED BY GOD

The Twelfth Original Mystery

I myself do nothing. The Holy Spirit accomplishes all through me.

WILLIAM BLAKE

When God breaks through all your nonsense and truly gets a hold on your heart, there is nothing that can stop you from feeling the joy. No matter what comes your way, whether it be physical sickness, personal attack, financial disaster, relational suffering, social injustice, family tragedy, or irrational inequity, God's love is there to lift you up. When you feel this truth penetrate all the way to your bones, then you are a heart of the spears.

Being a heart is a way of saying that you have lost your mind for God. You gave it up to find your soul. All that talk about the crossroads is mixed up. You go there to hand over your mind. Then you get handed your soul. When you find yourself at a crossroads, don't listen to trickster. Instead, make a heartfelt exchange with God.

Think of all the names of the world religions and their founding inspirational figures from Mohammed to Buddha, Mary, Jesus, Abraham, Black Elk, Saint Teresa of Avila, Hildegard von Bingen, Yeshe Tsogyal, Wei Huacun, George Fox, Confucius, Saint Catherine of Siena,

Swedenborg, Zoroaster, Mata Amritanandamayi, Rabia, Sri Aurobindo, Marudev, Esther, and Ruth. Every one of these individuals loved what was holy. Though their metaphors and cultural backgrounds are different, they shared the same devotion to being spiritually moved by their Creator. Every one of these names and their ways of worship should bring joy to your heart because they are inseparable from God's love.

You meet your rope when your feelings for God have taken over you. This is what the Bushmen mean by being awakened by n|om. The track to God is the rope that holds and pulls your heartstrings.

The same should be true for every person you have ever met. When your rope is strong, you see God's hand on every human being, even if that person is blind to the presence of anything holy. We are here to love, and that love has its origin in the holiest light of the cosmos. When your relationship to this divine light becomes concentrated and consecrated, it becomes a solid holy beam aimed at the sky. This is the track to God.

You meet your rope when your feelings for God have taken over you. This is what the Bushmen mean by being awakened by n|om. The track to God is the rope that holds and pulls your heartstrings. In the Kalahari, *!Xo kxao* means "I am an owner of God," that is, "I am the owner of the feeling of love for God." When you own God, God owns you. This is the same as saying: when you feel love for God, the Holy of Holies feels it and gifts you with more love.

The track to the higher realm is a love rope, what the Bushmen call *!hui*. When you get your rope, you are able to feel your way along the Highway to Heaven. This isn't a subtle intuition but a magnified pulling. You are emotionally grabbed and pulled as your dancing, happy feet never want to resist. There is no doubt when you are on the King's Highway because the celestial choir is singing and the heavenly band is playing. Absolutely no uncertainty exists when you dance down this aisle. It is the truest, purest, and surest way to reach your most desired spiritual home.

When you are on the rope, walking up the stairway, it is called *n!uan-tso*. This walk takes place in First Creation, where you feel no pain or suffering, only ecstatic joy and exhilaration. It may be deep suffering that brought you to the rope, but when you get on it, you are lifted to the highest realms. Your troubles fall away as you ascend into heavenly joy.

> **"Tell them that the greatest joy in life comes when**
> **you climb the rope to God," N!yae shouts out.**
> **"You haven't fully lived until you get on that rope."**

The rope renders you speechless. If you open your mouth, wild sounds come out. Bushmen call these n≠oahn, knowing that when the rope has a strong grip on you, you can only improvise the sounds made by n|om. The Bushmen have a word for feeling, *ta'msi*. But they also have a term for a very strong feeling, *ta'ma kaice g|aoh*. The latter is what must be brought forth to feel the love for God.

"Tell them that the greatest joy in life comes when you climb the rope to God," N!yae shouts out. "You haven't fully lived until you get on that rope."

I have climbed the rope many times, but it is not always a climb. When your rope is really strong, it's an elevator ride. You walk to the rope and as soon as you are near it, you float upward. The stronger your love, the thicker the rope. When it is as thick as an elevator cable, you get a free float trip. When it's thin, sing more and fall deeper into God's love. Then you can go up.

"Make sure they don't try a rope that is too thin. It might break, and then they will fall. Tell them that," Twa adds her advice for those outside the Kalahari. "They need a song to raise their hearts and to make the rope strong enough to climb. You can't get to God without a song. Please, please, remind them again of how we sing."

|Kunta Boo also has something to say: "Some of us were very lucky. God dropped the rope on us. The rope hit us on top of the head, and it felt like a lightning bolt. That's when you crack open and receive God's egg."

It's true. Some people are thrown to the ground in an experience of holy rapture. These folks are lucky enough to have the spiritual lightning open their mind and empty its contents so there is room for n|om to move in. N|om literally flows into you and cooks you whole, right there on the spot. Among the Bushmen, this direct hit from the Sky God happens to very few. It is the most extraordinary original mystery of them all. Being struck dead and resurrected by God is the oldest way of being enlisted in the n|om army, the special operations force for love. Though we don't know why, it usually happens to people between the ages of eighteen and twenty-one, and their life instantly becomes both lost and found at that moment. They know that this is the answer, but the rest of their life is spent figuring out how to help others articulate the right questions.

When I was nineteen years old, God struck me with n|om lightning. A spiritual fire in my belly gave birth to a glorious volcano that shot forth invisible, gravity-defying lava. It went straight up my spine and out the top of my head. There was no pain or fear. It was the most ecstatic joy and rapturous love imaginable, and I knew in an instant that this is what life is all about. It took place in a university chapel, and it lasted all night. Thankfully, no one called the police or an ambulance. I sat on a pew at the front of the church and felt God's love set me on fire, whirl me in a holy wind, and baptize me in the most sacred of waters.

All this was most likely precipitated by my intense involvement with passionate music during that time of my life. I was improvising jazz and composing love songs on the piano. Without knowing it, the music was constructing a highway to the ecstatic heavens. With a stirred heart filled with the sounds of longing, I hitchhiked myself along the most extraordinary love trip possible. My jam sessions turned me into love jelly, and that's all it took for the gods to gobble me up in a sweet and delicious way.

That was my entry into a moment of eternity. As my body shook and trembled, my heart multiplied and amplified. The concentrated love inside came out as a bright light that appeared directly in front of me as a large oval shape. I now know that it was what the Bushmen call God's ostrich egg. As I looked at this almost blinding luminosity, I saw Jesus. More important, I felt His love in a way that I can never forget and never stop feeling. I also witnessed the presence of other images of holiness.

At that time, I received my rope. It was so strong that it pulled me into the heart of God. There was no separation, and what had begun as observation quickly turned to immersion and absorption. I wept with joy. I learned that God is love—the almighty love that is the one and only originating mystery.

After that experience, it took me over a decade to find the Bushmen and to learn that this is how spirituality began. I would have been recognized as a cooked n|om-kxao in the Kalahari for seeing the ostrich egg. But I was an undergraduate student at an American university. I kept my mouth shut and did not tell anyone. This is what my inner voice advised. My adventures with n|om began on that night and, when I started searching for the tracks that led to the Kalahari, I met other people around the world who had also received a luminous egg. I finally arrived at the ancestral home in Mother Africa.

When you are given that luminous egg, it is the beginning of a journey to become a heart of the spears. Inside the egg are all the ropes, arrows of n|om, songs, and spiritual know-how needed to be a master of seiki, an owner of n|om, and an ambassador of the Holy Spirit. Unfortunately, there are no operating instructions inside the egg, and it takes years to find out that no instruction is needed. You simply allow the ropes to pull you. This is not an easy lesson. Your mind doesn't believe it to be true, so you study this and you follow that, hoping it will explain why you are spontaneously doing something without any knowing. Finally, you give up and find that it is not about understanding the original mysteries; it is about being pulled by them.

"You have to keep going back into the frying pan," Toma comments. "Even when you get that egg, you wake up the next morning as an ignorant baboon. You have to learn that the contents of the egg don't work unless you wake yourself up. Your feelings must trigger the ropes to pull you in the right direction."

I learned the hard way. My mind tried to understand, and I became a scholar and a professor. But the more I learned, the less I understood.

At the same time, I was beginning to understand that it wasn't about understanding. God continued to cook me. I resisted further, so the heat got turned up.

If a peek at heaven didn't work, then why not throw me into hell? I think that is what God did. I fell into a health crisis, a relationship calamity, an economic disaster, and one professional battle after another as I tried to find my way toward embodying this n|om know-how. Hell took its turn at cooking me, and it was not a pleasant experience. I wanted to die, and in a way, I did. I gave up trying to understand, stopped running away, abandoned embarrassment, and ended my separation from all of it. I finally stopped fighting my calling. I surrendered fully, without reservation and hesitation, to be a servant of God's love.

When I learned to wake up, the egg came back whenever it was needed, doing so at a second's notice. New visions of the egg appeared. They transmitted more of the peace that is beyond textbook understanding. I was given a holy cell phone. I even have God's email address. (You can call it the Lord's ecstatic-address.) I learned how to be a nutritious yolk rather than an egg head. In other words, I could help feed n|om to those who were hungry for it. I also learned how to cook others, scrambling, boiling, frying, poaching, and even barbecuing them. (I'm kidding about the barbecue part. Or maybe not.)

**You are inside a cocoon spun tightly by a
culture entranced by wordplay and trickster folly.
You need to be cracked open and un-spun.**

Now I am an elder, fully cooked, and am ready to begin now that I approach the beginning of my end. I have tried to tell you everything I know, but it seems that there is no end to what can be taught and felt about the infinite possibilities for God's creative expression and manifestation. At least you have been given a glimpse, and that may be enough to pop some of your bubbles. You are inside a cocoon spun tightly by a culture entranced by wordplay and trickster folly. You need to be cracked open and un-spun. You do not need psychobabble or spirit-babble. You need deprogramming. And there is a fortune to be made by someone enterprising enough to deprogram people from all the babble they are indoctrinated with. For now, start with yourself.

Tonight, wrap yourself with toilet paper. Even better, do it with a friend and wrap each other. Make yourself a mummy, then stand in front of a mirror and say out loud, "I am a mummy looking for my mommy." If that is too much absurdity for you, then start with a pencil. Wrap it with toilet paper and make it a pretend mummy. Stand it in front of a mirror and speak for it: "I am a fake mummy looking for my mommy." Now, if you're willing to do this with a pencil, then move toward a life form. Do it with a carrot. Wrap the carrot twenty-five times, stand in front of the mirror and say, "I am a twenty-five-carrot mummy looking for my mommy."

Why do this? Because you are a mummy, someone asleep who has been wrapped with too many words. All you need is a good peeling to get to your good feelings. Take off the cover and find out what lies behind the name. Meet your non-word self for the first time. Know that it wants to feel completely alive. It is soft enough to receive n|om. All it has been doing is looking for home. It wants its mommy. The Great Mother wants to hold you and nurse you into being an awakened heart. She is calling you to come home. "Come home, laddie. Come home."

Fall into the Kalahari circle. It is an unbroken circle of eternal love waiting to lift you toward God.

The Rope Is Pulling

There is nothing like the anticipation of a dance in the Kalahari. In the same way you can smell rain before it comes, your senses can tell you that a big dance storm is rolling in. As Bushmen spread word that there will be a dance, the n|om-kxaosi become excited and share their enthusiasm with one another. "Tonight we will visit God," N!yae tells me. "I can feel it. Can you?"

Yes, the rope is already feeling tight in my belly, and my heart is fluttering. The music has been present inside me all day long, and there is a sweet scent in the air. When your rope with God is tight, you smell a special sweet fragrance, sometimes like that which arises from an orange that has been peeled and squeezed.

The rope is already pulling. We hold on to each other before the community has gathered to start the fire. You can't always plan these things; they sometimes just happen. The same is true about a chick that hatches. The egg cracks when it is ready.

"Have you told them that we don't climb the rope alone?" N!yae wants to say a few more things before n|om takes away her ability to talk. "Tell them that we travel on this track with everyone by our side. We hold the hands of everyone we love and the ones they love. We walk on the road to God with everyone, hand in hand. The difference between the hearts of the spears and everyone else is that the others are asleep. They aren't aware that they are on the rope. They miss the heart of this experience."

N!yae is telling the absolute truth. A heart simply feels what is happening and walks with full awareness and presence. The spears of n|om awaken a heart to be fully engaged in the greatest Mardi Gras parade of them all—the festive march to the holy village. Rather than sleepwalk in a stupor, God wants us to enjoy what has been given to us at birth. The parade is filled with gifts. They float in front of our eyes.

Like a New Orleans parade, when a float goes by, shout out, "Throw me somethin', mista!" And the gifts will come because when n|om makes you feel it that strongly, your rope pulls it right out of the hands of spirit. It is released upon the sincere asking. Don't worry, you won't ask for the wrong thing; n|om has you in tune with what is right. N|om attraction brings the gifts that bring you further into God's love. They are the gifts that help you share the love with others. Go ahead, ask for a n|om gift. No need to be careful what you ask for when you are drinking n|om.

Love comes to wake us up. It doesn't abandon the words.
It grabs hold of the words and pulls them into our hearts.

Words are trance inductions. They hypnotize us to believe in anything suggested and manipulated by the verbal techniques of persuasion. Love comes to wake us up. It doesn't abandon the words. It grabs hold of the words and pulls them into our hearts. It spins the words, and our minds get spun as well. In the whirling is a dancer. In the dancer is a whirling.

N!yae is inviting you to hold her. |Kunta Boo, Ti!'ae, Toma, |Xoan, and G|ao'o are extending their hands and arms as well. Fall into the Kalahari circle. It is an unbroken circle of eternal love waiting to lift you toward God.

The music has begun. The rhythms are stirring. It is time to heal, have church, and party until you drop. God always has a hold on you. Wake up and feel it. Enter without concern of failure. Fail in order to take the first step toward entry. Do anything.

Shout out the name of your lucky number, cry over a falling leaf, make an unseen gesture, nod your head like a horse, stand up and turn around three times, laugh for no reason at all, slap the tip of your nose, scratch your fingernail, sing your name, play with your shoe, introduce yourself to a chair, kiss a book, write a letter to an angel, send a stamp to yourself, drink a single drop of lemonade, search for a staircase you have never climbed, replace your light bulb with one you have not tried before, change the thermostat setting of your home, surprise your loved one with a pet string, cork an empty bottle, pour dirt over your car hood, place a cartoon in your freezer, celebrate the birthday of a musician, try to think about the word *boring* until it becomes interesting, write a list of all the lists you will never make, go shopping for something that looks lonely and give it a home, pray to a blade of grass, roll over for a dog, shake hands with an invisible fairy, put wings on one of your fingers, place a Band-Aid over your television screen, talk to your phone book, make a pledge to be less obvious, open a drawer and imagine something else is inside, open a door and welcome God, open your oven and say goodbye to the devil, make a fire and ask it to beg for water, baptize your smallest toe and ask for its forgiveness, commit a random act of randomness, practice loving the word *hate* in order to help make it soft, tame a rock, walk your pencil, take your favorite book to a movie, visit a diner and order four eggs and four forks, crack open an egg and let it spill over your photograph, ask in order to perceive, act in order to crack, peel half an orange and half an apple, make a sign that points to heaven, deliver a thank-you note to a tombstone, visit a bar and drink a glass of air, look up and ask to be taken down the right road, look down and say thanks for what's above, say yes to every other answer, celebrate every odd question, clap your hands whenever your pet wakes up, enter your front door three times, announcing, "It's good to be home again."

Do these things in the name of Second Creation so that trickster can feel the love and be carried along the track that leads to God's party. "No one shall be left behind"—this is the motto of our pilgrimage to joy. "Kick everyone's behind"—this is our modus operandi. The meat must be insulted before it can be cooked. "Get behind God's love." This is the secret. Let the love pull you all the way to the sky village. "God is behind you." Fear not, God is holding, comforting, and pushing you forward.

When you realize what God is all about, ceremony and church become a blast. You attend to receive the greatest joy and peace. I hear the choir singing. People must be climbing already. Do you hear them? They have something for you to feel. Forget whether it has meaning. Feel it. Let it pull whatever is inside of you—that which is waiting for a new kind of movement in your life.

Be not dismayed whate'er betide,
God will take care of you;
Beneath his wings of love abide,
God will take care of you.

You will always find a reason to be dismayed. Something will show up to give you cause to worry; that's the way it is. But rather than stay down, hand yourself over to a higher power. Let God pull you up. You are taken care of, and there is a rope that can lift you. God will take care of you and bring you upstairs. The wings of love will carry you there.

God will take care of you,
Through every day, o'er all the way;
He will take care of you,
God will take care of you.

Those are all the words you need to know: God will take care of you. Let the now of the Tao be your wow know-how. Seriously, you are a joke. You can't do it all. Hand it over to the big-picture Sky Dude. Let the ropes do their job.

Through days of toil when heart doth fail,
God will take care of you;
When dangers fierce your path assail,
God will take care of you.

It can't be said enough: shit is going to happen. Why worry about it? Head to New Orleans and throw a party. When your heart is right, God will take care of the tab and call a cab.

All you may need he will provide,
God will take care of you;
Nothing you ask will be denied,
God will take care of you.

There is a shelter where you can get away from worry, sorrow, and dark nights of the soul. It's God's house, and it is located at Universal Heart Street. Get on that street and move in any direction. As long as you stay on track, you'll find your way home.

No matter what may be the test,
God will take care of you;
lean, weary one, upon his breast,
God will take care of you.

Where to Go to Meet—and Get Touched by—God

Here's the test: do you want the greatest ecstatic joy? Next test: do you want true love? Final exam: do you want to party with the Almighty? If you answered yes three times, then you have created another trinity. Three yeses entitle you to be a special guest at the Kalahari Sky Ranch N|om Resort.

"When we go up the rope to God's village, our ancestors meet us and take us to visit God, who can appear in any form. If you have a cunkuri, God may touch you. That is the ultimate n|om. Getting touched by God is the number-one gift we can ever receive. I have been touched by God, and I like it!"

Toma is talking about what Bushman n|om-kxaosi have experienced for thousands of years. They go up the rope and hope to get touched. Sometimes God gives them a new song or shows them a dance. God may be a man or a woman. Remember, God is a family of gods, and they are all beings of infinite love. They are formed to pull your heart into the cosmic rhythms and passions of ongoing ecstatic creation.

I met my grandfather in the sky village. He walked me along a path and introduced me to God. I was touched and super-zapped by n|om. God has come to me as a grandfather and as a grandmother. Once, God had many arms and hands, and spun like a top, enabling many hands to heal and shoot n|om. I met God as a child and as an elder; God can become all things in the sky village. Whatever form is the best fit for your heart at the time of your visit is how God will come to you. This is First Creation, the changing forms of eternity.

Simply love, and love complexly without complicating a thing. There is a season for this love. It is eternity.

Our God is a mighty mountain and fountain of love. Its ocean of bliss has many tributaries, and they reach out to us as fingers ready to point the way to what touches our heart. God wants to hold your hand. Help God and hold another hand. Become part of the holding, lifting, and pulling. Do so for the loving. Simply love, and love complexly without complicating a thing. There is a season for this love. It is eternity.

"Looks like you found the treasure, matey! It's about time you saw it. It was standing right in front of you. If you ask me, you're a squiffy buffoon who looks at the map rather than the territory. My hearty, it doesn't matter because you are now at Fiddler's Green, the pirate heaven where pirates go when they die. Here, the sweet trade is travelin' the high seas looking for the ropes and the love.

"Our sails are up for the wind, for she is a blowin'. The answer, my friend, is blowin' with this gale of a tale. The treasure you seek is inside your chest. It's your heart, dear matey. Arr, it's the heart that sings a chantey. Sing it and shiver me timbers! Sink me! Then hoist the Jolly Roger. We're on course for another round of the sweet trade. Yo-ho-ho and ahoy!"

Legend has it that there was once a great city in the Kalahari, perhaps more advanced and mysterious than Atlantis. Numerous expeditions have been carried out in hopes of uncovering where it is buried in the sand. Even Alan Paton, the famed South African writer, set out to discover its whereabouts. It is supposedly filled with gold and untold treasures, and stories about its existence make it one of the great myths of southern Africa.

When I first met the Zulu High Sanusi Vusamazulu Credo Mutwa, also known as the pope of African witch doctors, he consulted the ancestors. In an enhanced state of consciousness, he ceremonially announced that I had been to Africa before, many years ago:

257

Yes, back in the days of your country's civil war, there was a doctor. He healed many people. During the conflict that separated north from south, this doctor refused to take sides. He healed anyone, and spoke against that which divided men's hearts and caused them to fight against one another.

This man was asked to leave his country. He boarded a ship and set sail for the southernmost cape of the African coast. He arrived and traveled through the land, meeting the first people, the ones we know today as the Bushmen. They loved him and adopted him as one of their own. They gave him a name and taught him the old ways. He became a Bushman n|om-kxao and held all the mysteries of n|om. One of these mysteries was the location of the Lost City of the Kalahari. He followed the ancient track to it, and he never returned.

You, sir, are this man. You have come back to find who you are. You, sir, have been to the Lost City of the Kalahari. You, my dear friend, have returned home.

Now go share what you know and what you feel with every-one. It is good news. It is a testimony about the greatest love human beings can have for one another. It is about the coming together of the four winds. It is your destiny, and it has brought you to me as it has brought me to you.

I say these things for my ancestors. They are the great ones, the great kings, and the great queens. For them we dance and we become who they were meant to become.

Yes, I have witnessed the Lost City of the Kalahari. It is a holy place that exists in the spiritual landscape. It is the highest realm where the mysteries of n|om reside. The first name of this city was simply the Village in the Sky. Later explorers and adventurers, hearing about its treasures, began referring to it as the Lost City. All strong Bushman n|om-kxaosi visit this heavenly city to receive gifts from God. It is the highest and mightiest mystery school.

Let's get back on the rope again. I want to take you to the Lost City of the Kalahari so you can find your heart of hearts. There, I will introduce you to God. Who do you know that truly loves God? Is it a friend, relative, or someone you have heard about? Imagine her holding your hand. This will give you an extra boost because your partner is already being pulled. Maybe there is someone you would like to have meet God. Your heart aches for him to be touched by the divine. Hold on to these people, for they make your rope to God stronger.

Hop Aboard God's Elevator

Let's gather together, all of us, and push the button on God's elevator. *Ding, ding.* It's here, and the door has opened. After you, please. There's music in the elevator, but it's not elevator music. It has soul, and it feels like it is live and right in the midst of us. It actually sounds better than live music—it is music from the gods. They are jamming for our benefit. Have you noticed that this elevator is no longer an elevator? We are standing in the cosmos, and the movement of infinity has begun.

What is this? What is happening? We are not moving up; we are going down. Feeling kind of blue? Are you taking on the burdens of being a human being who isn't quite sure about how to live in this crazy world? Do you feel messed up? Let this ride take you farther down the shaft. The band is singing a lament, some blues for your pain and anguish. Fall to the floor as you feel the weight of the world resting on your shoulders. Even as you read this book, lie down on the floor. I'm serious. Lie down and feel heavy, my brothers and sisters. If not for you, then for those who suffer more than you. It can be a heavy ride getting from one day to another.

When you get down like this, you make company with all the pilgrims of the spirit in St. Vincent who are fasting for a rope, trying to get on board a spiritual journey by first feeling their lowly stature in the scheme of things. They, too, are on the mourning ground, experiencing the universe of suffering. We all suffer, and we are wired to feel the suffering of others. When you hit the point where you know, and I mean truly know with all your heart that you do not have a chance in hell of fixing your life or anyone else's by sheer cleverness or even professional skill, then and only then can you make a sincere phone call to

God. Ask God to help you. God will pick up the phone if your heart is sincere. I only have the letters, rather than the numbers, but they will work as well. Dial away to Glory Land: G-O-D-S-L-O-V-E.

Every time you hit one of those letters, notice that the music picks up its beat. You must have gotten through because the music is now starting to swing. God is present. Did you see that the light is starting to appear? The crack of dawn is arriving. God is here. This is your lesson: You can get to God by going either up or down. The Delta blues will take you there as well as Looney Tunes. Get heavy or lighten up. Both ways work.

The sun has risen, and the music is blaring away. It has changed to the sweet and happy sounds of a New Orleans brass band. The elevator door is opening. There's a street in front of you, and it has a parade. Follow the band. I'm sure it's heading to God's crib.

Someone is marching to Zion, beautiful, beautiful Zion. Others are on a soul train bound for Glory. There's also a ship crossing the Jordan, and those who have gone before us are waiting on the other side of the river. It is the final crossing. They are waving and pulling us across the water. I hear them sing the old spiritual:

'Tis the old ship of Zion, 'tis the ol' ship of Zion
'Tis the old ship of Zion, git on board, git on board
It has landed many a thousand
It was good for my dear Mother
It will take you home to glory

Feel its slow and steady driving pulse, and allow it to take over you. We'll hold on to each other and pull ourselves across the divide. We have landed. As it was good for others, it is good enough for you. As it was home to countless others, it is home enough for you. This is the glory of the crossing. This is what love can do. This is what God has in store for you.

Our Father God is pulling the whole world with his hands. That's right, as expected, he's got the whole world in his hands. And our Mother God is holding our hands, comforting and assuring us that we will be home soon. Home is where the love is. Home is God.

260

This river we are crossing is deep. It is as deep as that elevator ride took us. In the deepest water is the final crossing. Its currents bring everyone home.

Deep river, my home is over Jordan
Deep river,
Lord, I want to cross over into campground
Lord, I want to cross over into campground

My grandfather is on the bank of the other side. He loves this old spiritual. He, my father, and I used to sit in the living room and listen to a recording of it when I was a boy. He wept when he heard it play. It must have made him think of his own mother and father, and all those loved ones who crossed over before him.

I see there are folks who know you. They are weeping with joy and dancing as they sing. "Come, come," they say, greeting us on shore. "Come home. God is waiting to see you. Hurry, hurry, and don't wait another moment. Time is of the essence. You haven't got long."

Down the narrow track we go, as fast as we can move. There's no parade like a march to the Lost City of the Kalahari, the Zion of all Holy Cities. We are entering God's holy place.

God is the pulse beneath all beats, the breath inside each breath, the internal rhythm and harmony of all songs, and the heart of all hearts. God is doing something that goes past music and dance and all our senses. The great infinite source is beyond our ability to discern. It is beyond our ability to name. What we can be sure about, however, is that God loves us, and that we are created and changed by this love. In this creation, we are transformed over and over again with each breath, beat, pulse, song, and birth. We fall into God's heart.

God is the pulse beneath all beats,
the breath inside each breath,
the internal rhythm and harmony of all songs,
and the heart of all hearts.

Be inside God's walls; they are infinite. Pray inside God's Love. Sing within God's house. Here, you love everything when you love anything. "I pray inside the Lord. I love inside the Lord...." I remember the words spoken in another kabi. The anointment of n|om takes place inside the Creator. This is First Creation, where everything is everything.

We feel the touch of God, and one touch lasts a lifetime. Drop your guard and let your cover-up slide away. Enter into the final wisdom.

The Twelfth Mystery

It doesn't matter whether you go up or down. It is in the going and the returning, and the traversing through the ups and downs that lead to the breath of spiritual life. Do not be caught still; hell is not below. It is the still point going nowhere. Find God below and above, and in the movements that rock like a wave in the ocean. God is the motion, the wind, the current, and the whirling.

It cannot be this way unless there is love. It all comes down to one word: love.

Your holy books need to be edited; there is too much of man's hand inside these volumes. Each holy book, whether it is the Bible, Koran, Torah, or Upanishads, should only have one word—this four-lettered word that honors God's essence: love. This singular word is the title, author, text, and final commentary.

Now you know everything. You are a heart of the spears in the making. Get ready for the loving. Are you willing to love this truth into existence? Go home. You have more work to do.

As soon as possible, go purchase a small dictionary. Proceed to tear out every page except the page holding the word love. On that page, black out every word except love. After creating a dictionary with only one word, make a new cover. Paste it on the present cover. It should say, *The Word*. Carry your holy book—your absurdly cooked dictionary—around with you, waiting for people to ask about *The Word*. Open it up, and show them the word that matters most. Consider yourself the carrier of a one-word spirituality whose origin is inspired by the original spirituality of the First People of the Kalahari. Imagine that this word is all you need to say in order to send you to your truest home. Open the book every night before going to sleep. Say the word out loud and feel that it will take you to the heart of your longed-for home.

In a split second, we are shot faster than a shooting bullet and come back to ourselves. Like the Bushmen and all the ancestors before them, the last words you hear after a visit with God are, "Go home. You have more work to do."

In case you didn't hear it, I'll say it again: "Go home. You have more loving to do." I had to change it a bit. Otherwise, you'd lose the feeling for its truth.

In the name of all things ridiculously holy, go home and love God. Love yourself to death, and find life in loving others. Do it with the wisdom of a child and the madness of a saint. Come home to yourself and find the love that resides in your treasure chest.

"Ho-ho-ho, ninety-nine bottles of love on the wall; ninety-nine bottles of love. Take one down and pass it around, ninety-eight bottles of love on the wall. Ninety-eight bottles of love on the wall . . ."

"Go ahead, matey. Drink all the grog you want, but make sure you get it from the highest bar."

We are all Bushmen who are hunting for God's love. In your journey, you become the arrow, bow, poison, animal, meat, and excrement. One thing transforms into another, and in these changes, there is life that is inseparable from death. Feel the tapping. God is knocking on your door. If you open the door, you will see the track. Follow where it leads. With each step, you are called to the next movement. This is what it means to be pulled by God. This is how you find your way home.

"We need to open our hearts to each other so that your heart becomes my heart and my heart becomes your heart," N!yae says as she sits on the ground-trembling with n|om. "This is why we wake up each morning. N|om is hunting us as we track it down. Love is pulling on us as we yearn for it."

The world belongs to the ropes. In their crossings, we find God; in God, we find the original way of loving.

The original mysteries have been revealed. What will you do with them? Will you give your life to being a Kalahari fool for extreme love? Or will you keep on searching for a sophisticated answer held by fancy words?

I am no longer looking for the answer. The answer found me: I stumbled upon the gods in the Kalahari. They are as crazy as a giraffe dancing the ballet or an ostrich running for president. But they are as mighty as a roaring lion, and as sweet and beautiful as singing lovebirds. These original gods never intended for us to grow up; the Garden of Eden was only meant for children. The forbidden apple was nothing more than the apple on a teacher's desk—an invitation to hand our hearts over to a word-smitten world.

Please consider saying no to the apple and declaring yes to the original way of loving. Surrender yourself to the greatest insult imaginable: making fun of taking yourself too seriously. Party all night to lose your mind and find your heart. Shake your booty for the sake of being overtaken by n|om. I sing to you:

In the heart is found the universe.
Its grace is the human race.
Our only teacher is love
Peace of a soaring dove.
Embrace the Kalahari;
Own the ancestors.
They will introduce you to life,
The living of mystery
Freedom from mastery

With songs up your spine
Wisdom in your feet
Light in your heart,
Fire on your tongue,
Infinitely passionate breath.
I am asking you to join me in the greatest crusade of undoing
    the doing.
I am asking you to join me in the wildest celebration of kissing the
    Supreme Being.
I am asking you to become a flaming heart of the spear.
Piercing the lives of others,
Setting them on fire,
Inviting them to dine with mystery,
Embracing them with tender insults,
Awakening them with a vibration.
A movement between life and death,
A breathing of knowing and not knowing.
Welcome to the rock-and-roll spirited movement that has
    no reason.
But overflows with heart in every season.
The gods are crazy,
And full of everlasting delight,
Made especially for you and me.
Why?
Because we are created by love to become love.
This is how it began and how it continues,
With each and every
Beginning,
Turning,
Teasing,
Dying,
Living,
Loving.
Let us live to love.
And love to live.

For no other reason than
Shaking with the divine ecstasy of loving love.

Now I come back to myself.

BASIC GLOSSARY

|ae-N≠unhn: an ancestor who hands down God's water, the golden elixir

!aia: a waking up of feelings and being in a heightened state of emotion

!aaiha: a pulling doctor who helps keep the community well

arrows of n|om (tchisi): the way n|om is delivered to others; comparable to Cupid's transmission of love

cunkuri: a spiritual encounter with God

ecstatic pump: the pumping sensation associated with a healer's abdominal contractions during the act of healing

g||abesi: the lower part of the abdomen, where the Bushmen believe that arrows and nails of n|om reside once they enter the body

g||auan≠'angsi: the original ancestors

God's ostrich egg (!Xo dso'o-n!o): a visionary symbol—the egg cracks open as a means of giving one all the nails, arrows, and ropes of the Sky God; it also enables communication with other Bushman n|om-kxaosi

First Creation (≠Ain-≠aing≠ani): the world before words, a paradise of change and never-ending transformation

First Line: in a parade, especially in Mardi Gras, principal members of the organization that authorized the parade make up this line

God (G≠kao N!a'an): the source of all love; also refers to the gods, goddesses, and god's children and relatives who create and disperse love

God's water (!Xo g!u): the golden elixir or concentrated n|om in a liquid form for drinking

heart of the spears (g≠aqba-n!a'an): a fully cooked n|om-kxao; the highest state of a n|om being

insulting the meat: playful teasing that brings everyone to the same social level

kabi: a spiritual visit with your ancestors

library of mystery: the domain of experience where original spiritual wisdom is passed on

nails or needles of n|om (tchisis or ||auhsi): like an arrow of n|om, but typically delivered directly from the Creator God

n!o'an-ka|'ae: the original force that changes everything; that which creates

n|om: non-subtle universal life force

n|om hug: a vibrational hug that enables arrows of n|om to be exchanged

n|om-kxao (plural n|om-kxaosi): an owner of n|om, usually referring to a healer or spiritual elder; ownership means "own the feeling" for n|om

pulling (≠hoe): the term used for removing sickness and tiredness from another person

rope (!hui): a strongly felt bond of relationship with another

Second Creation (G!xoa): literally, "now there is speech"; the world that resulted after words were introduced and paradise ended

Second Line: in a parade, especially in Mardi Gras, the group of common folk who follow a parade and enjoy the festivities

seiki: old Japanese word for the non-subtle universal life force; it is arguably the same as n|om. Seiki jutsu is the art of working with the universal life force. Its greatest practitioner was Ikuko Osumi, sensei.

shaking medicine: the utilization of ecstatic joy and love as a means of healing and transformation

shaman: someone who embodies ecstasy that is expressed through a shaking body, heightened emotion, song catching, and visionary experience

spiritual classroom: the experiential realm where original spirituality is taught by the ancestors, gods, and other spiritual presences

tco-kxao: ecstatic shakers who transmit n|om to others; they are the strongest healers

thara: the ecstatic shaking that accompanies being filled with spirit

thuru: shape-shifting

trickster (|xuri kxao): an invention of language; trickster is sometimes called self, the inner mirage that relishes believing one is God

word souls: the songs and messages that shamans deliver while under the influence of divine inspiration

Dictionary of Original Spirituality

WORDS USED BY THE N|OM-KXAOSI

Compiled by

BEESA BOO AND BRADFORD KEENEY

To hear proper pronunciation, visit:
http://shakingmedicine.com/bushmen/dictionary.php

The distinct punctuation marks from the Ju/'hoan Bushman language are symbols for their particular click sounds. According to anthropologist and linguist Megan Biesele, they are pronounced as follows:

| a dental click that sounds like *tsk*, *tsk* and is made by putting the tongue behind the teeth

≠ an alveolar click, a soft pop made by putting the tongue behind the ridge that is located behind the front teeth

! an alveolar-palatal click, a sharp pop made by drawing the tongue down quickly from the roof of the mouth

|| a lateral click, a clucking sound similar to that made by the English when they urge on a horse

' a glottal stop, as in the Cockney English pronunciation of bottle

|'ana: acacia tree associated with giraffe in Second Creation

|'an-jukonaqnisi: kabi of receiving needles

|'haam-!'haam: spiderweb of n|om that covers the head of a n|om-kxao; it tries to stop healing as it blocks the n|om-kxao's ability to see sickness

|' hare: being very happy while dancing in one spot

|'u a !xui: an animal chasing its tail (a way of referring to changing circles)

|'ua-n|om: giving a needle to another person

|ae-N≠unhn: ancestor that sends down n|om drink from God; the drink is God's urine and looks like water

|Aqn-|aqnce: Sky God's wife's name, which means "Mother of Bees"

|xo' djxani: elephant dance

|xuri kxaosi: tricksters

||'ai and ||oqm: grass associated with oryx and gemsbock in Second Creation

||'ai djxani: grass dance

||'oara: women's tortoise shell for holding perfume

||an: when people hear a song from a faraway village or from the ancestors and feel they have to go to the dance

||auh: another word for needle

||auhsi: Sky God's needles of n|om

||hangn'ang: top of head where needles can be given; place where fully cooked needles (turned to steam) exit the body

||kaquh: fruit-bearing tree in the Sky God's village referred to as "the tree of death"

||xaece: when a n|om-kxao protects himself by pushing back another person's anger

||xoan: the heavy breathing sound of climbing the thread to God

!'han-n!ang: inside the waterhole where some n|om-kxaosi visit in a kabi

!'hana: man's dance stick used by n|om-kxao to give needles to others through pointing

!'huhn: name of the sound made when releasing sickness

!'oan: open up the heart (most important learning for a n|om-kxao)

!'uhn: n|om-kxao's sound made when pulling out sickness or dirty needles

!aaiha: a n|om-kxao who can heal by pulling out sickness

!ai: real death, which has nothing to do with !aia, the waking up of a n|om-kxao

!ai||aah: mask of death that looks like an animal head and, when placed on you, causes sickness

!aia: waking up your strongest feelings and being reborn

!ai-tcia: something dangerous and deadly, like poison, lightning, and serious illness

!ain-!'u: spot on back of the neck where pulled sickness may leave the n|om-kxao

!'haam: spider

!hui: thread or rope to God

!huijuasi: the "straight-line people" who aren't Bushmen (e.g., the white people)

!ka tsau |'an: the heart rises more

!kabi: when the n|om-kxao sees First Creation in the dance (seen as a constant whirling)

!kain: a form of g||auansi n|om, used by g||auansi to trick you into following a bad direction

!kau: feeling of shock on fingertips that means that a lion is near

!ku: God's tree that holds the medicine water

!kunsi: respect name for Gemsbock people

!oo: dance skirt

!un: dream

!xaua-khoe: ignorance caused by being selfish and greedy; the opposite of love

!Xo dso'o-n!o: God's ostrich egg

!Xo hui mi: "God help me"; words of common prayer

!Xo g!u: Sky God's medicine water

!Xo kxao: means "I am an owner of God," that is, "I am the owner of the feeling of love for God"

!Xo tci: gift from the Sky God

!Xon!a'an: Sky God

≠a'am|'an: tapping that ancestors and God make on the body

≠ahmi: refers to Bushmen as "circle people" and the circles around the sun and moon that remind people of important things

≠ahmia-khoe juasi: another way of referring to the circle people and seeing everything move in circles

≠Ain-≠aing≠ani: First Creation

≠ang: bush used to make medicine for men's tortoise shell (combined with animal fat) and used to heat a n|om-kxao in a dance (done by adding charcoal to medicine and smudging with the smoke); also used to help illness leave the body

≠ara-khoe: shaking of a n|om-kxao's heart onto another person's heart

≠**hoe:** pulling out the sickness with your hands

≠**hoe djxani:** healing dance

≠**oah djxani:** giraffe dance

≠**oah tchisi:** giraffe arrows of n|om

≠**um !xo kokxui:** the belief in God brought about by the love you feel for God

≠**uma-khoe:** sharing

≠**umsi !xo:** religious beliefs about God and healing

are: love, which is the most important word for a n|om-kxao

ca-ca: plant root used to protect boys and girls from dangerous n|om associated with a girl's menstruation or following delivery of a baby

cunkuri: a particular kabi when you see Sky God or ancestors

da'a: fire in the sky seen by n|om-kxao when traveling along a thread

djxani: dance

djxani-!uhsi: two n|om-kxaosi shaking together

djxani-kxao: a n|om-kxao who is dancing

dshau-n!a'anao||xai-g!oqma: old woman who makes scary sound in a dance

ega: "something for me," which is the message of the body tappings

g||a'inkodin: an original ancestor who stared at things and made them move

g||abesi soan: "the g||abesi is soft," that is, ready to receive needles

g||abesi tuih: the waking up of g||abesi and needles; one feels heat and tightness

g||aoah da'atzi: healing songs to quietly sing around a home fire

g||auan (plural **g||auansi**): ancestral spirit, trickster spirit, or spirit of God

g||auan ||koa !a'ansi: little g||auansi children from long ago

g||auan≠'angsi: the original ancestors

g||auan-n|hai: laughing caused by ancestors (ancestral spirits)

g||auansi tchi: arrows of sickness

g!a'ama-ju: when a n|om-kxao catches the sick feeling of an animal

g!a'ama-n!ausi: second experiential station of a n|om-kxao where the heart rises; this is when healing can take place

g!kun||homdima: woman in First Creation who first blew a horn

g!o'e djxani: oryx dance

g!oah: name of dance with song and n|om from G!oah plant

g!oah n|oma: n|om from G!oah plant

g!oahnaqnisi: G!oah needles of n|om

g!oan: plant whose roots are ground to a red powder and used by men for good luck in a hunt (a vertical line drawn between the eyes and a horzontal line drawn around upper arms)

g!oh: steam (needles fully cooked are also called g!oh)

g!xa maq: breathing out the soul

G!xoa: Second Creation, meaning "now there is speech"

g!xoa-g!xoa koarasi: the Knee Knee None people, creatures without knees about which little is known

g≠aihg≠aing≠ani: time when there was no speech (later called First Creation)

g≠aqba-n!a'an: "heart of the spears," the most powerful n|om-kxao

G≠kao N!a'an: respect name of Sky God

G≠kao Na'an: Father of the original ancestors

Gauh-!o: Mother of the original ancestors

gu-tsau: the clapping that lifts the dancer's legs in a dance

gua: beginning of !aia when you first feel the power of the fire

gua-gua: when the fire has big flames

hatce koe du kxui mi ≠'angsi: expression for "what is making me think this way?" which refers to how trickster enters the mind

ju ka g≠om: moment when a n|om-kxao so full of n|om that he can no longer speak, but can only sing

ju!kag!ua: the liquid around the heart caused by anger

kaakare: the dizziness of doctors after a dance (it is caused by n|om)

kabi: visitation or message from Sky God or ancestors which is different from a dream

kaoha-kxo: God's pot that he cooks a n|om-kxao in

kaqian: g||auansi n|om used to make you sick or die

kau-hariri: the actual sound made by an !aaiha when illness is pulled

kxae |xoa: soul (the living self with its memories)

kxae≠xaisi: seeing the feelings (what is meant by "seeing properly")

kxaetci!hun: tapping on body that means it is time for hunting

kxao-kxaoa!kui: ostrich feather of decoration for n|om-kxao

m||ara: g!oah n|om stick used by dancers in the past

maniju≠'angsi: turning against someone

manisi n!a'an-n!a'an: "the great turning around"; the beginning of Second Creation

maq: thread for any ancestral spirit, whether good or bad

maqdore: the strange wind used for attack and protection by a n|om-kxao

Mban!a'an: Great Father; how Sky God is addressed in prayer

mi-n|ai-dci: expression meaning "my head is wet from God's water"

n|haitzi'i: good feeling when laughing together with friends

n|o'oan: bush associated with eland in Second Creation

n|om-da'a: name of the fire inside the n|om-kxao

n|om-kxao: owner of n|om

n|om-tzi: singular n|om (for example, applied to a n|om-kxao who only has giraffe arrows)

n|om-tzisi: multiple n|om (for example, a n|om-kxao who has several kinds of arrows)

n|huin: spirit (breath)

n|huin n'ang: breathing in (bringing back) the soul

n||oq!'ae: bush used for making perfume; made of ground leaves and used to cool down a n|om-kxao in the dance

n!aih-|ho: place to make a fire for dancing and healing

n!aihsi: old word for needles (which carry and transmit n|om)

n!ang !xui: tail of an eland used by a n|om-kxao in the dance

n!ang djxani: eland dance

n!ang tchisi: other animal arrows of n|om

n!ang-n|aisi: eland-headed tribe

n!angsi: eland-headed people

n!ao: spirit of weather conditions at birth, giving good or bad luck to the person and the community

n!aroh-||xam: first experiential station of a n|om-kxao; this refers to experiencing the power of the fire, which is where you meet and deal with fear

n!aroh-ma: beginning learner of medicine

n!hai !oqru: very dangerous skinny green lion

n!hai djxani: lion dance

n!huru: aloe plant associated with eland in Second Creation

n!o'an-ka|'ae: the original force that changes everything

n!o'an-n|om: throwing a dirty arrow to hurt someone through black magic

n!uan-ju: refers to the spirit of an animal standing on top of a person to help heal them

n!uan-tso: standing or climbing on the thread to God

n≠ahn: camelthorn tree in the Sky God's village

n≠hang: a red pigment from the Sky God's special plant that the Sky God rubs on a person for protection (this takes place in a kabi)

n≠oahn: when the ancestors make strange sounds through the n|om-kxao

n≠u'uhan: someone pretending to be a n|om-kxao

n≠u'uhan-kxaosi: those who show off and boast about their n|om

qaqm: to awaken, used to refer to the cause of !aia (analogous to striking a match); when lit, the n|om-kxao is in gua, the first stage of !aia

san !auah: skin bag for holding perfume

san||ae: sinew, the old word for thread traveled on by a n|om-kxao

ta'ma kaice g|aoh: very strong feeling

ta'msi: feeling

tau: n|om string

tchi-n||han: sending a deadly animal like a snake to harm someone

tchisi: arrows of n|om

tci-dore: name for trickster that is used when one is angry with it

tci-n|oa ||ah jan: hat from Sky God that is received in a kabi

tco: respect name for n|om

tco-kxao: a n|om-kxao powerful enough to give others needles

tco-tcaq: sweat; for a n|om-kxao who is dancing, the sweat is a medicine used to help give needles to others

thara: shaking caused by n|om

thara n|om: the third experiential station of a n|om-kxao where needles are given

thuru: when a n|om-kxao changes form into an animal or anything else

tjin-kxuisi-tsa'an-tsa'an: the scary sound made by the old woman in a dance

tso: thread for lion thuru—that is, for changing into a lion

waqdom: tortoise shell to wear in dance that is decorated with bullet shells to scare lions and g||auansi away

xaam: respect name of the lion

xaro: gift

xuru a o n|om ga: man's tortoise shell for holding medicine

zo: bee, which has tremendous n|om